What is the

What is the Future?

John Urry

polity

First published in 2016 by Polity Press

Polity Press
65 Bridge Street
Cambridge CB2 1UR, UK

Polity Press
350 Main Street
Malden, MA 02148, USA

ISBN-13: 978-0-7456-9653-9
ISBN-13: 978-0-7456-9654-6 (pb)

A catalogue record for this book is available from the British Library.

Library of Congress Cataloging-in-Publication Data

Names: Urry, John, author.
Title: What is the future? / John Urry.
Description: Cambridge, UK; Malden, MA: Polity Press, 2016. | Includes bibliographical references and index.
Identifiers: LCCN 2016001400 (print) I LCCN 2016009666 (ebook) | ISBN 9780745696539 (hardback) | ISBN 9780745696546 (pbk.) | ISBN 9780745696560 (Mobi) | ISBN 9780745696577 (Epub)
Subjects: LCSH: Future, The. | Forecasting. | Civilization–Forecasting. | Sociology.
Classification: LCC CB161 .U77 2016 (print) | LCC CB161 (ebook) | DDC 303.49–dc23
LC record available at http://lccn.loc.gov/2016001400

Typeset in 11 on 13 pt Sabon
by Toppan Best-set Premedia Limited
Printed and bound in Great Britain by CPI Group (UK) Ltd, Croydon

For further information on Polity, visit our website:
politybooks.com

Contents

Preface

I am very grateful to many colleagues who have stimulated my interest and thinking about social futures. I gained great insight from the work of the much-missed Ulrich Beck.

My thinking here was co-developed with Thomas Birtchnell and this is reflected in various joint articles and books, including the research reported below in Chapter 7. See our forthcoming book *A New Industrial Future? 3D Printing and the Reconfiguring of Production, Distribution and Consumption* (Routledge). I am also very grateful to other friends and colleagues who contributed in general or specifically commented on the manuscript, including Barbara Adam, Ian Aspin, Alan Beattie, Mike Berners-Lee, Paula Bialski, David Bissell, Rebecca Braun, Monika Büscher, Javier Caletrio, Rachel Cooper, Andrew Curry, Joe Deville, Pennie Drinkall, Nick Dunn, Anthony Elliott, Carlos Galviz, James Hale, Michael Hulme, Bob Jessop, Glenn Lyons, Astrid Nordin, Lynne Pearce, Serena Pollastri, Cosmin Popan, Katerina Psarikidou, Satya Savitzky, Andrew Sayer, Mimi Sheller, Elizabeth Shove, Richard Slaughter, Ken Smith, Nicola Spurling, Bron Szerszynski, Richard Tutton, David Tyfield, Amy Urry, Tom Urry, Sylvia Walby, Becky Willis and Linda Woodhead.

I am also grateful for EPSRC grant EP/J017698/1, which is part of the EPSRC Liveable Cities Programme directed by Chris Rogers at the University of Birmingham.

Institute for Social Futures, Lancaster University

1

Introduction: The Future Has Arrived

Welcome to the future

In 1994, the magazine *New Scientist* devoted a special issue to the subject of *Futures*, observing how the future is a foreign country since they do things differently there (*New Scientist* 1947, 5 October 1994). The Editorial argued that the increasingly complex nature of the world made it even more important to know the future so as to understand the present better. Somewhat similarly, John F. Kennedy said, quite close to his assassination in 1963, that: 'Change is the law of life. And those who look only to the past or present are certain to miss the future' (Kennedy Address 1963).

The future has most definitely arrived but what exactly it is remains a mystery, perhaps the greatest of mysteries. Futures are now everywhere. Thinking and anticipating the future are essential for almost all organizations and societies. Futures are on most contemporary agendas – many hold the future to be a better guide to what to do in the present than what happened in the past. States, corporations, universities, cities, NGOs and individuals believe they cannot miss the future; that foreign country is now everywhere.

Yet at the same time futures are unpredictable, uncertain and often unknowable, the outcome of many known and especially 'unknown unknowns'. Garrett Hardin once maintained 'We can never do merely one thing': the one thing that would produce a single clear set of future outcomes (1972: 38). We do, in effect, many 'things', even when we think we are doing just one, and these many things have varied and unpredictable consequences for the future.

Thus, the first reason for writing a book on futures is to demonstrate the many efforts made, in the past and now, to anticipate, visualize and elaborate the future(s) within various domains of human activity. Powerful social institutions and thinkers are developing various kinds of anticipatory discourses and techniques (see Szerszynski 2016, on anticipation). This futures orientation is big and significant business for companies like Google or Shell, environmental organizations such as the Intergovernmental Panel on Climate Change (IPCC) or Forum for the Future, government bodies like Foresight in the UK or the European Strategy and Policy Analysis System (ESPAS) in the EU, military organizations such as the Pentagon, academic bodies such as the Oxford Martin School or the Tyndall Centre, and very many others. Some of those futures anticipated by these organizations have performative consequences, certain of which will be documented and examined below.

Specific methods have been developed for envisaging, visualizing and assessing potential futures. Some of these originated from scenario planning exercises that Hermann Kahn initiated at the Rand Corporation during the 1950s (Son 2015: 124). He especially promoted the development of alternative scenarios, noting how they enabled the imagining of different future possibilities. Also, many imagined future worlds have been developed within literature, art, film, TV, computer games and so on. These often involved spectacular future technologies such as time-travel, personal flying machines, roads and trains in the sky, teleportation, robots, walking upon water, off-earth communities, vacuum powered propulsion, driverless trains, equal utopias, as well as many dark dystopic futures (see the amusing www.bbc.co.uk/news/magazine-20913249). This book will document and assess some of these ways in which organizations, intellectuals, scientists, artists, policy makers and technologists have developed, or are developing, futures.

The future also seems to be appearing ever more quickly, something first analysed in depth in Toffler's *Future Shock* (1970). He described exponential rates of technological and social transformation. In recent decades, 'Moore's Law' meant that world computing power (the number of transistors in an integrated circuit) doubled every two years. Today's smartphones possess the computing power once found in large mainframe computers, as well as possessing 'magical' affordances housed within a 'ready-to-hand' small machine which no one knew they 'needed' only twenty years ago. Some indeed argue that the future has almost disappeared, being transformed into an 'extended present' with no long-term futures (Nowotny 1994). And many people feel that they themselves have no 'future', since opportunities, hopes and dreams seem endlessly dashed, especially during times of 'austerity'.

A sense of a disappearing future is also found within new financial 'products' that are based upon computerized high-frequency trading occurring in millionths of a second (Gore 2013). Actions happening beyond the speed of thought involve movements of money and information that cannot be grasped by human minds, even by the 'flash boys' working in finance (Lewis 2015). In such an accelerating world, financial futures arrive before they have been understood by the relevant actors. This is a kind of nanosecond 'future shock' in which efforts to slow down decision-making even to transactions taking a whole second are rejected by financial institutions (Gore 2013: 16–17).

Moreover, futures are incredibly contested, saturated with conflicting social interests. Over two centuries ago, Edmund Burke argued that a society should be seen as a: 'partnership not only between those who are living, but between those who are living, those who are dead, and those who are to be born' (Burke [1790] quoted in Beinhocker 2006: 454). Burke points to the interests of unborn members of a society and how they need a powerful 'voice' to counter societies and lives being based only upon the interests of the living.

The environmental movement has played a major role in developing this idea of an inter-generational global commons, as set out in the Brundtland Commission's iconic Report on *Our Common Future* (1987). Environmentalism deploys generational rhetoric to argue for the interests of children, grandchildren and those not yet born (see Hansen 2011; www.gaiafoundation.org/earth-law-network/alliance-future-generations). Interestingly Hungary initiated the position of the Parliamentary Commissioner for Future Generations (www.ajbh.hu/en/web/ajbh-en/dr.-marcel-szabo), while a Future Generations Commissioner for Wales was established by 2015 legislation to act as an advocate for future generations.

However, most societal processes mould futures to the interests of current generations. Those yet to be born generally possess no voice in what we can call the 'parliament of generations'. Or, as Adam expresses it, future generations cannot charge the current generation for the use made of their present. Future generations have no voice or vote to register their interests and must accept most of what is handed down to them (Adam 2010: 369).

There are though moments when this power of the present generation is contested and efforts are made by governments and NGOs to form 'imagined communities' that do stretch across generations and seek a 'common future'. Such moments of generational solidarity can transform social and political debate, laying down new institutions and structures of feeling. One moment when this happened in some societies was during 1970. On 22 April 1970, 20 million Americans demonstrated for a healthy, sustainable environment. This first Earth Day led to the creation of the United States Environmental Protection Agency, the passing of various environmental Acts, the founding of Greenpeace and the publication of many iconic texts. At such moments, the long-term or glacial future functioned as a powerful structure of feeling (see Lash, Urry 1994). The future became democratized. But these moments are unusual. Overall, the arguments in this book are oriented to democratizing futures.

Rejecting the future

However, even though there are many social conflicts over futures, social science was reluctant to enter this futures world and has made a limited contribution to its theorization and analysis (but see Bell, Wau 1971; Young 1968). This reluctance partly resulted from how Marx, the most significant nineteenth-century social scientist, was apparently mistaken in 'predicting' that capitalism would engender worldwide revolution led by the industrial working class. Marx argued: 'The philosophers have only interpreted the world, in various ways; the point is to change it' (Marx 1962[1845]: 405). He expected that steam-powered factories, large industrial cities, railways and worker immiseration would lead the industrial proletariat to develop into a 'class-for-itself' and thus revolutionize the capitalist world. The proletarian class and its transformative power would overthrow capitalism and realize 'communism' through the effects of global capitalist expansion.

But in fact worldwide social revolution did not start in societies with the most advanced capitalist political economies, such as Britain or Germany. It commenced in Tsarist Russia in 1917, it did not initially involve a large organized industrial working class and the Bolshevik revolution resulted not in communism or even socialism in one country but, according to many critics such as Karl Popper, a new barbarism.

However, Marx's earlier 1840s writings instead emphasized how capitalist societies in fact involved much uncertainty and unpredictability. In *The Manifesto of the Communist Party*, written when he was just thirty, Marx (and Engels) described a modern world of transience and movement, arguing that all fixed, fast-frozen relationships were swept away in capitalist modernity: all that is solid melts into air (Berman 1983; Marx, Engels 1952[1848]). This vision of an uncertain capitalist modernity meant that, in terms of analysis from the 1840s it was impossible to develop a specified blueprint of the future, and indeed Marx and Engels generally argued against utopian future visions.

Nevertheless this apparent 'failure' of Marxist analysis to get the future right was used by many social analysts to reject the proposal that social science should make predictions or establish planned blueprints for the future. Utopian imagining and the fostering of alternative worlds were heavily critiqued especially during the Cold War period in western societies (Popper 1960; Kumar 1991). Social science turned its back on developing and analysing possible futures (but see Bell, Wau 1971). A few social scientists, such as Lefebvre, Bauman and Olin Wright, argued that utopias can hold a powerful mirror to existing societies as they demonstrate limitations of the present (Bauman 1976; Levitas 1990; Pinder 2015). This positing of a utopia has often been emancipatory, enabling people to break with the dominance of what seem to be unchanging forms of social life within the present. But, in general, utopian social science has been rare.

In fact, studies of alternative futures which emerged over the past seventy or so years were mainly developed outside 'social science' as such (see Son's periodization, 2015). Future studies was developed as a specialized and increasingly professionalized discipline, generating its own journals, key books, iconic figures, global bodies (http://foresightinternational.com.au), professional organizations (such as the Association of Professional Futurists) and founding texts (see www.wfsf.org/; Son 2015: 122). Futurist thinking immediately after 1945 often reflected Cold War debates and issues, with Kahn said to be the model for Dr Strangelove in the 1964 movie (see www.newyorker.com/magazine/2005/06/27/fat-man). Much of this futurist thinking was tied to powerful military and corporate agendas in which computers in particular were viewed as instruments of the Cold War (Turner 2006: 1). This futures thinking was normally funded from outside the academy and subsequently mainly developed within private thinktanks such as those established by Alvin Toffler (1970), and later Jeremy Rifkin (2009), Al Gore (2013) and many others. By the late 1970s, there were an astonishing 178 futures-related journals (Son 2015: 125).

Futures work also developed partly because of the growing significance of the environmental movement and related sciences in the decades after 1970 (see Schumacher's prescient *Small is Beautiful*, 1973). The *Limits to Growth* debates as well as the 1973 oil crisis involved developing computer-models, some involving doomsday scenarios, others techno-optimistic futures (Meadows, Meadows, Randers, Behrens 1972; Son 2015: 126). Such increasing concern with the issue of climate change led to General Circulation Models. By the early 1990s, these computerized models simulated the consequences of increases in CO_2 upon mean global climate at various points in the future. These predictions were incorporated into the major reports of the increasingly influential Intergovernmental Panel on Climate Change (IPCC) that appeared every few years after the first was published in 1990. These reports warned that, if societies continued with the practices and policies of 'business as usual', then the likely global future was a continued and significant warming of the earth's climate and hence the very opposite of maintaining business as usual (see Chapter 9 below).

Social sciences and the future

This book argues that different social futures are fateful for people's lives in the present. It also argues that the terrain of future studies should be reclaimed for social science and, in a way, for people in their day-to-day lives. There is much theory and research in social science that is pertinent to anticipating futures, but this linking has not often been achieved. This book seeks to 'mainstream' the future, which is too important to be left to states, corporations or technologists. Future visions have powerful consequences and social science needs to be central in disentangling, debating and delivering those futures. Hence we should develop what will be termed here 'social futures' – this notion having some similarity with the idea of an 'integral future' (Bell, Wau 1971; Slaughter 2012). The book shows how analyses of 'social institutions, practices and lives' should be core to theories and methods of potential futures. The time of the future is now, and the social sciences and the social world should not miss it.

This is firstly because social science is significant in helping to deconstruct a single notion of 'time'. Adam and colleagues show that there are varied forms of time as different societies and social institutions are built around contrasting time regimes (Abbott 2001; Adam 1990, 1995). Temporal regimes of calculation and disciplining, such as those within a monastery or contemporary finance, matter greatly to people's lives within different societies (see Canales 2009, on the historical significance of being able to measure a tenth of a second). Adam shows the importance of the historic shift from time as lived and experienced to time that is standardized and de-contextualized (Adam 2010).

Relatedly, social science elaborates how multiple futures are related to these different time regimes. According to Adam and Groves, futures are told, tamed, traded, transformed, traversed, thought, tended and transcended (2007). Especially significant is trading in futures, which involves a major break in the trajectory taken by societies. In many religions, it was considered a sin to charge interest on money lent into the future since the future belonged to God and not the people (Adam, Groves 2007: 9). However, within European societies, God's gift was transformed into a future made, intervened in and traded. Thus there was 'a change in the ownership of the future from gods to people', with many profound consequences for social life (Adam 2010: 365).

The future has often been viewed as empty and abstracted from context; as a result an 'empty future is there for the taking, open to commodification, colonization and control... When the future is decontextualized and depersonalized we can use and abuse it without feeling guilt or remorse' (Adam, Groves 2007: 13). The future has indeed been used and abused – seeing the future as empty makes it ready for exploitation since those in the future cannot get their own back for the future world that they will inherit.

Social science also examines the dangers of extrapolating the future from what is the present. Knowing the future necessitates examining various 'pasts' and developing ways of understanding how past, present and future are mutually intertwined. It is sometimes maintained that we can distinguish between planning, preparation, invention and co-producing the future, especially through what Riel Miller terms a 'futures literacy' (2011). He argues that developing this literacy as to potential futures enables the present to be better understood. The point he says is not to test present assumptions against some predictive future, but to use the future to question, unpack, invent what is going on and what can be done within the present. More generally, here people's anticipation of the future can have profound consequences for the present. In this book, we see many examples of the anticipatory character of contemporary society and its many consequences for the present (Szerszynski 2016).

Variations in time and possible anticipated futures also stem from how social systems can be characterized by discontinuity, change and unpredictability. Prigogine argues from the perspective of complexity science that futures are the effect of multiple unstable, complex adaptive systems and their often cascading interdependencies (1997). This 'end of certainty' has implications for future social worlds, as described in detail by Al Gore (2013).

Social studies of technology show that future economic and social innovations are rarely the outcome of linear processes but involve unpredictable combinations of elements, as elaborated by

Arthur in the context of 'new' technologies (2013). Similarly, futurist Ray Kurzweil said: 'most inventions fail not because the R&D department can't get them to work, but because the timing is wrong – not all of the enabling factors are at play where they are needed. Inventing is a lot like surfing: you have to anticipate and catch the wave at just the right moment' (http://crnano.org/interview.kurzweil.htm). I examine below various moments when the specific future was unanticipated since the wave was not caught 'at the right moment'.

Social studies of innovation show how futures are unpredictable because technologies are 'moving' around and exerting often unintended consequences, synchronizing with varied elements and occasionally forming a new system. Such systems are in 'process' and not pre-determined in their organization or effects. Many 'old' technologies do not simply disappear but survive through path-dependent relationships, combining with the 'new' in a reconfigured and unpredicted cluster. An interesting example of this has been the enduring importance of the 'technology' of paper even within 'high-tech' offices. The reference to 'technologies' indexes how the view of social science that is deployed here is based upon the contingent assembling of social *and* material elements (see Part 2).

Further, some futures are in a way built into contemporary societies, such as the idea of developing 'smart cities' which can help to bring such cities into being. Such a notion is performative (see http://smartcities.media.mit.edu). Powerful actors seeking to realize the future they envisaged often deploy complex rhetorical imaginaries and visions of a future 'heaven'. These actors perform or produce that future, while characterizing those who oppose this heavenly future as 'Luddite' (Law, Urry 2004, on enacting the social).

One kind of example of 'making the future' is found in 'predict and provide' models extensively deployed in planning and financing major transport infrastructures. Such a model proceeds as follows. Analysts conduct research on levels of congestion in a road system and predict further increasing demand for roadspace in an area; it is argued that this new roadspace must be provided through building a new infrastructure, justified since it will save valuable time; but this in turn results in more traffic filling up the new roadspace; and this leads to the further predicted demand for more roadspace, which is then provided, and so on. The prediction is realized and appears 'correct', so leading to further future demand (see Lyons 2015).

There are also some very long-term futures now being envisioned. Kurzweil emphasizes the law of accelerating returns resulting from enhanced computing and technological power. These exponential rates of change will result in a 'singularity', a moment when human biology merges with genetics, nanotechnology and robotics (Kurzweil 2006; see the 2010 movie *The Singularity is Near*). Kurzweil describes how, after the singularity, there will be no distinction between humans and machines. At the predicted date of the singularity (2045), computer-based intelligence will significantly exceed the sum total of human brainpower – so, in effect, creating a new species. It should not be presumed that humans are the evolutionary end-point. As media futurist Marshal McLuhan once said, 'First we build the tools, then they build us.' Exponential change brings the future so much closer. Yet if we see change as only 'linear', then Kurzweil says we will miss what is already in process, and, through exponential rates of change, the future will arrive much sooner than predicted (see Gore 2013: 240; www.technologyreview.com/view/425733/paul-allen-the-singularity-isnt-near).

Kurzweil's view of the singularity is broadly benign (he is now working for Google!). But other futures are more dystopic. Often the pursuit of short-term interests in the present results in unintended and highly perverse effects in the future. Social science analysis shows how futures are often the opposite of what is planned and imagined. Once the genie has been let out of the bottle, it cannot be returned and the stage is set for 'locked-in', path-dependent patterns, developing into the future and often the opposite of what were intended.

Some social scientists explore whether there will be a 'reversal' of many gains achieved in the 'rich North' over previous decades. A significant trend of social science writing, policy interventions, and filmic and literary thinking is a 'new catastrophism'. Some even talk of the future disappearance of western societies, drawing analogies between the fall of Roman and Mayan civilizations and the potential collapse of societies in the contemporary world, especially because of intersecting energy and environmental crises (Diamond 2005; see Chapter 3 below). One response to this fear for the future is that some of those working in Silicon Valley developed the Long Now Foundation to think about and plan very long-term futures (over the next 10,000 years; http://longnow.org).

Especially significant in this book is examining the power to make futures. A key question for social science is who or what owns the future – this capacity to own futures being central in how power works. I noted above that the future was once thought to be God's, with this belief powerfully constraining the growth of capitalism and the money economy (see Le Goff 1980). Making money from investing in the future through charging interest was forbidden in much of the world. But during the Middle Ages this restriction on trading in the future was relaxed within the Christian world, but not within Islam. In the 'west', trading the future rapidly became an activity from which much money could be made, and powerful interests were generated in and through trading the future.

Another important notion here is the sense of the future as a private matter that is cared about and nurtured by each individual person. So, although some aspects are similar to what others experience, each person hopes for, plans, plots and anticipates their own future. Much literature and many media representations presume the future is private and personal and no-one else's business. People in the 'modern' world are often exhorted to 'dream the impossible dream' especially to reinvent themselves (Elliott 2013). The implication then is that, if the impossible does not arrive, it is that person's own fault. Their dreams or their ambitions or their achievements were just not good enough.

In some recent formulations, it is presumed that the future is shared. It is often stated that the future is something owned together, and what 'we' want will somehow be realized. The future is public, held in common. All those in a society are said to participate in this common future. However, Jaron Lanier strongly disputes whether the future is such a commons, describing the power of large international computer companies, the 'server sirens' possessing 'ultra-influential' computers whereby information is turned into exceptional wealth. As Lanier writes: 'You can't see as much of the server as it can see of you' (2013: 63; Keen 2015).

The future is thus 'corporatized', especially by turning almost everything into a monetized commodity (Lewis 2015; Srnicek,

Williams 2015). One kind of future is that imagined and laid out by thinktanks and corporate futurists, particularly those working for Silicon Valley companies. This corporate world generates a kind of digital utopianism (Turner 2006). Lanier argues how this reflects the general corporate takeover of much of the world, especially since the growth of neo-liberal discourse and practice from around 1980, first within the US and Britain and then throughout much of the world (Klein 2007). Interestingly the Occupy movement challenged this corporatizing of the future through their counter-slogan 'Occupy the Future'; the malign power of large corporations is also a theme of much science fiction.

Future argument

Thus, thinking and planning futures is widespread, fateful and problematic. We have already seen that one problem lies in ignoring social science research and concepts, although almost all future visions concern ways in which social life and social institutions might or will be different. Such social characteristics are seen in much futures thinking as less significant than 'technologies' and their capacity to bend humans to their character. This book shows how it is necessary to avoid the Scylla of technological determinism of the future, but also the Charybdis of completely open futures. The future is neither fully determined, nor empty and open.

Moreover, thinking futures is a way of bringing back a way of planning, but under a new name. Issues are now so big and wicked that there has to be some planning of futures. But what is involved here cannot be termed 'planning' since that has become an ideologically contaminated term from the era of organized capitalism and social democracy. Such a notion was critiqued both from the communitarian/ecological left and from most of the right.

But thinking futures is necessary, given the many long-term processes involved in social futures. And once one is thinking futures, then public bodies and NGOs must be incorporated into the process. Indeed, they often have to be key coordinators within the processes of anticipating and making futures. It is hard to imagine developing policies to deal with, say, climate change without, in effect, 'planning' (as climate change sceptics are well aware). Thus within contemporary disorganized capitalism, futures thinking is a major way of bringing the state and civil society back in from the cold. Moreover, if we focus upon social futures, this forces a transcendence of both markets and technologies. 'Social futures' problematize both autonomous markets and the march of technology. They authorize the participation of a range of many relevant actors including states and civil society in making futures. Thinking and democratizing futures involves what we might call 'post-modern planning' in the contemporary era of civil society, global change, wicked problems, the limits of markets, multiple 'unknown unknowns' and so on.

We will also see below that it is necessary to distinguish between three kinds of futures: the probable, the possible, and the preferable – distinctions drawn from Wendell Bell (Bell, Wau 1971; see Kicker 2009). What is preferable may turn out to be the least probable. At the very least, that a particular future is preferable is no guarantee that it is the most probable. It is often presumed that, because a particular future is preferable to the present, then it will be realized, since the members of that society will see it has to be brought about. But there is no guarantee that what is best is what actually develops, even if there is widespread agreement in a given society that it is the most desirable of possible futures.

Part 1 of this book thus identifies and charts numerous ways in which organizations, writers, futurists, technologists and thinkers have anticipated, described, imagined and produced futures, including various utopias as well as dystopias. These various future visions and models of society, various 'past futures', are described and assessed in the next chapter. Some social futures are identified that have much contemporary resonance. Then Chapter 2 documents a striking change within the rich North from around the turn of the century, following the optimism for the future of the 'roaring' 1990s. This change in the structure of feeling, the 'new catastrophism' within contemporary social thought, is carefully documented. Central to deliberation about the future 'collapse of societies' was complexity thinking, especially in characterizing the cascading interplay between systems.

The second part turns directly to such complexity thinking in order to steer the tricky course between determinism and openness. Complexity analyses involve notions of path-dependence, lock-in, thresholds, positive feedback loops, tipping points and phase transitions. Systems are seen as dynamic, processual, unpredictable and interdependent. Particular emphasis is placed on shifts that recalibrate the balance, nature and functioning of economies and cultures in, and between, societies. They make the world different although no one necessarily planned or envisaged such a shift or even really noticed it at the time. This illustrates the wickedness of problems in the world of futures. These chapters explore the complex conditions for innovating new sociomaterial systems as well as assessing some of the main methods that have been developed to grasp different social futures.

In Part 3, some of these various methods and theories are deployed to examine what futures might develop within case-studies of uncertain, contested and socially powerful futures. In each, scenarios are developed. These case-studies concern the potential formation of global manufacturing and transportation in the light of the growth of 3D printing; changing forms of mobilities within cities in a potential post-carbon world; and the many futures implicated in global climate change. In these chapters, various scenarios are developed, and through backcasting the relative probabilities of different futures are assessed. Central to these chapters is the importance of complex systems thinking, multiple futures, and system lock-ins. They draw upon much social science and related domains of research.

In the concluding chapter, attention is directed to the future analyses of futures. It is shown that plausible futures must be analytically embedded within multiple social institutions, practices and movements. Complexity thinking should be deployed to examine futures made up of unstable, complex and interdependent adaptive systems. There are powerful physical and social systems, and yet they are also fragile and often characterized by innovation, unpredictability and possible reversal. And thinking futures makes one understand that things could be otherwise, that outcomes are not necessarily determined and hence there is the need to develop capacities for future-forming interdisciplinary research (see www.lancaster.ac.uk/social-futures). The chapter details the many unintended, perverse and wicked problems that arise in examining, making and assessing multiple futures, as this book documents.

PART 1

A BRIEF HISTORY OF THE FUTURE

2

Past Futures

Introduction

Although it is impossible to 'know' what the future has in store for us, most recorded societies developed procedures and discourses through which they believed the future could be anticipated, talked about and in some sense known. And this is so whether that perceived future was in the hands of gods or humans. People imagined, predicted, divined, prophesied and told many different futures, good and bad.

How these assemblages of the future were achieved tells us much about a society's workings. The forms of future anticipation have many implications for the nature of each society and especially regarding how relations of power are structured and flow. A key element of power is thus power to determine – to produce – the future, out of the many ways it is imagined, organized, materialized and distributed. Science fiction author William Gibson reputedly said: 'The future is already here – it's just not very evenly distributed.'

This chapter begins with a short history of how the 'future' has been told, by whom and with what consequences. It then examines 'social futures', presenting a short account of utopian and dystopian future societies. This history sets out many themes encountered in subsequent chapters which concern the complex issues of imagining future *societies* and not just the future fate of a particular person or institution.

Telling the future

In most known societies, the future has been extensively imagined and foretold. Often these processes of future-making were entrusted to 'specialists of the future', these varying across different historical and geographical contexts. Such specialists included prophets, diviners, seers, oracles, witches, technologists, sages, astrologers, clairvoyants, novelists, wizards, futurologists, fortune tellers and so on. These specialists often drew upon specific bodies of 'expert' knowledge, often a mix of the spiritual and secular. Those believed to be able to foretell the future through recourse to a body of expert knowledge were much sought after and well rewarded. These future specialists have also been heavily punished if their anticipation of the future presented 'bad news' for the powerful, or if the future they prophesied turned out to be 'mistaken'.

Moreover, the evidence for what the nature of the future will be has often been highly contested; most belief systems built in mechanisms to explain why the predicted outcome did not on a particular occasion materialize, without this failure undermining the overall system of beliefs. This is true even in the case of scientific theories which purport to predict the future results of an experiment but which can often be 'rescued' if the anticipated future does not occur in the laboratory or field site. This process of saving the prediction is a key issue in the philosophy of science and especially in whether a failed prediction should lead to the 'falsification' of the overall theory, as Karl Popper famously advocated (see Lakatos, Musgrave 1970).

Some foretelling of the future related to what was expected to happen to particular individuals in a society, especially monarchs, emperors or corporate leaders, who often employed their personal teller of the future. Other anticipated futures related to the future fortunes of most people, often through systems of astrology, clairvoyance or fortune telling. Some future telling involved prophesying potential large-scale religious, spiritual or earthly events, often lying far off in a distant future. A few futures have been 'good news', a possible utopia. Others told of terrible catastrophes – as in 'the end of the world is nigh' – which were often designed to transform the present through warning of the terrors of what would ensue if humans did not act in radically different ways.

There are hundreds of ways of telling the future (Adam, Groves 2007: chs. 1, 2). Methods have ranged from interpreting people's dreams to observing the state of the human liver, which in Mesopotamia was seen as the seat of life.

In much Greek mythology, fate was thought to be pre-set. Although oracles, such as the one at Delphi, were believed to know the future, they could not intervene and change what was going to happen. Much Greek mythology was based on the tragedy of those knowing the future but not being able to change it (Adam, Groves 2007: 4–5). Cassandra famously forewarned the Trojans not to accept the Greek gift of the Trojan horse but she was ignored, and Greek troops inside the wooden horse captured Troy. Although Cassandra knew what was going to happen, she could not prevent these tragic events. In Chapter 9, I examine other examples where people believe they know the future of global climate change but where this is widely ignored; this is sometimes seen as a contemporary example of the 'Cassandra syndrome'.

Druidic interpretations of the future have been historically significant. Druids drew inspiration from bird flight, the shape of clouds, particular trees and other features of the natural world. Based upon a long period of specialized training, Druids were regarded as prophets and magicians, many becoming influential royal advisers. It was believed that Druids could read minds and predict future events using sophisticated powers of prophecy and magic. There are some parallels with today's reading of 'strange weather', which climate scientists increasingly take as evidence of future climate change, this resting upon their arcane customs (Szerszynski 2010).

In many societies, key texts were crucial in prophesying the future. The Old Testament told of many events that would come to pass, including those occurring in Christ's life, while prophecies of the end of the world were frequent within the New Testament. Prophets were thought to draw their authority to know the future through privileged access to the word of God. Many disagreements occurred as to whether particular prophets possessed this power to know God's word.

The most common predictions of human fate were based on astrology, on the movement of stars and of the gods associated with those stars. Indian, Chinese and Mayan cultures developed elaborate systems for predicting events on earth drawn from such celestial observations. In the west, astrology most often consisted of a system of horoscopes used to interpret aspects of an individual's personality. Future events were predicted based upon the position of the sun, moon and other celestial objects at the time that a person was born. Most professional astrologers relied upon these systems (see www.astrology.org.uk). And for almost all its history, astrology was considered to be a scholarly tradition interconnected with similar scientific systems such as astronomy, alchemy, meteorology and medicine. Even after astronomy developed, the power of astrology over the past two millennia has been striking. There has been much debate about the astrological predictions that were made by the sixteenth-century seer Nostradamus, who supposedly foresaw many wars, earthquakes and other disasters in the future (see the amusing www.nostradamus.org).

There are thus some powerful discourses involved in prophesying or divining the future. Most of these prophecies related to what will happen to individuals in the future, to telling the fortunes of particular people. They involved individuals gaining knowledge of what the gods or fate had in store for them or for other individuals. It was thought that such futures could be known but mostly not altered, even if people were aware of their likely fate.

Some social futures

Over the past few centuries, more complex accounts of possible futures appeared, considering here mainly European examples. These often presented quite detailed analyses of future societies. Moreover, they often sought to change what was happening in the present through warnings or inducements. Some accounts of the future became enduring classics of western literature, reflecting in part the historical period in which they were written. These tales constructed models of future societies, of utopian and dystopian worlds. Some terms in these texts entered language, and they structure lay and social scientific discourses about futures, often centuries after the texts originally appeared.

It has been argued that utopian writing could only emerge once the apparent certainties of the mediaeval period began to dissolve. From the sixteenth century onwards, it became possible to assess and critique how society as a whole was organized (Kumar 1987, 1991). Some key texts began to develop this, beginning with Thomas More's *Utopia* (1516; reprinted Andrews 1901). This was the first work that described a whole alternative society rather than just the ideal version of one element. *Utopia* was published just after Machiavelli's *The Prince*. This birth of a modern utopia occurred 500 years ago (1516) as a single Christianity was beginning to fragment through the Reformation that convulsed the Catholic Church across Europe (Kumar 1987: 22).

Anticipating social thought written in subsequent centuries, Thomas More details the City of Man, not the City of God. In this, he initiates a new literary genre and 'method' for thinking futures. *Utopia* is a description of a roughly egalitarian society in full operation. Writing rather like a modern social scientist, More describes in *Utopia* the 'mutual intercourse of this people, their commerce, and the rules by which all things are distributed between them' (Andrews 1901: 173).

The island of Utopia is made up of 54 roughly uniform cities, each constituted of 6,000 households with 10 to 16 adults. In order that numbers are roughly even, populations are re-distributed between households and towns. If the island experiences overpopulation, new colonies are established elsewhere. There is only one way to access the island of Utopia, serving as both entrance and exit.

There is no private property on Utopia, goods are stored in warehouses and people request what they need and when. In this society, need, not income, is the main basis of the economy. Work is undertaken so as to create useful products; and wasteful luxury items are not produced. There is no unnecessary work. Women do roughly the same work as men. Unemployment is eradicated, and the length of the working day is no more than 6 hours. There are also free hospitals, euthanasia, priests are allowed to marry, and divorce is permitted. Interestingly, meals are taken in community dining halls, with cooking being undertaken by different households in turn. There is uniform clothing. Such a utopia is seen as safe, with no locks being needed on the houses. The ownership of houses rotates between citizens every ten years.

Travel on the island is possible if 'any man has a mind to visit his friends that live in some other town, or desires to travel and see the rest of the country' (Andrews 1901: 178). This presents a 'modern' orientation to travel, in which friendship and the desire to gaze on other places are seen as legitimate reasons for it. In Utopia people are granted the means of travel, the provisions for the journey and an internal passport. Anyone found without a passport will be returned to their home. Privacy in Utopia is not regarded as freedom; there are no taverns and places for private gatherings. Everyone remains in full view of everyone else and is obliged to behave well. Centuries later, Jane Jacobs referred to the importance within effective urban design and regulation of there being 'eyes on the street' (1992[1961]).

The toleration of other religious ideas is enshrined in a universal prayer that all Utopians recite. But scholars can become the ruling officials or priests, and there are slaves. Overall, Utopians detest war. If they feel that countries friendly to them have been wronged, they will send military aid. However, they try to capture rather than kill their enemies. Utopians are upset if victory is achieved through bloodshed. The main purpose of war is to achieve the state that would have obtained if there had been no war.

Most commentators consider More's *Utopia* as the founding text in a significant line of 'social futures', Marx interestingly praising More as a 'communist hero'. By contrast, H. G. Wells considered Francis Bacon's *New Atlantis*, published a century later in 1627, as the first modern Utopia (Andrews 1901; Kumar 1987: 198–9).

New Atlantis described the customs found on a utopian island and especially in its state-sponsored scientific institution, Salomon's House, viewed as the eye of the kingdom. Here there are many instruments, processes and methods of scientific research. In one scene from the New Atlantis, the Head of Salomon's House shows a European visitor the scientific background, with experiments conducted using the Baconian method. These experiments are designed to understand and conquer nature and then to apply that knowledge to improve society.

Somewhat similar views were developed by the eighteenth-century scientist the Marquis de Condorcet. He gazed into the 'ocean of futurity' and anticipated the development of a progressive future world that would be based upon equality, enlightenment and societies orchestrated under the benign direction of a world body of scientists (Kumar 1987: 44). Science would dynamically develop as a collective force, transforming and improving the world.

More generally, the novelist Anatole France wrote of the positive power of utopian thinking. He maintained that: 'Without the Utopians of other times, men would still live in caves, miserable and naked...Out of generous dreams come beneficial realities. Utopia is the principle of all progress, and the essay into a better future' (quoted Mumford 1922: 22). Before the nineteenth century, the future was rarely understood as a very different place, as an undiscovered country. But during the nineteenth century, many ideas were developed, with detailed visions of future utopias emerging (Armytage 1968). Most futurists saw the dynamic role of new science and technology and especially the way that steam engines and electricity would enable progress to a different and better future world (Kumar 1987: ch. 1; Morus 2014).

Some utopias were seen as close to being realized, rather than far off in the distant future. Examples included Marx's notion of 'true communism' stemming from class struggle, as well as the free market utopia of John Bright and Richard Cobden (Kumar 1987: 46–9). Robert Owen's early nineteenth-century development of a model factory village in New Lanark in Scotland was especially significant. This 'real utopia' in turn spawned other utopias over the century. Owen's account of New Lanark Mills was entitled *A New View of Society* (1970[1813/14]). He critiqued the competitive and alienating character of industrial capitalism and advocated instead relatively small 'Villages of Cooperation'. Each such village had a population of around 1,000. In such communities there were large public buildings, cooperatives, playgrounds, public kitchens, lecture rooms and schools. Owen thought these villages of cooperation would help ameliorate the 'depreciating' effects of new technologies and machines (Owen 1970[1813/14]: 53; see Wright 2010, on some recent 'real utopias' many of them being similarly small in scale).

A related late nineteenth-century utopia was William Morris's *News from Nowhere*, which presents a vision of the ideal society (1890). In this imagined society, a literal *Nowhere*, people are freed from the burdens of industrialization and find harmony in their organic coexistence with the natural world. Morris saw machinery as reducing some of the more painful aspects of labour although he does not presume any transformation of the domestic division of tasks. People's material surroundings are described as pleasant, generous and beautiful, a kind of pastoral and simple idyll (Levitas 2013: 80). In discussing William Morris, Levitas distinguishes between utopia as a closed system and utopia as an heuristic device for examining and critiquing contemporary societies (2013: 114–15). According to Levitas, even Morris's method of writing and publishing emphasized openness and participation rather than a fixed and closed utopian blueprint.

Other nineteenth-century utopias presented much more dynamic visions of future worlds, some especially involving extensive travel, adventure and movement. Examples included H. G. Wells's account of 'time travel' and a 'world brain', and Jules Verne's *Around the World in Eighty Days* (2008[1873]). Other visions of the future presented conflicts between mankind and a more advanced extraterrestrial race that is thought to live elsewhere on earth or in space. H. G. Wells's *The War of the Worlds* was the first example of this genre and generated many subsequent books and other mediated visions (2005[1898]).

Most nineteenth-century works were broadly optimistic about the power and progressive quality of advances in science and technology, the iconic 1851 Great Exhibition in London displaying such a utopian vision. Oscar Wilde famously wrote at the turn of the century that: 'a map of the world which does not include Utopia is not worth even glancing at, for it leaves out the one country at which Humanity is always landing' (2001[1900]: 141). H. G. Wells was described as 'utopianism incarnate' (Kumar 1987: ch. 6, on much variation in his writings). He thought sociology should examine the utopian, since 'Sociology is the description of the Ideal Society and its relation to existing societies' (Wells 1914: 200).

This description of the ideal society is illustrated in Wells's *A Modern Utopia* (2011[1905]). He contrasts this modern utopia with older static notions – for him utopia is full of change and innovation. He conceived of world-wide mobility with vast trains moving above the earth at 200–300 miles per hour (Kumar 1987: 194). The utopia cannot be static. There are no reasons for privacy, with language, coinage, customs and laws all shared. There is a world state which is the sole landowner and which owns all sources of energy. Humanity is almost entirely liberated from physical labour. Design is efficient, simple and functional. The scientific spirit pervades the social organization of this utopia. Few limits are placed upon the invasion of human life by machines drawn from the latest developments in science and technology. There is an index of the world population kept in a vast building, with a record card documenting much information about each individual, including their patterns of travel.

However, H. G. Wells's *The Invisible Man* presents a much less optimistic vision. Here the perverted scientist Griffin discovers the secret of invisibility and this enables his paranoid pursuit of total power (Kumar 1987: 184–5). This unintended power of the machine over humans was an enduring theme in many anticipated futures, following Mary Shelley's early nineteenth-century story of the monstrous figure created by Swiss scientist Victor Frankenstein (2000[1818]). Frankenstein conducts experiments within the very new space of the scientific laboratory. He rejects the laws of nature regarding how life is naturally created. In the laboratory he creates a new person – the subtitle of the story being *The Modern Prometheus*. However, Frankenstein is horrified at what he assembles from diverse body parts. He abandons his creation but then gets punished by it. This theme of the 'scientific monster' created by human activity that then goes wildly out of control and returns to haunt its creator is found in much subsequent science fiction, such as the classic *Blade Runner* (film first released in 1982).

Mary Shelley's *The Last Man*, set at the end of the twenty-first century, is often said to be the first work of 'apocalyptic' fiction. The novel describes a group of survivors struggling to live with a plague rapidly spreading from country to country (1826). Shelley describes the 'vast cities of America, the fertile plains of Hindostan, the crowded abodes of the Chinese, are menaced with utter ruin. Where late the busy multitudes assembled for pleasure or profit, now only the sound of wailing and misery is heard. The air is empoisoned, and each human being inhales death' (www.gutenberg.org/cache/epub/18247/pg18247-images.html).

The problematic relationship between humans and machines was also elaborated in Samuel Butler's *Erewhon*, and especially 'The book of the machines' (Butler 2005[1872]), appearing soon after Charles Darwin's *On the Origin of Species*. Butler warned that when it comes to the survival of the fittest, human beings may one day lose control over the machines that they themselves created. He argued that the human body in its present shape took many millions of years to emerge. It did not develop nearly as rapidly as modern machines were advancing; there seem no limits to their rate of improvement. Butler warned that one day machines might develop the capacity for 'thought', or what we would now term artificial intelligence.

Machines were seen as potentially evolving, self-organizing and able to take over the world. Butler presciently wrote: 'what I fear is the extraordinary rapidity with which they are becoming something very different to what they are at present. No class of beings have in any time past made so rapid a movement forward. Should not that movement be jealously watched, and checked while we can still check it?' (2005[1872]: ch. 13; Armytage 1968: 52–4). In the society of Erewhon (anagram of *nowhere*), the anti-mechanists did rise up in revolt and destroyed the machines. Butler maintained that it was necessary to eliminate the more advanced machines being developed at the end of the nineteenth century.

E. M. Forster also presented a future world where science and technology enslave humans to machines, or what he calls the Machine. The brilliant short story 'The Machine stops' describes a future society with many echoes in subsequent science fiction and in the digital worlds that have developed since the mid-1990s (1985[1909]). This story was partly designed as a counter-blast to Wells' positive anticipation of machine civilization and a world-state (see analysis in Foster 2015: 217–21).

Forster describes a future characterized by atomized and immobile people whose lives are governed by the Machine. More or less everyone lives under the ground in tiny isolated cells and communicates across the world through the Machine. There are some airships but mostly people do not physically travel since they have no need to meet other people. Everyone is totally dependent on the Machine, with the one remaining physical book *The Book of the Machine* published by the Central Committee of this world society.

These people living under the ground in cells are unable to touch or smell others or have any sense of space. Since there is almost no travel, people connect via the threads of the Machine, so enabling aural and visual contact with the thousands of others that each person appears to 'know' (rather like today's Facebook links). What is described as the 'clumsy system of public gatherings' (meetings) has long since been abandoned. Some letters are transmitted through the 'pneumatic post', similar to systems found in shops in the first half of the twentieth century, but mostly life *is* the Machine. Forster presents a persuasive dark future.

Like almost everyone else, the central character, Vashti, is repulsed by the surface of the earth and is unable to comprehend life beyond the Machine. Her room contains nothing much but buttons which, when pressed, deliver water, heat, music, clothing, food and especially communications with others. As a result, Forster writes, she is 'in touch with all that she cared for in the world' (1985[1909]: 111). She is described as a 'swaddled lump of flesh…with a face as white as a fungus' (1985[1909]: 108). She never leaves her tiny room, never gets into the fresh air, never does any exercise and is what we now call morbidly obese. And, like most others in this society except her 'son' and a few others, Vashti is perfectly content with this dependence upon the Machine. All are contented participants in a Machine-organized life.

Forster would appear to have foreseen a kind of internet, although the Machine is described in mechanical rather than digital terms. He describes how research in this society involves re-digesting what people already know from the vast archives of the Machine – what we now describe as the internet or the Cloud. In this society, researchers are not allowed to go to the surface of the earth in order to conduct research. One lecturer justified the recycling of ideas: 'beware of first-hand ideas…generation is being formed that is "absolutely colorless"' (Forster 1985[1909]: 131). Rather like the web, the Machine cannot communicate nuances of expression, only a general idea of others that is said to be 'good enough' for practical purposes (Forster 1985[1909]: 110; see Carr 2010, on the digital shallowing of experience).

But, one day, her son contacts Vashti's and asks her to go and speak to him. He emphasizes that this communication should be undertaken 'not through the wearisome Machine'. Reluctantly, Vashti undertakes a two-day airship journey to the other side of the earth to talk with her son, a most unusual event (Forster 1985[1909]: 109).

As with the world presented by Forster, people today are enmeshed by the power of the Machine, by the billions of connections through the internet of things (www.brookings.edu/blogs/techtank/posts/2015/06/9-future-of-iot-part-2). There is a machine-dependence, and if the Machine fails then civilization will break down. Without the internet, there would be no food, water, phone calls, credit card payments or communications. Somewhat similarly to Forster, Nye writes, of today, 'Subtract electricity [or oil or computers] for more than one week from the networks sustaining American cities and suburbs, and they risk becoming uninhabitable' (2010: 131; Foster 2015: 219).

At the culmination of Forster's story, a terrible Machine failure in fact occurs. All power breaks down, food ceases to arrive and air no longer circulates. Vashti is horrified when she looks outside her cubicle during the Machine's final days. She sees people crawling about a catacomb of tombs. They are screaming, whimpering, gasping for breath, touching each other. These earthy bodies repel her – this is her worst nightmare. She closes the door and sits waiting for the end. There are horrible cracks and rumblings. The light begins to ebb and she realizes that civilization's long day is closing as power grinds to a halt. Society collapses as it is no longer powered up with sufficient energy (Urry 2014b).

But her dying son has told her that the Homeless are waiting on the surface of the earth – what we now call the multitude (Hardt, Negri 2006). These, excluded by the party, are hiding in the mist and ferns and waiting for the end of the Machine. And they are ready to start afresh, waiting to recapture life, to touch, to talk, to sense, but not through the ubiquitous Machine whose time has ended (Forster 1985: 139–40). The story finishes with this possibility of human redemption that can only be achieved beyond the Machine, by those who have been cast out on the margins, away from the Machine. John Foster uses this idea to argue that 'hope for a human future lies in those who have been able to see it for what it is, and who have maintained in spite of it their contact with the *essential* wild' (2015: 221).

A contrasting dystopia to Forster's is Aldous Huxley's *Brave New World* (1991[1932]). Huxley was struck when visiting the US in 1926 by how a population could be rendered docile through mass advertising, psychological conditioning, consumerism and hedonism. He also presumed that scientific advance would eventually give powers to humans that were previously the preserve of gods. The World State of *Brave New World* is built upon the principles of Henry Ford's assembly line: mass production, homogeneity, predictability and consuming new consumer goods. America, he thought, is the future – but a terrifying future. Ford is revered as the deity of this new society, and 'Fordism' is its ideology. The conveyor belt of production is producing not only goods as developed by Henry Ford, but also human beings. The principle of mass production is being applied to human biology (Kumar 1987: 245).

Huxley describes how, from birth, citizens are conditioned to value consuming goods. Constant consumption and near-universal employment to meet material demands are the basis of a stable World State. There is also mass production of children through what we now know as in-vitro fertilization. Huxley describes how child development works to ensure that children have carefully controlled capacities, so enabling them to fit without complaint into one or other of the five castes of this world. Children are subjected to Pavlovian conditioning from birth, nobody gets ill, everyone has the same lifespan (about sixty years, at which point they painlessly die), there is no marriage or sexual fidelity, and wars are no more.

Thus, there is a benevolent dictatorship in which subjects are programmed to enjoy their subjugation through various kinds of conditioning and the drug soma. This hallucinogenic drug developed by the World State ensures that users enjoy hangover-free holidays. The rulers of *Brave New World* thus solve the problem of making people love their servitude. Huxley subsequently wrote that: 'In *Brave New World* non-stop distractions of the most fascinating nature...are deliberately used as instruments of policy, for the purpose of preventing people from paying too much attention to the realities of their social and political situation' (1965[1958]: 36–7). Overall, Huxley feared that people would be provided with so much entertainment, consumerism and drug-induced intoxication that everyone would be rendered passive and happy, unaware that they were in effect 'controlled'. The film *The Truman Show* (1998), in which the lead character lives in a perfect reality TV show, is a contemporary version of *Brave New World*. Many later commentators developed Huxley's idea that consumerism is the new opium of the masses.

The control of the population occurs somewhat differently in perhaps the greatest dystopian novel, Orwell's *Nineteen Eighty-Four* (2008[1949]). On the first page, Winston Smith observes the ubiquitous posters that state 'Big Brother is watching you.' Surveillance of the population occurs through what are called 'telescreens' located in people's residences and offices (apart from those of the powerless proles who make up 85 per cent of the population).

This tele-screen functions as both a television/computer screen for people watching in their rooms *and* as the means by which the state observes and hears all that happens within each room (see http://rt.com/uk/230699-samsung-tv-listens-privacy, on how this is actually now possible). As with contemporary CCTV cameras, there is no way of knowing whether one is being watched. Residents are located in an electronic panopticon. Orwell presciently writes: 'You had to live – did live, from habit that became instinct – in the assumption that every sound you made was overheard, and except in darkness, every movement scrutinised' (2008[1949]: 5). And there is what is called 'face-crime' – this is the adoption of an improper expression on one's face when watching the tele-screen as ever more improbable facts get transmitted (Orwell 2008[1949]: 65).

Prefiguring what is now understood as voice recognition software, Orwell also describes how almost all writing involves dictating into the 'speak-write' machine. Writing by hand has become more or less redundant. There are even novel-writing machines.

When Smith is at work in the Ministry of Truth, various pneumatic tubes supply hard copies (as we would say) of the texts that are read on screen. He then marks up the hard copies, such as newspaper reports, changing texts to rewrite history. These are then sent back down the pneumatic tubes. Incidentally, when pneumatic tubes first came into use in the late nineteenth century, they symbolized technological progress and it was widely thought they would become ubiquitous. Jules Verne's dystopic *Paris in the Twentieth Century* describes suspended pneumatic tube trains stretching across the oceans (1996[1863 but not published until 1994]). Others envisaged submarine tubes carrying people faster than aircraft, while some analysts thought that food might be supplied to each home along pneumatic tubes.

When Winston Smith sets out to produce a diary, he writes by hand in a notebook using an old-fashioned pen. He does this so there is no record in the speak-write of what he is trying to write. Writing a diary is not itself illegal since there are no laws, Orwell here alluding to the lack of the rule of law in Fascist countries or in the Soviet Union. *Nineteen Eighty-Four* was written between

1946 and 1948 in the era of totalitarian one-party rule in which the distorting power of propaganda was becoming clear. Orwell critiques the various technologies of propaganda and control. Subsequently, we have grown familiar with the idea that modern states and corporations deploy versions of Newspeak.

Orwell writes of how Newspeak is designed to '*diminish* the range of thought, and this purpose was indirectly assisted by cutting the choice of words down to a minimum' (2008[1949]: 313). One consequence of systematic word-elimination is that all sorts of 'facts' fade away into a 'shadow-world' (Orwell 2008[1949]: 44, 290). This is similar to the way that people disappear in *Nineteen Eighty-Four* and get immediately written out of history by officials. In the end, Winston Smith, working for the Ministry of Truth, is himself written out of history.

According to Orwell, the goal of this society is power itself – to establish and sustain the dictatorship, the society ruled by the priests of power. And this power is realized by controlling people's minds. People do not know who the members of that regime of power are. Winston Smith is subjected to a seven-year period of surveillance. After a prolonged struggle, at the end he is a broken man. He wins the victory over himself by happily learning to love Big Brother, and finally proclaims that two and two do indeed make five (Orwell 2008: 311). *Nineteen Eighty-Four* dissects mechanisms though which power will be organized in the future, and especially the dangerous role new surveillance 'technologies' play in probable new worlds of power.

The final dystopic future here derives from a different genre: Charlotte Perkins Gilman's short story 'Yellow wallpaper' (1892; www.publicbookshelf.com/romance/wallpaper/yellow-wallpaper). This story is also concerned with confinement and control, but where the confinement is exercised by the narrator's husband. The story depicts the effects of being confined upon the narrator's mental health and her consequential descent into psychosis. With nothing to stimulate her, she becomes obsessed by the pattern and colour of the yellow wallpaper in the room where she is staying and from which, because of her husband's power, she cannot escape. At the end, she imagines there are women creeping around behind the wallpaper pattern and believes that she is one of them. She locks herself in the room, now the only place where she feels safe, and refuses to leave. Subsequent feminist science fiction examines many parallel accounts of patriarchal confinement and the possibilities of alternative 'feminist' futures.

Conclusion

So, I have set out here some brief moments in imagining futures that developed in the English language up to the middle of the last century. The chapter examined various 'social futures', presenting a short history of anticipating utopian and dystopian future societies. It established many themes that are developed in subsequent chapters engaging with how to imagine future societies.

Although it is impossible to 'know' what the future has in store for us, most societies thus developed procedures and discourses through which the future could be anticipated, talked about and in some sense known, whether that perceived future was in the hands of gods or of humans. People have imagined, predicted, divined, prophesied and told the future. These forms of future anticipation in the past – what can be termed 'past futures' – provide some key terms and issues in subsequent future-making. The second chapter in Part 1 explores an astonishing number of new dystopic futures that emerged in the early years of the current century. We thus turn to the new catastrophism in social thought.

3

New Catastrophic Futures

Economic growth and its other

During the 1990s in the 'west', it seemed that a new bright future was coming into being. This was an optimistic utopic globalization based upon the rapidly increasing movement of money, people, ideas, images, information and objects. This scale of movement and strong economic growth were seen as transforming societies through notions of a shared planet, new businesses, international friendship, cosmopolitan polities, international understanding and a greater openness of information and communications. This was an increasingly borderless world with new experiences, technologies, products, travel-possibilities and opportunities (Ohmae 1990). Especially significant was the digital utopianism of the web that led to unexpected virtual worlds and very many novel economic and social opportunities (Turner 2006).

This 1990s 'global optimism' promised a progressive open future. Joseph Stiglitz talked of the 'roaring [nineteen] nineties' in the west (2004, 2007). Having 'won' the Cold War, the west set about making the rest of the world into a utopia of borderlessness, global consumerism and choice, with food, products, bodies, places, services, friends, family and experiences set out for display, purchase and use. It looked like for many in the west and elsewhere, economic growth and a borderless world were here to stay.

But the 1990s were not in fact the harbinger of such a long-term, optimistic and borderless utopia. The 1990s were more like a *fin de siècle*, of intense opulence and decadence, combined with the anticipation of doom-laden catastrophe. And catastrophe arrived on 11 September 2001 with the dramatic attack on the Twin Towers of the New York World Trade Center (as well as the dotcom crash of 2000–2). This mediatized ending of the decadent 'roaring nineties' and its utopic imaginary in turn engendered various apocalyptic visions for the new century. The images of New York on 11 September were more dystopic than had ever been created in the mass media (Urry 2002). But those images were soon surpassed by another dystopia engendered by the 'shock and awe' bombing of Baghdad at the beginning of the Iraq War in 2003. Former US Private Roy Scranton described his personal experience of this bombing as literally being present at 'the end of the world' (2013).

It thus turned out that there are many dark dystopic sides to globalization. Migrating across borders are terrorists rejecting a utopia of western choice, environmental risks, military power, medical pandemics, trafficked women, drug smuggling, international crime, outsourced work, slave trading, pornography, asylum seekers, gambling, smuggled workers, movements of waste, financial risks and vast untaxed flows of money. Each of these flows has been documented by new kinds of 'mobile' research (Urry 2014a; see Kloppenburg 2013 on drug smuggling).

The significance of these flows came to engender what can be termed a 'new catastrophism' in social thinking. A torrent of social science dystopic analysis developed, much loosely based upon a complex systems perspective. The 'causes' of catastrophe lie with the systemic and often perverse effects of human activities as these cascade across financial, climate, religious, food, water, security and energy systems (Walby 2015).

Especially important here are long-term shifts in societies – what Fernand Braudel described as the 'longue durée' – counterposing these to a short-term focus upon events. Braudel talks of 'history whose passage is almost imperceptible, that of man [*sic*] in relationship to his environment, a history in which all change is slow, a history of constant repetition' (1972: 20). Historical shifts are often only identifiable in retrospect. What turn out to be tectonic shifts in the fault lines of society are often only noticed well after the shifts started to occur. We should not be taken in by the confusion of events but focus upon long-term and often imperceptible shifts.

And these long-term shifts can involve what Raymond Williams termed 'structures of feeling'. He explains:

> 'feeling' is chosen to emphasize a distinction from more formal concepts of 'world view' or 'ideology'. It is not only that we must go beyond formally held and systematic beliefs . . . we are concerned with meanings and values as they are actively lived and felt . . . not feeling against thought, but thought as felt and feeling as thought: practical consciousness of a present kind, in a living and interrelating continuity. We are then defining these elements as a 'structure': as a set, with specific, internal relations, at once interlocking and in tension. (Williams 1977: 132)

Thus, a crucial difficulty in anticipating futures lies in long-term shifts in structures of feeling, of thought as felt and feeling as thought. So when I argue for seeing futures as 'social', it is also to emphasize how there can be changes over the *longue durée*, tectonic shifts in the structures of feeling that are often hard to identify by those living through that particular period. Although few notice such changes as they occur, these may nevertheless turn out to have long-term consequences. (See Turner 2006, on some of these tectonic shifts since World War II.)

Such structures of feeling are a bit like 'dark matter', which is said to be by far the commonest feature of the universe. Such dark matter cannot be observed but it affects other matter through gravitational pull. Analogously, changes in the structure of feeling affect the power of social groups and social institutions and yet are hard to identity, document and – especially – measure. Anticipations of the future depend on identifying shifts in the *longue durée*, particularly in the structures of feeling which, like dark matter, can alter the gravitational pull of different systems and hence the power, weight and significance of social institutions, groups and practices.

I thus suggest that a striking change of the structure of feeling or *Zeitgeist* within the rich North emerges after the optimism of the roaring 1990s was blown away. This long-term catastrophism within much social and scientific thought can be seen in many texts dating from 2003 onwards. In the English-language world, these include: *Our Final Century* (Rees 2003), *Collapse: How Societies Choose to Fail or Survive* (Diamond 2005), *Catastrophes and Lesser Calamities: The Causes of Mass Extinctions* (Hallam 2005), *The Party's Over: Oil, War and the Fate of Industrial Society* (Heinberg 2005), *The Next World War: Tribes, Cities, Nations, and Ecological Decline* (Woodbridge 2005), *The Upside of Down: Catastrophe, Creativity, and the Renewal of Civilization* (Homer-Dixon 2006), *The Long Emergency: Surviving the Converging Catastrophes of the 21st Century* (Kunstler 2006), *The Revenge of Gaia* (Lovelock 2006), *Global Catastrophes: A Very Short Introduction* (McGuire 2006), *Heat: How to Stop the Planet from Burning* (Monbiot 2006), *When the Rivers Run Dry* (Pearce 2006), *The Suicidal Planet: How to Prevent Global Climate Catastrophe* (Hillman, Fawcett, Raja 2007), *The Shock Doctrine: The Rise of Disaster Capitalism* (Klein 2007), *Field Notes from a Catastrophe: A Frontline Report on Climate Change* (Kolbert 2007), *Winds of Change: Climate, Weather and the Destruction of Civilizations* (Linden 2007), *Dirt: The Erosion of Civilizations* (Montgomery 2007), *With Speed and Violence: Why Scientists Fear Tipping Points in Climate Change* (Pearce 2007), *The Next Catastrophe* (Perrow 2007), *The Eye of the Storm: An Integral Perspective on Sustainable Development and Climate Change Response* (Riedy 2007), *The Last Oil Shock* (Strahan 2007), *An Uncertain Future: Law Enforcement, National Security and Climate Change* (Abbott 2008), *Climatic Cataclysm: The Foreign Policy and National Security Implications of Climate Change* (Campbell 2008), *Reinventing Collapse: The Soviet Example and American Prospects* (Orlov 2008), *Global Catastrophes and Trends: The Next Fifty Years* (Smil 2008), *World at Risk* (Beck 2009), *Time's Up! An Uncivilized Solution to a Global Crisis* (Farnish 2009), *Hot, Flat and Crowded* (Friedman 2009), *Why We Disagree About Climate Change* (Hulme 2009), *Down to the Wire: Confronting Climate Collapse* (Orr 2009), *The Empathic Civilization: The Race to Global Consciousness in a World in Crisis* (Rifkin 2009), *Climate Refugees* (Collectif Argos 2010), *Requiem for a Species* (Hamilton 2010), *The Post-Carbon Reader* (Heinberg, Lerch 2010), *The Vanishing Face of Gaia: A Final Warning* (Lovelock 2010), *Fool's Gold: How Unrestrained Greed Corrupted a Dream, Shattered Global Markets and Unleashed a Catastrophe* (Tett 2010), *Storms of my Grandchildren: The Truth about the Coming Climate Catastrophe and*

Our Last Chance to Save Humanity (Hansen 2011), *Tropic of Chaos* (Parenti 2011), *Living in the End Times: Updated New Edition* (Žižek 2011), *Convergence of Catastrophes* (Faye 2012), *The Great Disruption: How the Climate Crisis Will Transform the Global Economy* (Gilding 2012), *The Burning Question: We Can't Burn Half the World's Oil, Coal and Gas. So How Do We Quit?* (Berners-Lee, Clark 2013), *Unburnable Carbon 2013: Wasted Capital and Stranded Assets* (Carbon Tracker 2013), *Does Capitalism Have a Future?* (Wallerstein, Collins, Mann, Derluguian, Calhoun 2013), *The Knowledge: How to Rebuild our World from Scratch* (Dartnell 2014), *Crisis Without End? The Unravelling of Western Prosperity* (Gamble 2014), *This Changes Everything: Capitalism vs. the Climate* (Klein 2014), *After Fukushima: The Equivalence of Catastrophes* (Nancy 2014), *The Collapse of Western Civilization: A View from the Future* (Oreskes, Conway 2014), *The Resilience Dividend: Being Strong in a World Where Things Go Wrong* (Rodin 2014), *The Sixth Extinction: An Unnatural History* (Kolbert 2015), *In Catastrophic Times: Resisting the Coming Barbarism* (Stengers 2015) and *Crime and the Imaginary of Disaster: Post-Apocalyptic Fictions and the Crisis of Social Order* (Yar 2015).

Over the same period various universities established research centres/programmes concerned with the potential collapse of human societies. These include The Centre for the Study of Existential Risk in Cambridge (see http://cser.org/resources-reading; www.newstatesman.com/sci-tech/2014/09/apocalypse-soon-scientists-preparing-end-times), Oxford's Future of Humanity Institute (www.fhi.ox.ac.uk) and Princeton's Global Systemic Risk Project (www.princeton.edu/piirs/research-communities/global-systemic-risk).

There has also been a growth in new financial instruments known as catastrophe bonds or 'cat bonds' concerning extremely rare events – buyers of these bonds in effect sell 'catastrophe insurance' (Appadurai 2013: 296–8). Teams of mathematicians are employed by hedge funds to quantify the risks of unexpected events when the past and the present are poor guides to the likelihood of a potential but statistically rare catastrophe occurring in the future.

This catastrophist structure of feeling is reflected in many films, books and art exhibitions. Naomi Klein notes that such dystopian writing is currently all the rage (http://bostinno.streetwise.co/2014/12/26/the-divergent-effect-dystopia-genre-reflects-climate-change-fears). Carroll refers to many current cultural interventions as indicating diverse 'temples of doom' (2008; Beckett 2011). One example is Ian McEwan's *Solar*, in which the Nobel Prize-winning climate scientist Michael Beard apocalyptically states that: 'the basic science is in. We either slow down, and then stop, or face an economic and human catastrophe on a grand scale within our grandchildren's lifetime' (2010: 149). Other examples of dystopic books and films include Cormac McCarthy's *The Road* (2006), Alfonso Cuarón's film *Children of Men* (2006), Marcel Theroux's *Far North* (2009), Franny Armstrong's film *The Age of Stupid* (2009), Margaret Atwood's *The Year of the Flood* (2010), *The Hunger Games* (2012), Nathaniel Rich's *Odds against Tomorrow* (2013), *The Giver* (2014), *Divergent* (2014) and *Mad Max – Fury Road* (2015). Queenan argues that we are 'living in a golden age of dystopian films... a tsunami of dystopian films' (www.theguardian.com/film/2015/mar/19/dystopian-films-blade-runner-insurgent-future-grim).

Another example is Sarah Hall's *The Carhullan Army* which represents Britain as being in a state of depression following global economic collapse and extensive flooding (2007). Oil and bio-fuels are rationed, electricity is metered and tinned food is shipped from charities in the US. Following a census almost all citizens are herded into urban centres. But away from London there is the Carhullan Army settlement, a final bastion of feminism. A girl escapes the confines of her repressive marriage to find an isolated group of women living as 'un-officials' on the edge in Carhullan, a remote northern farm. One character states: 'I'm not interested in London. London's finished. We're no longer the nation we were. If you think about it, there's no central command. We're back to being a country of local regimes' (Hall 2007: 104). However, those living in Carhullan are forced into backbreaking subsistence farming under autocratic leadership. The alternative to the regime in London thus behaves much like the regime people had escaped from. This tragic outcome provides the context for interpreting the portrayal of immobile lives organized around a rugged subsistence farming lived out on bleak northern hills.

Collapsing society?

Many of these dystopias present the thesis that there is nothing automatic about human societies and their continuous improvement and progress. Societies can collapse. These texts problematize the idea that conditions of life are inexorably improving; according to Greer, we are moving to a condition that is *After Progress* (2015). These texts point to the possibility of systemic reversal, some deploying the language of austerity, and show that this is directly affecting people's lives and levels of consumption, leading to the loss of a 'future' for younger generations, and threats to the notion of public interest (www.austerityfutures.org.uk).

Dartnell interestingly examines the consequences of all human knowledge being lost because of this catastrophic collapse of societies (2014). He explores what would have to occur in order to rebuild our world from scratch, starting from first principles. He describes the time and resources that would be needed for this, bringing out the interdependence and social character of the many forms of knowledge that make contemporary life possible. He illustrates this by considering one of the simplest technological artefacts, a pencil, which requires an astonishing array and ordering of different forms of knowledge in order for it to be assembled (Dartnell 2014: 4; and see Allwood, Cullen 2012).

Dartnell's book in turn raises the issue of what a society is in the first place, and what its spatial, temporal and resource preconditions are. Simmel put the point well when asking 'how is society possible?' (1910). This question was much discussed in sociology during the middle years of the last century. Talcott Parsons, in particular, argued that sociology should be concerned with the ways that societies secure order, this often being described as the Hobbesian problem of social order (Parsons 1968[1937]).

Hobbes maintained that, in the state of nature:

> there is no place for industry, because the fruit thereof is uncertain, and consequently no culture of the earth, no navigation nor use of the commodities that may be imported by sea, no commodious building, no instruments of moving and removing such things as

> require much force, no knowledge of the face of the earth; no account of time, no arts, no letters, no society, and, which is worst of all, continual fear and danger of violent death, and the life of man solitary, poor, nasty, brutish, and short. (www.bartleby.com/34/5/13.html)

Hobbes argued that a powerful Leviathan is necessary to overcome a war of all against all. People would be willing to give up liberty through agreeing a social contract with the Leviathan if this were to ensure industry, culture, arts and so on, to stop lives being potentially nasty, brutish and short.

By contrast, Parsons argued that the problem of order is not solved through a powerful Leviathan but rather through the members of a society sharing norms and values in common (1968[1937]). Such normative consensus ensured that societies were integrated and would not collapse. Parsons emphasized how 'American or western' values and norms are crucial to solving this problem of order, making society possible and ensuring people's lives are not nasty, brutish and short. Parsons' formulation here is based upon seeing a strong division between the individual and societal levels of analysis. Later sociology critiqued this division emphasizing more the co-constitution of individuals and societies. Writers such as Norbert Elias argued that individuals and societies are not separate entities but embedded within 'figurations' or networks of social relations (2012[1939]).

Many of the catastrophist texts listed above proposed that social order will break down since we have neither an effective Leviathan nor shared norms and values. Also, most of these texts further claim that people, societies *and* material conditions co-constitute the conditions for human life. Gregory Bateson once argued that 'the unit of survival is *organism* plus *environment*...the organism that destroys its environment destroys itself' (cited in Welsh 2010: 34). Social practices thus take place in and through a material environment, something examined within the Marxist tradition of social theory. But this notion of the material-dependence of societies was largely ignored by social science during the twentieth century. It was presumed that there were no finite limits and perverse consequences resulting from exploiting the earth's resources and, especially, the 'energy environment' within which human societies are embedded.

These catastrophist analyses mostly demonstrate that human life did not 'solve' the problems brought about by the problematic resource-base of contemporary societies. According to Rifkin, this is because such societies presupposed energy resources that would unproblematically power ever greater levels of consumption and communications (2009). Central to dystopic accounts is the intractable 'problem of energy', of societies not being safely, securely and sustainably 'energized'. Energy provides oxygen for societies – and without the right energy in the right places over the long term, then communications and societies die (Motesharrei, Rivas, Kalnay 2014).

The fossil fuels of coal, gas and oil account for over four-fifths of current energy use. The techniques of burning these fossil fuels and converting heat into energy were the most important transformations in the world economy and society over the past three centuries (Urry 2014b). Indeed, 'western' civilization was not inherently superior to civilizations elsewhere. But it was the rapid exploitation of the climate-changing carbon resources of coal, oil and gas that contingently enabled energy converters in the 'west' to determine the earth's trajectory and initiate a distinct new phase of geological time, as discussed below.

The importance of the human species and its energy environment has led analysts to think more generally about human societies and other species. Here there has been a major debate between uniformitarianism and catastrophism. *Uniformitarianism* is the assumption that the same natural laws and processes have always operated, they apply everywhere and there are no striking breaks or disjunctures in history. By contrast, *catastrophism* argues that there are gaps and disjunctures in the history of the planet. Thus, particular species disappear; indeed 98 per cent of all species that have lived on earth are now said to be extinct. It is estimated that species extinction is now occurring at the fastest ever rate (Hallam 2005).

Over the past decade or so, catastrophism gained wider acceptance, partly through an improved understanding of the scale of past mass extinctions. Especially significant was the 10-kilometre-wide asteroid that struck the earth 65 million years ago, at the end of the Cretaceous period. This asteroid brought about the equivalent of a nuclear winter and wiped out about 70 per cent of all species on earth, including the dinosaurs that had been the dominant species. There is debate as to whether there was also widespread volcanic activity at the time that contributed to this highly significant extinction.

Along with some science fiction writing, academic commentators increasingly argue that human societies could disappear (see Kolbert 2015). It seems incorrect to posit that human societies constitute given and unchanging elements upon the earth. A bifurcation could be reached, with the catastrophic collapse of human societies were they to pass a tipping point. A social catastrophist discourse has rapidly developed since the start of this century, with various analysts elaborating the thesis of societal collapse, although most of these analyses emphasize not asteroids but 'man-made' transformations.

This idea of collapse drew upon archaeologist Joseph Tainter's *The Collapse of Complex Societies*. In this, he argued that, 'however much we like to think of ourselves as something special in world history, in fact industrial societies are subject to the same principles that caused earlier societies to collapse' (Tainter 1988: 216). In various ways, societies became more complex in response to short-term problems. The causes of societal collapse were thought to be endogenous economic/social/resource processes rather than external shocks. Growing complexity demanded ever more high-quality energy, but such increased energy normally involved diminishing returns. An evolving combination of energy and environmental problems unpredictably reinforced each other across domains and resulted in some societies collapsing and disappearing.

Like many contemporary writers, Tainter drew analogies between today's societies and two other traumatic historical events: the fall of the Roman Empire, and the collapse of Mayan civilization in the Yucatán peninsula in central America in AD 800. On the second of these, Mayan civilization had lasted for at least 500 years, and over that period complex technologies, mathematics, astronomy, architecture and culture were developed. But at the height of its powers, Mayan civilization appears to have stopped. Monuments were no longer built, palaces were burnt, lakes silted up, cities came to be abandoned and 90–99 per cent of the population of some millions vanished (Motesharrei, Rivas, Kalnay 2014: 91). Mayan civilization was like a car being driven faster and faster until it blew up and disappeared almost overnight. This Mayan experience is similar to what a complex systems analysis of the population of a species also reveals. Populations can rapidly rise and equally rapidly fall. There is nothing linear about the population size of a species living within a specific environment (May 1974; see Chapter 4 below).

Some commentators argue that most civilizations only last a few hundred years. 'Western civilization', we might say, has survived 600 years since the Renaissance. So, like the powerful Mayan civilization, it could come to an 'end'. A very rapidly increasing population is appearing to outstrip its energy resources, especially given increasing demands for energy as societies are more complex and need exponentially more energy (Motesharrei, Rivas, Kalnay 2014). Previous societies collapsed because systems were not in place to ensure the continued 'energizing' of their population at the moment that those societies were at the height of their powers. Societies appear to fail at their peak and not after a long period of weakness (Carroll 2008).

What are the lessons here for the current century? Before the oil and electricity age, the population of the world was around 2 billion. But with the oiling and electrifying of society during the last century, world population trebled to 6 billion. Heinberg considers that this world population of 6 billion might collapse back to 2 billion during the current century, returning to the population size of 1900, before the fateful upscaling of energy (2005: 196). Such a population decline would be analogous to the scale of societal collapse experienced in the falls of Roman and Mayan civilizations. Many catastrophist analysts develop an energy-inflected social science (Tyfield, Urry 2014). They examine relationships between social institutions and practices and the resource base and unintended environmental consequences.

Various bleak analyses thus proclaim that a new dark age is on its way, often using alarmist language and the notion of catastrophe. Lord Martin Rees, former President of the UK's Royal Society, provocatively states that the chances of the human race surviving the twenty-first century are 1 in 2 (2003). A key text is Jared Diamond's best-selling *Collapse* which attempts to explain why so many past societies fell, leaving behind ruined or abandoned temples, pyramids and monuments (2015). Why did societies that were as powerful as the Khmer Empire or the Maya abandon sites into which they had invested such effort over centuries?

Diamond's answer is that it was environmental problems that brought about such 'collapse' through 'ecocide': partially self-inflicted ecological disaster. Eight environmental processes were especially responsible: deforestation and habitat destruction; soil problems; water management problems; over-hunting; over-fishing; effects of introduced species on native species; human population growth; and the increased per-capita impact of people. Diamond's account emphasizes how populations grew and stretched natural resources, particularly energy resources, to breaking point, especially at the moment that such societies were at their height.

He goes on to argue that, in the twenty-first century, human-caused climate change, the build-up of toxic chemicals in the environment, and energy shortages will produce abrupt, potentially catastrophic, reversal or decline. This will involve increases of global temperatures that make much plant, animal and human life impossible, the running out of oil, the increased lack of resilience of many societies, a global failure of economy and finance, population collapse, increasing resource wars, and huge food shortages. In short, these interdependent social–ecological processes constitute a perfect storm, analogous to what seems to have produced 'societal collapse' within previous civilizations. Contradictions working slowly and imperceptibly over time brought down apparently dominant systems based upon what had seemed to be sufficient supplies of energy.

A catastrophist thesis was once elaborated as the first item on a 10 p.m. BBC 1 news programme (Urry 2011: ch. 1). The lengthy BBC news report argued that by 2030 the world could be confronted by a catastrophic 'perfect storm' caused by the interdependent effects of runaway climate change, huge water, food and energy shortages, and population growth. The analysis of such a potential perfect storm was illustrated by reports from correspondents on worldwide developments showing that such a storm was already being formed. This BBC report suggested that, without reversing various systems, the world would race into multiple interlocking catastrophes, with the result that much of the population would be poorer, less mobile, hungrier and fighting for increasingly scarce resources.

Reinforcing this catastrophist kind of analysis is the way that many commentators refer to the current period of geological history as the *anthropocene*. This is characterized by soaring carbon dioxide levels, a quantum step upward in erosion, widespread species extinction, ecosystem disturbance and acidification of the oceans. To speak of the anthropocene is to see this as a finite period of geological history. Analysts thus show that physical worlds are full of change, paradox and contradiction, with no unchanging order. Slavoj Žižek writes how 'Nature is one big catastrophe. Oil, our main source of energy – can you even imagine what kind of ultra-unthinkable ecological catastrophe must have happened on earth in order that we have these reserves of oil …Nature is not Mother Earth…Nature is imbalanced' (www.democracynow.org/2008/5/12/world_renowned_philosopher_slavoj_zizek_on).

As will be elaborated in Chapter 4, some notions from complexity theory are developed in this book. It is presumed here that there are no unchanging stable states to which there is a process of equilibrium-establishing movement. Physical worlds and societies are characterized by 'the strange combination of the unpredictable and the rule-bound that governs so much of our lives' (Ball 2004: 283). So there are patterned, regular and rule-bound systems; these rule-bound workings can come to generate various unintended effects; and unpredictable events disrupt and abruptly transform what appear to be rule-bound and enduring patterns. This is a view which emphasizes networks of people, of systems, of societies as fundamentally historical, and with no necessary movement towards equilibrium. The 'normal' state is imbalance. Thus, in relationship to population, the numbers of a species show extreme unevenness, with populations rapidly rising when introduced into a given area and then almost as rapidly falling. There may be periods of boom and bust. Systems are thus 'complex', with population trajectories sensitive to initial conditions and to historical processes (May 1974: xiv–xv).

In these various texts, policies never straightforwardly restore equilibrium as policy makers often claim. Indeed, interventions can generate the opposite, or almost the opposite, of what is intended. So decisions aiming to generate one outcome, because of the operation of a complex system, generate multiple unintended effects, different from those that had been sought (Urry 2003). One reason for this is the importance of small but potentially major changes often described as 'black swans' – rare, unexpected and highly improbable events, but which have huge impacts. A recent example of such a black swan has been the dramatically declining cost of the means of violence (Walby 2009). It has been normal to argue, following Max Weber, that the 'state' is a community that successfully claims the monopoly on the legitimate use of physical force within a given territory (1948[1919]). Because of this monopoly, modern nation-states are legitimately able to impose their will, to keep the peace, to protect their populations and to pass laws which apply to all. This notion of the state was based on the increasing scale, cost and organized complexity of the means of physical force. States would become more powerful, legitimate and able to control borders against other states. The first part of the twentieth century saw a system of nation-states develop in which each state increasingly appeared to possess a monopoly on physical coercion over the members of its 'imagined community' of the national society, as Anderson describes it (1991).

However, many catastrophist texts emphasize that in recent decades global processes disrupted national societies that no longer can be governed by powerful and legitimate national states possessing a monopoly over the means of physical violence (Urry 2000). There has been a dramatic fall in the cost of the means of violence. Many of these have turned into capitalist commodities and become remarkably cheaper through economies of scale made possible by new materials and novel sites for selling weapons, especially supermarkets and the internet. Weapons are objects of consumer choice and style. It is reported in the US that the semi-automatic AR-15 is especially 'fashionable' since it was used by the perpetrator of the worst ever American schoolyard massacre in Newtown, Connecticut (in December 2013). Since then the AR-15 has been selling fast, the gun that many Americans apparently hanker after (www.nytimes.com/2013/02/03/business/the-ar-15-the-most-wanted-gun-in-america.html?_r=0; Walby 2009).

And many other guns, pistols, rockets, drones and bombs are available for purchase on the internet, only a click or two away. There is no monopoly on the means of violence. Huge damage can be done to conventional states because of the growth of cheap means of violence, which has helped to proliferate many 'new wars' (Hardt, Negri 2006; Kaldor 1999). The new wars examined in these catastrophist texts undermine conventional distinctions between the internal and the external, aggression and repression, local and global. New wars are based more on identity than territory; there are lengthy guerrilla and/or terror campaigns; insurgents often come from other countries or continents; resistant armies may be funded through international crime; they use much cheaper and lighter weaponry but it is often as sophisticated as that deployed by regular soldiers; there are many informal fighters, including children; and there tends to be no formal declaration of war or peace. At the same time, much regular military and security activity by official 'states' has been outsourced to private security corporations that are cheaper and less governed by strict rules of engagement. New wars are currently being fought across much of the Middle East and north Africa.

New wars proliferated the possibilities for violence and 'insecurity' within most societies. It is not that more people are killed or injured than in the huge state wars of the first half of the last century (especially the Great War of 1914–18). But war and violence can happen in very many places and at very many times, as Hardt and Negri describe (2006). And war is less specific and identifiable, overlapping and intersecting with crime, terrorism, drugs, rape and other forms of interpersonal violence. Some societies institutionalize warfare and violence, which continue for long and indeterminate periods of time. There may be little likelihood of states being able to end the violence, especially if they are themselves corrupt and viewed as little better than clusters of private interests, or are dependent upon other corrupt states.

Attention has been paid here to the means of violence and its likely lack of legitimacy. States are often unable to resolve the systemic contradictions that intersecting systems engender. States can be weak and illegitimate, especially in being unable to deal resiliently with the systemic, unpredictable and cascading challenges they often now encounter.

Catastrophic cascades

Analysts have identified various kinds of conditions which, in their cascading interdependence, can engender catastrophic change (Walby 2015). Catastrophes stem from the way that systems interact with each other and especially those systems ruled through market mechanisms. Karl Polanyi presciently wrote in the 1940s about the potential 'demolition' of society: 'To allow the market mechanism to be the sole director of the fate of human beings and their natural environment...would result in the demolition of society...Nature would be reduced to its elements, neighborhoods and landscapes defiled, rivers polluted, military safety jeopardized, the power to produce food and raw materials destroyed' (1954[1944]: 73). Polanyi effectively captures the interdependent character of systems and the ways in which domination by markets would be potentially catastrophic.

Homer-Dixon develops this thesis: 'I think the kind of crisis we might see would be a result of systems that are kind of stressed to the max already...societies face crisis when they're hit by multiple shocks simultaneously or they're affected by multiple stresses simultaneously' (2006: 1). Human and physical systems exist in states of dynamic tension. Systems may reverberate against each other and generate cascading impacts. It is the simultaneity of converging system shifts that creates significant change. Such processes may overload a fragile global ordering, creating the possibility of cascading failure.

Some writers especially link potential failure to the massive and accelerating increase in international transactions beginning in the late 1970s (see research at Princeton on global systemic risk: www.princeton.edu/piirs/research-communities/global-systemic-risk). These connections necessitated a complex and interdependent system of global nodes and links. But such interdependence caused systemic risk to increase exponentially. Tangible risks in systems such as energy exploration and production, electricity transmission, computer networks, healthcare, food and water supplies, transportation networks, commerce and finance now threaten global political, economic and financial systems. The following are some of the systemic global risks that various texts show catastrophically reverberating against each other in this century of global interdependence, generating much 'systemic instability'.

First, the world's human population is growing exponentially. Just 10,000 years ago, there were around 1 million people, by 1800 1 billion, by 1900 2 billion, and by 2000 6 billion. The world population is currently expected to reach 9.1 billion by 2050 (Emmott 2013). A rapidly rising population disproportionately adds to the global consumption of energy and raw materials, as well as worsening environmental carrying capacity.

Second, much of this population growth takes place within large cities. Mega-cities include the Greater Tokyo Area with around 38 million people, Seoul with 26 million, Delhi with 25 million, Shanghai with 24 million, Mexico City with 21 million, and so on (Urry, Birtchnell, Caletrio, Pollastri 2014). Such cities are the largest structures that have ever been created upon earth. The growing populations of these mega-cities are exposed to many hazards, including food and energy shortages, absence of clean drinking water and sanitation, lack of safe and reliable transportation, and poor air quality that breaches World Health Organization standards (see striking images from Beijing: www.theguardian.com/cities/2014/dec/16/beijing-airpocalypse-city-almost-uninhabitable-pollution-china?CMP=share_btn_tw). By 2050, it is anticipated that around 70 per cent of the world's population will live in cities.

Third, food production for this rapidly growing urban population depends upon hydrocarbon fuels to fertilize and irrigate crops, to harvest and process them, and to transport them to those in the cities, and more generally to people whose diets presuppose exceptionally lengthy food miles. Oil shortages would mean that 'food could be priced out of the reach of the majority of our population. Hunger could become commonplace in every corner of the world, including your own neighbourhood' (Pfeiffer 2006: 2). More generally, there will be food protests as a result of climate change-related flooding, desertification and generally rising costs, combined with the tendency for 'richer' societies to appropriate land in 'poor' societies that should be ensuring food security for its residents. Harvey characterizes these relationships in terms of the 'food–energy–climate change trilemma' (2014).

Fourth, according to Schumacher: 'There is no substitute for energy. The whole edifice of modern society is built upon it.... it is not "just another commodity" but the precondition of all commodities, a basic factor equal with air, water, and earth' (quoted in Kirk 1982: 1–2). This 'basic factor' structures the social, temporal and spatial organization of societies and 'life' itself. And, since the eighteenth century, energy has progressively presupposed systems that involve extracting, burning and distributing fossil fuel-based energy. There are two huge problems, which many of these texts document: some sources of that fuel, especially oil, are getting more difficult to extract as easy oil has been mostly used up; and the burning of such a fossil fuel changes the world's climate (Urry 2013b).

Furthermore, there are growing insecurities in the systems supplying clean usable water. There are huge demands from growing populations, especially in mega-cities, that have to buy and transport water from outside the city. Around 1.2 billion people, or almost one-fifth of the world's population, live where water is physically scarce. Another 1.6 billion people, or almost one quarter of the world's population, face water shortages due to cost (see www.un.org/waterforlifedecade/scarcity.shtml). Some commentators use the term 'peak ecological water' to refer to the fact that only 0.007 per cent of water on earth is freshwater that can be used by humans (Pfeiffer 2006: 15).

In addition, the economic and financial systems in the global North collapsed in October 2008, although commentators had presumed that the world's production, financial, real estate, consumption and income systems could not do so. The economy-society flipped over, from increasing prosperity and richer lives for many in the prosperous North, to increasing misery for many. Moreover, even now, the systems have not been significantly reformed and, according to Gamble, this is a 'crisis without end' (2014). There has not been a reversal of the financialization of most economies, so many instabilities remain within the banking and finance sectors (Haldane, May 2011). It is significant that a 'worldwide recession' is one scenario used by the Bank of England in order to 'stress test' the robustness of major UK banks (www.bbc.co.uk/news/business-32116356).

Finally, richer societies increasingly break away from poorer nations into relatively protected enclaves (north America, Europe, parts of Asia). Outside such fortified enclaves, there are 'wild zones' which the rich and powerful move over or exit from as fast as possible. These wild zones are left to ethnic, tribal or religious 'multitudes', although from time to time they try to enter the protected zones as, variously, refugees, drug or people traffickers, slaves, terrorists and so on (Hardt, Negri 2006). Bleak, impoverished societies face regular breakdowns of civil order and a crippling incapacity to resolve system crises. Their populations regularly try to jump over offshored barriers in order to enter the safe zones (with increasing numbers dying en route).

Moreover, states are often 'vulnerable' and poorly able to cope with potential system crises or the wicked problems of droughts, heat waves, extreme weather events, flooding, desertification, mobile diseases, dust storms, famines and energy and water shortages (Abbott 2008; Leichenko, Thomas, Baines 2010). Even in prosperous societies, states, corporations and relief organizations are generally ineffective in responding to systems impacting upon each other, as in New Orleans in 2005, the nuclear collapse in Fukushima in Japan in 2011, or Hurricane Sandy that occurred in New York / New Jersey in 2012. It is especially difficult to assemble in such an unpredicted crisis a sufficiently resilient network that can reverse the catastrophic interdependence of cascading systems. This is especially the case given the declining costs of the means of violence, as noted above. Rodin argues that it is necessary to prepare cities around the world for catastrophe and not presume that there are unchanging states of equilibrium, since it is clear that on occasions 'things go wrong' (2014).

Furthermore, the growth of inequality over the past three to four decades makes it more difficult to orchestrate resilient responses. On the basis of mathematical modelling, Motesharrei, Rivas and Kalnay show how societal collapse is more likely where the levels of economic inequality are pronounced and it is hard to mobilize appropriate income and material resources to respond to structural crises (2014; Piketty 2014). According to Davis these system crises are going to get more intense, so that by 2030 'the convergent effects of climate change, peak oil, peak water, and an additional 1.5 billion people on the planet will produce negative synergies probably beyond our imagination' (2010: 17). Likewise, Kunstler describes multiple vulnerabilities: 'At peak and just beyond, there is massive potential for system failures of all kinds, social, economic, and political. Peak is quite literally a tipping point. Beyond peak, things unravel and the center does not hold. Beyond peak, all bets are off about civilization's future' (2006: 65).

Lovelock concludes his analysis of these multiple systems and positive feedbacks with the question 'is our civilization doomed, and will this century mark its end with a massive decline in population, leaving a few survivors in a torrid society ruled by warlords on a hostile and disabled planet?' (2006: 151). There could be a more generalized 'peaking' here, not only of oil and water but of American power, European welfare states and 'western life' more generally. A catastrophic future would involve the intersecting impact of these system problems, combined with a plummeting standard of living, a forced re-localization of economy-and-society, and weak national or global forms of governance. Oreskes and Conway maintain that the 'great collapse' of 'Western Civilization' is the most likely future outcome (2014; see Slaughter 2003).

Thus, there are a striking set of writings and other cultural interventions conveying visions of dystopic future worlds. Brunn and Wakefield review recent major art exhibitions and installations and conclude: 'Catastrophe is everywhere and ever-present.... A civilization already in ruins...we are already living in a post-apocalyptic condition' (http://societyandspace.com/material/article-extras/theme-section-a-new-apparatus-technology-government-and-the-resilient-city/bruce-braun-and-stephanie-wakefield-inhabiting-the-postapocalytic-city; also see Nancy 2014).

Dangers of catastrophism

These writings and exhibitions thus describe the catastrophic consequences of processes cascading across the interlinked systems of energy, environment, economy, population, food, water, migration and governance. However, some commentators maintain that there is danger in these 'new catastrophist' writings. What is sometimes termed 'cli-fi' shows readers and viewers that future environmental catastrophe is inevitable and nothing can be done to combat impending disaster (see www.dissentmagazine.org/article/cli-fi-birth-of-a-genre). Klein for one argues that catastrophism induces a problematic fatalism about the future. In contrast, she argues, people should be actively planning viable alternatives. Alternatives to climate change are possible and it is crucial not to see catastrophe as inevitable, since this will make people quiescent in facing the future (Klein 2014).

Another danger of catastrophist thinking is that it may induce powerful interests to mobilize for the planetary technological fix of a very large-scale scheme of geo-engineering. Such a global social experiment could be presented as the last possible way of keeping the high-energy systems functioning (Klein 2014: 258). Most states would assess that they would have to sign up to such a short-circuited reworking of the future, although it may have worse consequences than the problem it is trying to fix (see Chapter 9 below).

So, dystopias and indeed utopias are partly performative, helping to realize the kind of future being envisaged, as noted by Slaughter (2003). William Gibson commented that he omitted certain dystopian notions from his novels because he did not want to be responsible for helping to bring them about. By contrast, Gill notes how the film and TV series *Star Trek* is said to have inspired Motorola's development of the first mobile phones during the 1970s (see https://christopherharpertill.wordpress.com/2014/12/08/should-sociology-try-to-predict-the-future-in-order-to-produce-a-better-one). Visions of futures, whether dystopic or utopic, may indeed engender futures, as they are part performative and not merely analytic or 'representational'.

PART 2

COMPLEX SYSTEMS AND THE FUTURE

4

Time and Complex Systems

Social science and the future

Central to many of the texts examined in the last chapter was complex systems thinking. This part of the book develops such notions in greater depth, beginning with time and complexity. I begin by noting how within social science there are three main approaches to anticipating social futures.

First, and most powerful is the individualistic model of human action, in which theories and methods emphasize the capacity of individuals to behave in some sense rationally, or at least independently of others, so as to determine what to do and why. This individualistic model is used in much social science to explain many kinds of human actions, including the futures people are likely to generate through their actions in the present. In this approach, it is believed that futures are best changed through modifying how each individual behaves by altering the basket of rewards and punishments relating to different kinds of activities. This model of humans minimizes the power of 'social ties', seeing individuals as relatively autonomous. The conception of the individual can range from the 'rational' individual that is the basis of much economics, to individuals with a 'lack of individual self-control' often deployed in accounts of why people engage in 'crime'.

This individualistic approach is critiqued by some social science theory and research, as well as recent behavioural economics. These all show the profound significance of 'others' that form each person's desires, capacities and judgements for action. These others may be near or far, few or plentiful, connected with each other or unconnected (Ormerod 2012). Social institutions, networks and groups construct, mould and orchestrate human actions. Marx famously argued that people make their own history, but they do so not under circumstances of their own choosing since the 'tradition of the dead generations weighs like a nightmare on the minds of the living' (Marx 1973[1852]: 146). Futures appear to depend in part upon social patterns and practices that are 'external' to each individual and in which traditions or experiences from the past weigh heavily upon the minds and actions of the living.

A second set of theories emphasizes the importance of relatively fixed and enduring economic and social structures. There are various versions of this approach, ranging from those focusing upon social institutions such as family or education, to analyses of capitalism as a system of exploitation and power. In these various analyses, the future is treated as the outcome of relatively fixed and self-correcting social structures; anticipations of the future are based upon a 'business as usual' model of existing structures.

There have been many critiques of this structural position. Keynes highlighted the possibility of a 'chronic condition of sub-normal activity' in which feedback mechanisms are unable to restore equilibrium (1936: 249; Beinhocker 2006: ch. 3). Moreover, structural analyses neglect internal sources of change which over time undermine a system's persistence. For example, Marx and Engels describe the endogenous contradictions at the heart of bourgeois society. They talk of 'the sorcerer, who is no longer able to control the powers of the nether world whom he has called up by his spells' (Marx, Engels 1888[1848]: 58). Many social groups resist their society, seeking to make their own futures, often against the 'traditions of the dead generations'. Social structural accounts fail to build social conflict, unpredictability and system reversal into their analyses of how different futures may or may not materialize.

The third approach is that of complexity theory, now present within many disciplines. It is an emerging paradigm within the social sciences (on sociology, see Urry 2003, 2005). A complex systems approach brings out that the future cannot be reduced either to the actions of individual actors or to persisting social structures. Complexity overcomes the limitations of both individualistic and social structural approaches while maintaining elements of both. The rest of this chapter sets out some elements of such complex systems thinking in relationship to time.

The complexity turn

It is presumed that there are powerful physical and social systems stretching over time–space, often into distant futures. Yet such systems are characterized by innovation, unpredictability and reversal. Although systems possess emergent properties, these are not unchanging and stable. Complex systems thinking thus emphasizes how systems are dynamic, processual and unpredictable. They are open, with energy and matter flowing in and out. Many 'sciences' understand how systems in the physical world are emergent, dynamic and self-organizing. An early example of such systems thinking with regard to the climate future was the classic *The Limits to Growth* (Meadows, Meadows, Randers, Behrens 1972; see Gell-Mann 1995; Kauffman 1993; Prigogine 1997).

Unlike cybernetic analysis that developed during and after World War II, subsequent complexity theorists emphasize the importance of positive feedbacks that move systems away from equilibrium. Small changes may bring about big, non-linear system shifts (Arthur 2013: 3–5). Systems are characterized by a lack of proportionality, or 'non-linearity', between apparent 'causes' and 'effects' (Nicolis 1995). Such small causes are mostly unpredictable, difficult to foresee, although in hindsight they may be explicable. So while systems can be stabilized for long periods through 'lock-ins', certain small causes can prompt or tip the emergence of new 'paths'. Systems are thus not fully stabilized; they are sometimes characterized as 'metastable'.

Complexity emphasizes how there are multiple forms of 'organization', of complex adaptive systems, which evolve, adapt and self-organize. Each system demonstrates properties not necessarily present within individual elements. The properties of the system are emergent without a directing hand. These emergent properties can involve conflict, change and transformation. Thus, systems adapt and evolve as they self-organize over time. Such complex interactions are like a person walking through a maze where the walls rearrange themselves as the person moves through it. New steps have then to be taken to adapt to the walls of the maze that change in response to each person's walk through the maze. Complex systems theory involves studying the consequences of the dynamic and partially unpredictable interactions between elements making up any system.

While commentators often emphasize the accelerating nature of change within the modern world, this is misleading, since some systems can be stabilized for long periods. Systems survive through path-dependence, a process model in which systems develop via 'lock-in' but where only certain small causes are necessary to tip the initiation of the 'path'. Such lock-ins mean that the 'surrounding' social institutions matter a great deal in how systems develop over the long term, once they have been set onto a particular path (North 1990: 104; the classic example of lock-in is the layout of the QWERTY keyboard). Systems can endure even though there are strong forces that 'should' undermine their irreversible, locked-in character (Arthur 1994; Mahoney 2000). Hence, futures are not to be understood as 'empty'.

Such systems are both robust and fragile (Ormerod 2012: 18). Prigogine argues that:

> If the world were formed by stable dynamical systems, it would be radically different from the one we observe around us. It would be a static, predictable world, but we would not be here to make the predictions. In our world, we discover fluctuations, bifurcations, and instabilities at all levels. Stable systems leading to certitude correspond only to idealizations, or approximations. (1997: 55)

Change is non-linear; there is no necessary proportionality between 'causes' and 'effects'; the individual and statistical levels of analysis are not equivalent; and system effects do not result from adding together individual components.

Moreover, time is not viewed as a dimension along which systems move. Rather, systems are constituted through their becoming, through process, through what the philosopher A. N. Whitehead and others termed the 'arrow of time' (1929). There is thus no distinction in complexity thinking between states of equilibrium and growth states – all systems are dynamic and processual, with new structures developing and others disappearing in ways that are often difficult to anticipate.

In particular there can be moments of heightened openness, when the die is less cast and various futures are 'on the table'. It is not that such change is uncaused, but it is less reducible to locked-in pre-existing systems. Although, as argued above, there are long-term path-dependencies, no system is fixed for ever. According to Abbott, there is 'the possibility for a pattern of actions to occur to put the key in the lock and make a major turning point occur' (2001: 257).

Major turning points are what physicists term 'phase transitions', as when water turns into ice (Arthur 2013: 10–11; Nicolis 1995). This is 'uncertainty', not mere risk, and such transitions are enormously difficult to 'predict'. Climate scientists debate whether a phase transition will occur if global temperatures increase by a few degrees over the next few decades such that much of the ice at the Poles will turn into water.

Laszlo refers to momentous 'chaos points' when systems tip from one path to another (2006). In the global North, the period around 1990 was such a moment when many political, informational and communicational systems simultaneously adapted, co-evolved and resulted in a generalized 'chaos point'. The conjuncture of conditions included the 'birth' of the internet, the disappearance of Soviet communism, new patterns of 24-hour real-time global news reporting, 24/7 on-line trading on major financial markets, the rapid spread of mobile telephony, and 'cheaper' business models within many modes of transport and communications (Urry 2007: 5–7).

Thus, if a system passes a threshold, change can be not gradual but dramatic. Switches occur through positive feedback and what Arthur describes as 'the propagation of change through interconnected behaviour' (2013: 11). An example of this is Keynes' analysis of a fall in consumer confidence which then cascades through a population and generates major economic and social crises via positive feedback mechanisms (1936). The system turns over, in the way the internet grew dramatically from the early 1990s onwards, with billions of people and organizations adapting and co-evolving with it (Gore 2013). Another example was how in the mid-1990s, almost overnight, office workers found that they 'needed' a fax machine and purchases of them skyrocketed for a few years. It rapidly became the fashion to send and receive faxes, so office communications were transformed with each office imitating every other office. Copying what others did made good sense, this being one of Keynes' 'rules of thumb' for how people should operate within much economic and social life (see Ormerod 2012: 94–7). Imitating others, and hence herding, is often 'rational' for each individual and crucial to imagining and realizing a certain future – in this case, of all offices being linked together through networked fax machines.

But while copying others may be optimal for individual people or offices, this can have problematic system consequences. Herding magnifies the probability of system failure. In relationship to financial systems, Haldane and May argue that 'excessive homogeneity within a financial system – all the banks doing the same thing – can minimise risk for each individual bank, but maximise the probability of the entire system collapsing' (2011: 353). Thus, similar herding behaviour makes system failure more likely, as happened almost overnight during the finance and banking crash in August 2008, as Ormerod shows (2012: 101–2).

One further feature of tightly coupled systems is that they are characterized by relatively routine 'normal accidents' (Perrow 2007): processes happen very fast and cannot be turned off, the failed parts cannot be isolated and there is no other way to keep the system going. With such tightly coupled systems, recovery from the initial disturbance, which may have been relatively trivial, is impossible. The consequences spread quickly, chaotically and irreversibly throughout the system. This can produce accidents, as cascade effects generate intermittent 'breakdowns', rendering cities, for example, as dysfunctional (Nye 2010).

So far I have used the term 'system' whether the system is physical/material or social. However, Latour and others show that many formulations of the idea of the system in social science are too *social* (1993). These formulations are purified of crucial heterogeneous material elements such as machines, texts, metals, technologies, physical environments, plastic, weather and so on. Thus, I take systems in the contemporary world to be economic, physical, technological, political and social. Systems should not be reduced to any of these individual 'factors'. They are sociomaterial; power is as much material/technological as it is social.

Societies are thus presumed to be a set of contingently assembled and interdependent sociomaterial systems locked together in relations of power, and with each typically providing conditions of existence for the others. And the 'material' is immensely complex – a book, for example, being made of at least ten basic materials (Allwood, Cullen 2012: 12).

Thus, interdependent complex systems consist of cascades, self-restoring patterns, apparently stable regimes that suddenly collapse, punctuated equilibria, 'butterfly effects' and thresholds (Axelrod, Cohen 1999). These complexity effects mean that one cannot read off, predict or produce a clear and knowable account of the future. Thompson and Beck explore some conceptual and policy implications of this viewpoint, and advocate clumsy rather than elegant solutions to problems. This is the best that can be achieved in a situation of 'decision-making under conditions of contradictory certainties' (Thompson, Beck 2014).

Thompson and Beck provide provocative accounts of two clumsy solutions which had not been originally envisaged by public or corporate decision-makers. The first was the building of Arsenal's Emirates football stadium in a previously unnoticed stretch of land in north London. This only happened following a campaign mounted by well-organized local residents who forced this possibility onto local agendas. The second was the construction of a hydroelectric-powered ropeway to transport milk from remote inaccessible villages to the rapidly developing city of Kathmandu in Nepal, a solution that was strongly opposed by hierarchical actors but which in the end generated many benefits for villagers and the 'environment'. In both cases, the clumsy outcome emerged in a disruptive fashion, particularly from the forceful pressure of social groups who had originally not been part of the formal future-making process.

A related case is that of Malibu, although here the protest of citizens causes the problem. This is the wildfire capital of north America (Davis 2000). There is a non-linear relationship between the age structure of vegetation and the intensity of fires. Fifty-year-old trees burn fifty times more intensely than twenty-year-old trees. However, because of the power of influential residents living in the Malibu region, since 1919 the local policy has been one of 'total fire suppression'. This means that smaller fires that are beneficial in recycling nutrients are forbidden. Most trees in the area are older, and *more* intense in the fires they generate. So the policy of limiting small fires results in larger fires subsequently occurring. Further, the extreme fires transform the chemical structure of the soil, turning it into a water-repellent layer which accelerates subsequent sheet flooding and erosion (Davis 2000: 100–3). Extreme fire events and massive flooding follow from the elegant intervention to prevent the limited fires that would otherwise be a routine feature of the Malibu eco-system.

Thompson and Beck thus maintain that clumsy solutions are required where there are irreconcilable problems, as with fires in Malibu. Such contradictory processes generate hugely complex global challenges through what are sometimes known as 'wicked problems' (Brown, Harris, Russell 2010; Bunders, Bunders, Zweekhorst 2015; Rittel, Webber 1973). These problems occur where: there are multiple 'causes' and 'solutions'; there are long-term lock-ins and complex interdependencies between processes; the effort to solve one problem reveals or creates other problems; solutions depend on how each issue is framed, and vice versa; different stakeholders have radically different frames for understanding what actually is *the* problem and the solution; the constraints that the problem is subject to and the resources needed to solve it change over time; each problem is never definitively solved but returns, albeit in different ways in different places, since there is no 'stopping rule'; and there may be no solution, as such, to the problem (Thompson, Beck 2014: 8–10; Tutton 2016).

So in the case of wicked problems such as climate change – as opposed to 'simpler' problems of the 'hole in the ozone layer' – there is no permanent way of getting the right policies in the right place at the right time. Acting in a particular way can change the situation, so that policies are not now appropriate even if they once were (Thompson, Beck 2014: 31). Thomson and Beck emphasize how path-dependence means that societies can be locked in to what is the 'wrong' technology for that period, but one that cannot be escaped from. And, we may add, a given technology can be locked out, although it can turn out with hindsight to have been the best game in town. They make a strong case for keeping technologies 'flexible' since no one knows what lies round the corner, so that what was optimal at one moment may be non-optimal at another. They argue that if 'the market can no longer be relied upon always to bring us onto the most efficient technological path then we are going to find ourselves locked in to some horrendously wasteful lines of development' (Thompson, Beck 2014: 34).

Bunders, Bunders and Zweekhorst indeed maintain that climate change is an example of a super-wicked problem (2015: 22–3). In the case of super-wicked problems, there are extra issues: time is running out to find a 'solution', there is no central orchestrating authority, those seeking to solve the issue are also in part causing it, and there is what can be called 'hyperbolic discounting', which massively favours immediate rewards over rewards arriving much later.

Relatedly, potential system failure is often the product of cascading interdependence; and this may be avoided through a much greater 'modularity' of systems (Haldane, May 2011 – Haldane is Chief Economist at the Bank of England). Haldane and May describe how system resilience stems from gaps or firewalls existing between the elements of a system. This is the exact opposite of what hierarchical actors, such as corporations or planners, normally maintain (Thompson, Beck 2014). Haldane and May argue that the greater the gaps, the less the dangers of herding, contagion and cascades infecting a whole network.

Arthur maintains that analysis has to be history-specific, case-based and concerned with process. He quotes the Keynesian economist Joan Robinson who, in 1973, argued that 'once we admit that an economy exists in time, that history goes one way, from the irrevocable past into the unknown future, the concept of equilibrium…becomes untenable' (quoted Arthur 2013: 18). She points to the significance of history, time and process in examining complex systems. I turn now to a brief analysis of time, this being crucial to analysing multiple futures.

Times

It is difficult to understand time. Unlike some aspects of space, time is invisible to the senses and can only be viewed through indicators of its passage, such as sundials, clocks and calendars. Moreover, divisions of the day, week, year, decade, century and millennium often engender powerful emotional sentiments (Elias 2007[1984]; Urry 2000: ch. 5). Further, as noted in Chapter 1, there is no single time but many times. In addition, there is a long dispute as to whether time is an absolute entity, possessing its own nature or particularity as Newton maintained, or whether time is, as Leibniz argued, an order of successions. It is also disputed whether time possesses directionality. Is there an arrow of time, as presumed above, such that effects result directly from time's passage, or is time reversible and there is no distinction between past and future, as Newton and Einstein presumed (Coveney, Highfield 1990)?

These different kinds of time can be further specified through the philosophical distinction between the A- and B-series of time (McTaggart 1927). The B-series is the sense of time as 'before and after'. Events are separate from each other and strung out along the dimension of time, such that they can always be located before or after each other. Each event is separate and never changes its relationship to the other events. Time is taken to be an infinite succession of identical instants, each identifiable as before or after the other. Statements about such phenomena are timelessly true. Many analysts have presumed that the physical world can be examined through the prism of the B-series, often termed clock- or calendar-time.

This can be distinguished from the A-series, which involves the relationships of 'past-to-present-to-future'. Here, past events are seen as being in part retained within the present and then carried forward into the future. Moreover, the present is not seen as an instant but as having duration. The past is not simply back there but comes to be incorporated into that present, as well as embodying certain expectations of the future. Coleridge captures the movement of present and future when writing:

> In the atmosphere, so often do the spirits
> Of great events stride on before the events,
> And in to-day already walks tomorrow.

Other writers developed the A-series. George Herbert Mead adopts a consistently 'temporal' viewpoint, regarding the abstract time of clocks and calendars, of the B-series, as nothing more than a 'manner of speaking'. For Mead, what is 'real' is the present, as established in *The Philosophy of the Present* (1959[1934]). What we take to be the past is reconstructed within the present; each moment of the past is recreated afresh. So there is no 'past' back there. Emergence transforms the past and gives sense and direction to the future. This emergence stems from interactions between people and the environment, humans being indissolubly part of nature, roughly as they are taken to be in this book.

Martin Heidegger stresses, in *Being and Time*, that philosophy must return to the question of 'Being' (1962[1927]). Central to Heidegger's ontology of Being is time which expresses the nature of what human subjects are. Humans find meaning in their temporality. Being is made visible in its temporal character, and in particular the movement from birth towards death. This view of time is not as a perimeter but rather as permeating each person's being. Birth and death as future are necessarily connected, forming a unity. Significantly, feminist critics have argued how this Heideggerian notion of 'being unto death' signifies a masculinist approach to time. It excludes women's concerns, such as birth and the apparently time-generating capacity of procreation, as well as the need to protect the environment for future generations, for the 'children of our children' (Adam 1995: 94).

Social scientists have typically insisted that there is a radical distinction between natural and social time. However, what social scientists have treated as the specifically 'human' aspects of time are in fact characteristic of the physical world. Adam argues that 'Past, present, and future, historical time, the qualitative experience of time, the structuring of "undifferentiated change" into episodes, all are established as integral time aspects of the subject matter of the natural sciences' (1990: 150). Complex systems thinking emphasizes the importance of history, time and emergence.

Twentieth-century science transformed the times of nature. Einstein showed that there is no fixed or absolute time independent of the system to which it refers. Time or *Eigenzeit* is thus a local, internal feature of any system of observation and measurement. Further, time and space are not separate from each other but are fused into a four-dimensional time–space curved under the influence of mass. Quantum physicists describe a virtual state in which electrons seem to try out instantaneously all possible futures before settling into particular patterns. Quantum behaviour is mysteriously instantaneous.

Thermodynamics showed the irreversible flow of time. Rather than there being time-symmetry and reversibility, thermodynamics is consistent with the A-series. This arrow of time results from how all systems show a loss of organization and an increase in randomness or disorder over time. Such positive entropy results from the Second Law of Thermodynamics; negative entropy involves a thermal disequilibrium characterized by evolutionary growth and increased complexity. All energy transformations are irreversible and directional.

The clearest example of irreversibility is the cosmological arrow of time. Laws of nature are historical. The irreversibility of time brings order out of chaos (Prigogine, Stengers 1984: 292). Thus, Hawking summarizes: 'Space and time are now dynamic qualities: when a body moves, or a force acts, it affects the curvature of space and time – and in turn the structure of space–time affects the way in which bodies move and forces act' (1988: 33, and throughout). Complex systems thinking presupposes that there are similar notions of time across the physical and social sciences and the various sociomaterial systems examined below.

Networks

Also crucial to complex systems are 'networks'. Complexity scientist Fritjof Capra argues that networks are the key to late twentieth-century advances concerned with the 'web of life... Whenever we look at life, we look at networks' (1996: 82). Castells likewise argues that networks: 'constitute the new social morphology of our societies, and the diffusion of networking logic substantially modifies the operation and outcomes in processes of production, experience, power, and culture... the network society, characterized by the pre-eminence of social morphology over social action' (1996: 469). And according to complexity economist Paul Ormerod, when contemporary challenges such as future climate change are examined, we see it is necessary to bring about dramatic mass behaviour change, but this will not stem from individual-based incentives. Rather, it is social networks that help to innovate changes in human behaviour and hence in future systems. Networks are central to futures, according to Ormerod (2012).

In social science, the analysis of networks was especially developed with Granovetter's account of the 'strength of weak ties' (1983, 1985; Albert, Barabási 2000; Watts 1999, 2003). He showed that 84 per cent of those people searching for a job acquired one not through someone they knew well but through a person they knew slightly and only saw occasionally. The *weak* ties of acquaintanceship and informational flow were central to successful job hunting. This strength of weak ties also applies to the spreading of a rumour, joining a social movement, initiating a new sociomaterial system and so on (Barabási 2002: 43; Burt 1992: 24–7; Gladwell 2002; Ormerod 2012). The weak ties connecting people to the outside world provided a bridge other than the 'clump' of people's close friends and family. Bridges were formed through weak rather than strong ties.

But most people live in 'clumps' of close friends and family. Barabási maintains: 'we live in a small world. Our world is small because society is a very dense web' (2002: 30). But if people were only connected to this small group of close friends and family then there would be a large separation of the world's 7 billion population. In fact, it only takes a few long-range random links or weak ties connecting these 'clumps' of fifty neighbours to greatly reduce the degree of separation of people around the world. This is known as the 'small world' phenomenon. A number of long-range random links, if combined with densely knit clumps, produce a low degree of separation of each person from everyone else on the planet. This patterning of networks and the low level of separation of people worldwide is one reason why future diseases, rumours, information and innovations can spread rapidly (Watts 1999, 2003).

The internet appears to be patterned like this, with each person 'present' with geographically remote other people through just a few clicks (Buchanan 2002: 118–19). Its architecture means that information travels from one point to any other point with only a handful of steps. However, there is a major difference between most social networks and the networks of the web. In the former, there is a normal or Gaussian distribution of people across the world with the overwhelming majority relatively weakly connected and only a few moderately connected and powerful. This is an egalitarian network characterized by a normal distribution of people and the number of links each person possesses (Ormerod 2012: 156).

By contrast, websites are not normally distributed. A few nodes possess an enormous number of links and are totally dominant. These hubs carry most traffic, with a skewed or 'power law' distribution (Watts 2003: 107). The web consists of a relatively few exceptionally well-connected hubs that utterly dominate the networks – unlike the 'democratic' small worlds networks (Buchanan 2002). The web is an aristocratic network stemming from 'the flocking sociology of the World Wide Web' (Barabási, quoted Buchanan 2002: 85). There is thus a hidden order of the web, the power law distribution, even though much of the web's development was unplanned, uncontrolled and anarchic, seemingly the opposite of order (Ormerod 2012: 160).

This aristocratic order can be seen in other aspects of contemporary life. An aristocratic system is one in which the rich get richer and have disproportionate influence, while the poor get poorer (see Ormerod 2012: 162). Global financial flows through London and New York are a good example of the aristocratic network. Another example is that of global brands that demonstrate increasing returns magnifying and expanding power through use (Klein 2000). Generally, the 'rich' are connectors, bridges or hubs that dominate networks and are crucial for making futures.

Innovations stem from such networks, and especially from the 'trading zones' between networks. This was important in the history of cyberspace, as shown in detail by Turner (2006; see Castells 2001; Lanier 2013). Such networks exhibit self-organization: 'millions of interactions occur simultaneously – where everyone changes the state of everyone else' (Strogatz 2003: 34). Moreover, in these complex networks, 'Enormous numbers of components keep changing their state from moment to moment, looping back on one another in ways that can't be studied by examining any one part in isolation…These phenomena…are fundamentally *nonlinear*' (Strogatz 2003: 286; italics in original).

Innovation processes, as discussed in the next chapter, often involve powerful connectors (individuals or organizations), possessing a disproportionate number of social ties within and especially across networks, seeking out and exploiting 'structural holes' (Burt 1992). Gladwell notes the importance of 'word of mouth' social interactions in systems tipping (2002: 264–5). The non-linear outcomes involve three processes: events and phenomena are contagious, little causes can have big effects, and changes can happen abruptly at a moment as the system switches – with, for example, every modern person believing they now 'need' a mobile/smart phone partly because they actually do, since most other people also possess them. The notions of social contagion and tipping points presuppose a very small number of extremely powerful connectors located at key points within certain networked relationships. Such connectors possess many social ties and, because of this concentration, systems suddenly tip. In the development of networked computing, Stewart Brand, who initiated *The Whole Earth Catalogue* in 1968, was one of those key connectors of networks (see Turner 2006).

So fashion is central as it emerges and spreads through networks within a population, as with networked computer use in developing so-called cyberspace. Also, fashion can be crucial in linking networks, in enabling synchronization between what can seem to be distant realms of social practice. Ormerod notes how fashions often seem to emerge from nowhere in particular, but, once they have emerged, they can grow, expand and transform multiple domains of economic and social life (2012; Turner 2006). Partly what happens is that people imitate others; Ormerod notes how preferences 'are no longer fixed. Instead they change and evolve over time, as the impact of people on your various social networks alters your own behaviour' (2012: 33). So herding behaviour stems from networks and may on occasions generate a massive transformation of the future, especially if networked relations develop unexpectedly incorporating and enhancing many new domains of practice, as happened through the growth of what has been called 'digital utopianism' (Turner 2006).

Conclusion

This chapter has established a range of concepts and arguments that are the building blocks for thinking about futures. The first point is that there are varied notions of time and hence of futures. It has been shown that time should be viewed as historical, with past and future being deeply intertwined with the present. This notion of time, the A-series, is broadly consistent with that found within the physical sciences.

Second, such a notion of time is part of a complex systems analysis of societies. This involves the importance of systems that endure, but also of unpredictability and uncertainty. Key within such a complexity analysis are notions of path-dependence, lock-in, thresholds, positive feedback loops, tipping points and phase transitions. This set of concepts is used below in exploring and anticipating varied futures.

Third, it has been argued that such systems are neither social nor physical but sociomaterial. Systems are to be understood as being in relations of power with each other, with each constituting the environment for the others. Power in a society depends upon the respective powers of each such sociomaterial system and their organization. Especially significant is the capacity of each such system to make, or to control, its own future.

Fourth, complex systems are constituted of multiple networks and these stretch relationships through time–space. It will be seen in the next chapter that such networks are crucial in analysing various kinds of innovation, especially of sociomaterial systems. These typically involve certain ideas or objects becoming highly desired, matters of fashion and fad. Fashions can grow, expand and transform economic and social life as people often imitate what others are doing, using or believing.

Finally, it is almost impossible for social groups to anticipate exactly what will bring about appropriate system change, especially because of the 'wickedness' of problems. There are often no elegant solutions. While groups seek to innovate projects of change, it is hard to ensure that intended outcomes will occur. Knowing what will generate desired global change is often impossible, although social groups struggle to achieve their goals. They have to believe what they say the future is. But there are always unintended consequences stretching across time and space and stemming from economic, social and political innovation; and these consequences themselves engender further adaptive and evolving system consequences. We noted above how Hardin maintained that we can never do merely one thing which will produce a clear set of anticipated and successful outcomes (1972: 38; see Chapter 1). These issues are now examined in the next chapter in Part 2, concerned with innovating the future in a world of systems.

5

Innovating Futures

Systems

The last chapter described how futures depend upon complex systems that make the world go round. And much of the time these systems work away without people whose actions presuppose such systems being aware they are elements of such a system (or systems). Systems mostly operate 'behind the scenes'. Examples include those systems responsible for delivering luggage at airports, or energy to houses, food to supermarkets or images to TVs. Most people are unaware of the 'systemness' of their daily practices and how they 'bear' systems as they go about their weekly shop or commute or daily shower or participation in a cultural event. People can be said to 'bear' such system relations; – this notion generalizing Marx's thesis that people are *Träger* (bearers) of class relations and not their originators.

Indeed, it is only when a disruptive event occurs that people often realize this system-dependence. Disruptive events include the uncharged battery, the misremembered password, the small mechanical fault that shuts down power stations and produces cascading outages, credit cards that stop giving credit, and volcanic ash clouds such as those from the Eyjafjallajökull volcano in Iceland that grounded planes in 2010 (Birtchnell, Büscher 2011). Disruptive events often interlink with system failures that cascade from system to system. The futuristic TV series *The Last*

Enemy involved a mathematician devising systems that would link together many databases (BBC 2008). But, for various reasons, he came to be excluded from this system of systems as his enemies (former friends) deactivated his RFID (Radio Frequency IDentification) implant. All the systems failed and he was transformed into a virtual – and hence physical – outcast.

In the previous chapter it was seen how wicked problems increase the need not for elegant policies and solutions but for those which are 'clumsy'. This involves greater reliance on horizontal actors and a lack of seamless integration. The implications of this will now be explored in relationship to anticipating 'socio-material' innovations of and for the future.

Innovating

Central to many future scenarios are novel and unexpected socio-material systems. But in developing anticipations of the future we should resist a technology-first analysis – technologies do not develop only for endogenous reasons. Nor do they then transform the economic and social landscape in their own image once they have been developed. Technologies are embedded within many forms of economic, social and political life, as Hughes showed in the case of electrical power systems (1983). Such systems are not autonomous, or free from the influence of non-technical factors. Overall, Hughes shows the impact society has on how electrical systems developed, especially through the notion of 'style'. Tutton expresses this in terms of how there are many 'entanglements of matter and meaning' in future-making (2016; Adam, Groves 2007).

Moreover, it is not a foregone conclusion that the best innovation will be the one that ultimately shapes the future. Innovation involves processes that are different from the linear notions often spoken about and promoted by policy makers. They typically describe innovation as a top-down process developed and implemented by hierarchical actors, resulting from the brilliance of an entrepreneur, or the chance 'discovery' of a new technology, or the system of knowledge-creation put in place by far-sighted policy makers. If only the conditions are right, then policy makers maintain that the innovation will materialize and the future will be successfully remade.

But innovating a new system is non-linear and unpredictable. Systems hover in a state of self-organized criticality where what matters is not the average behaviour of people or institutions. Key are unexpected rare events which have potentially huge impacts upon physical and/or social systems (Taleb 2007). Such outliers make history jump, not crawl. Arthur maintains that a new system typically involves a novel combination of *existing* elements, of machinery, text, technology, materials and organization (2009, 2013). Innovation involves *combining* isolated elements into a new system, often over a lengthy period, such new systems being not technological or economic or social or political but all of these. Often there is some outlying 'event' which provokes the new assemblage and transforms the future.

System innovation involves the co-evolution of numerous interrelated elements; there are changes in both demand *and* supply sides; many agents are involved; long-term processes occur over decades; and the innovation is not caused by a single 'policy' or 'object'. This combinatory character of innovation makes it hard to say exactly when an innovation process begins – when a small innovation emerges that in retrospect was the 'green shoot' of a system innovation that engenders a new *longue durée* (Tuomi 2003).

Moreover, technologies are often 'on the move', and exert intended and unintended consequences as they synchronize with other elements in a putative new system. Such a system is in 'process' and not pre-determined in organization or effects. Many 'old' technologies do not disappear but live on through path-dependence and get combined with the 'new' in some reconfigured cluster. An example of this is the importance of the 'technology' of paper even within 'high-tech' offices, reflecting what Edgerton terms the 'shock of the old' (2006).

New systems form, often assembled from apparently unconnected innovations initiated within geographically distant locations. Changes happen so that the actions of many agents, both producers and consumers, gradually 'beat to the same drum' across time and space (Strogatz 2003). It is immensely difficult to anticipate or manage into the future. Agents will not know the likely outcome, scale or impact of each 'innovation' since they depend upon what is happening elsewhere. This is well shown in the history of 'cyberculture', which developed through many kinds of networking and synchronization on the east and west coasts of the US in the decades after 1945. Turner especially documents the role of both Cold War computing and the counterculture in facilitating what he calls 'digital utopianism' (2006).

And systems that seem at one moment so locked-in can wash away. Strogatz maintains that a 'network appears highly stable and resistant to outside disturbances. Then another seed comes along, seemingly indistinguishable from the others before it, yet this one triggers a massive cascade. In other words, near this second tipping point, fads are rare but gigantic when they do occur' (2003: 33). A new 'fashion' may take the future world by storm, and then it becomes hard to imagine what the world was like before that storm.

Geels especially highlights the importance of 'niches' for system transitions. He plots the different possible pathways through which niches can develop into 'regimes' and ultimately future 'landscapes' (Geels 2014). Such niche-innovations build up internal momentum through learning processes, price/performance improvements and engendering support from powerful groups. Changes at the landscape level create pressures on the regime; while destabilization of the regime creates windows of opportunity for diffusing niche-innovations into the future. Such innovations struggle with the existing regime but can, on contingent occasions, come together to become a new regime. Geels, though, brings out many ways in which the already powerful resist system transitions, such as the resistances there currently are to developing a 'green economy' regime (2014).

Overall, Geels elaborates how system innovations 'are not merely about changes in technical products, but also about policy, user practices, infrastructure, industry structures and symbolic meaning etc.' (2006: 165). As seen in the previous chapter, networks are core to innovation since 'Innovation does not happen "out there" in the world of objects, but in society and in minds' (Tuomi 2003: 5). Innovations thus presuppose a societal as well as a business model. It is only if a potential innovation comes to be successfully inserted within specific social practices that it will become core as people's lives get reorganized around it. Innovations thus presuppose transformations in underlying social practices. New practices can be difficult to engender by hierarchical policy imposition or by commercial advertising, as in the cases described by Thompson and Beck (2014). Ormerod maintains that the world is much less controllable than 'rational' planners believe. Policy for the future is very difficult to get 'right', as shown in Chapter 4 in examining various clumsy solutions to system problems (Ormerod 2012: 265).

Systems are thus not reducible to, nor explained by, 'new technologies' in themselves. Rather as already noted, there are 'instabilities' or 'ambivalences' of technologies. According to Arthur: 'novel technologies call forth further novel technologies...It follows that a novel technology is not just a one-time disruption to equilibrium...The result is not occasional disruption but ongoing waves of disruption causing disruption' (2013: 5). These may also open up opportunities for 'radical innovations' through creating pressure upon the existing regime (Geels 2010). Innovations may be 'bottom-up', emerging unexpectedly from left-field, from experimenters or alternative groups. This was how the 'car system' developed in the late nineteenth century with none of the early experimenters or tinkerers having much idea of what the resulting car system would look like or that it would in the end exert systemic domination across the globe (Dennis, Urry 2009; Franz 2005).

According to Arthur, a 'combination' of elements leading to a future system typically takes three to four decades to develop (2009). Likewise, Nye notes how past regime change usually took forty or more years. It involves reorganizing society over decades, including its transportation system, population distribution and the nature of work and of the practices of social life (Nye 2014). Indeed, innovations do not develop rapidly: 'A revolution does not arrive until we reorganize our activities...around its technologies, and until those technologies adapt themselves to us. For this to happen, the new domain must gather adherents and prestige. It must find purposes and uses...This time is likely to be decades, not years. And during this time the old technology lives on', generally locking out the new (Arthur 2009: 157).

An example of the problematic character of policy development can be seen in the 'need' for people to reduce their carbon footprint. It is often argued that if only humans understood this need better through more education, then they would pursue rational policies to reduce their future carbon footprint and save the earth from irreversible climate change and long-term energy insecurity.

This kind of argument is normally derived from an individualistic 'behaviour change' policy programme focusing upon rational actors being encouraged or nudged to think and behave differently. However, Shove and colleagues strongly argue against this model of behaviour change that is based upon the dominant paradigm of 'ABC' – attitude, behaviour and choice. Shove shows that it is necessary to transform or replace high-carbon social practices, and only in that more radical way will future energy 'demand' and CO_2 emissions be significantly reduced (Shove 2010).

Innovations likely to be important in the future must also confront the momentum of existing systems since the future is not at all empty. Such momentum makes it difficult to reverse systems in which most people are strongly embedded through social networks, and in which large global corporations have interests in the 'business as usual' of, for example, 'carbon capitalism' (Urry 2013b). Societal change can be glacially slow, as seen in the persistence of the car system that dates from the late nineteenth century.

This slowness of change stems from many limits on futures. Such limits include cognitive and non-cognitive human capacities, the embedded practices and traditions within each society, the power and conserving effect of national and international states, interlocking global processes operating on multiple scales, the relative fixity of the built environment, various economic, technological and social path-dependencies, the emissions already in the atmosphere, and large-scale enduring economic–technological, social, environmental and political inequalities around the globe. These powerful features of the landscape make only certain futures possible at any moment in time.

Thus the future is not just waiting to be transformed. Futurist Buckminster Fuller explained that it is very difficult to change and innovate what lies in the future: 'You never change anything by fighting the existing reality. To change something, build a new model that makes the existing model obsolete.' This is effectively what happened in the case of mobile phones, which were developed as a new model alongside landline phones but did not challenge them directly. It was only much later that mobile phone technology made the existing telephone model partially obsolete.

It is also almost impossible for social groups to anticipate what exactly will generate desired change. We noted that, while many groups seek to realize change, it is enormously hard to ensure a preferred future. Analogies can be drawn with political movements for change. The mid-nineteenth-century essayist Alexander Herzen famously said that revolutions devour their own children. There are many examples of revolutionary change resulting in outcomes so different from what was actually planned. These unintended effects are sometimes destructive of the interests of those who brought about the initial change; it is hard to 'control the future'.

Thus, knowing what will produce desired future change is almost impossible. This is so although many economic and social innovators are seeking to do exactly that: to transform the world in a specific way. There are many unintended consequences of economic, social and political innovation stretching across time and space; and these consequences themselves engender further adaptive and evolving system consequences. Systems in which humans are 'bearers' of social relations possess features that make knowing and bringing about proposed futures exceptionally difficult. How is it possible to anticipate the range of unintended consequences of any particular innovation, especially to avoid revolutionary changes devouring themselves?

Moreover, transformation often involves what Schumpeter termed 'creative destruction', waves of destruction causing further disruptions within and across systems (1942). Any new system must develop its own 'momentum' so as to underpin further change, innovation and new power relations with multiple positive feedbacks. These power dynamics are essential for sociomaterial transition, but are enormously hard to bring about intentionally.

But if a new momentum does get established, then benefits flow throughout networks and result in extensive 'increasing returns' to scale (Arthur 1994). Such 'externalities' across networked relationships generate, through positive feedback mechanisms, non-linear increases in output and income (as occurred with the arrival of fax machines in every 'office' during the mid-1990s). The 'networked economy' changes how economies and their reward systems operate, on occasions spreading huge non-linear gains and benefits. Increasing returns result from improved coordination between entities and organizational learning across relevant networks (Benkler 2007). Such economic and social benefits can lock in the new system and generate extensive forward momentum.

It thus also follows that tipping points onto a new path usually do not stem from linear changes within existing firms, industries, practices and economies. The economy is driven by the entry and exit of firms, by their emergent effects, rather than by individual companies innovating over and over again (except maybe Apple; see Atherton 2005; Beinhocker 2006). Innovation mostly stems from the entry of new corporations, entrepreneurs, governments, NGOs and so on. Often it is the newer, smaller companies and organizations taking advantage of niches that enable the 'incubation for radical innovations able to develop in relative isolation' (Mitchell 2010: 89).

Also, many entities implicated within innovation processes are not market-based, such as users or households, consumers, NGOs and especially states and international organizations. Mazzucato, particularly, shows the importance of the entrepreneurial state (2015). She demonstrates that all the innovations that made the iPhone 'smart' were in fact government-funded: the internet, GPS, touch-screen display and voice-activated Siri. She also argues that the green revolution today is missing patient public-sector financing that enabled the IT revolution to get 'off the ground' twenty to thirty years ago.

Von Hippel describes how so-called 'users' of goods and/or services come to be part of, and help to generate, services and products (2006). Central in innovative activity are often 'disrupters', who are opposed to the prevailing 'spirit of capitalism' (Boltanski, Chiapello 2007) and to 'incremental innovations' realized along predictable, well-established trajectories (Geels, Schot 2007).

This analysis bears some similarity to what is now called 'responsible innovation', developing institutional capacities to help researchers anticipate possible future impacts and implications, to open up such questions to broader and more inclusive dialogue, to encourage reflection on the motivations for and potential implications of research, and to use these processes to influence innovation in a responsive manner (Macnaghten et al. 2015: 92).

But often there is just no effective synchronization of the potential elements of a new system. The innovation remains a 'niche' or disappears over time. And there are of course many examples of 'failed systems'. The anarchy of innovation does not result in all necessary elements being present, synchronized and assembled.

An example of a 'failed' system was the Aramis rapid transit system that was developed during the 1960s and 1970s in France (Latour 1996). This could have been a major advance in personal rapid transit – combining the efficiency of a subway with the flexibility of the private automobile. But in the end, the system of electronic couplings proved too complex and expensive and plans were jettisoned in 1987. At the time there was no extensive 'digitization' of movement that, combined with the electronically and mechanically engineered rapid transit units, could have assembled Aramis as a viable mobility system. Thirty years later, after the growth of digitization, a somewhat similar rapid transit system is now operating within specific niches, such as Heathrow Airport and central Milton Keynes. It has some potential to become a more extensive system in the future although it is unlikely from what is currently known that it will be powerful enough to displace the car system (Druce-McFadden 2013).

'Small' technologies

This and other examples show how there are very varied 'human' and 'non-human' elements that get drawn into and become part of a system. For example, many technologies that have nothing to do with 'transport' were transformed into elements of mobility systems – such as locks and keys, waterproof clothing, disposable cups, magazines, maps, clocks, mobiles and so on. We have seen how new systems generally involve 'combinations' of many pre-existing elements that are ambivalent in their nature and functioning. They become elements of different systems as disparate and ambivalent elements are contingently combined. Powerful effects follow as these elements are not necessarily fixed in place but move about and may find themselves assembled into one system or another.

Some of these elements may be 'small' but with big consequences. Examples of such a small change include the stirrup that was invented during the Chinese Jin dynasty. Without stirrups the military system based on the horse could not have spread around the world and, for over a millennium or so, consolidated societies based upon rapid horse-based movement and military power.

Another significant small innovation was the car key and lock, which meant that possessions could be locked inside cars; this greatly aided the spreading of the car system as being more than a mere means of physical movement between A and B. A contemporary small change has been the rise of the standardized credit card that facilitates new forms of movement away from home and work, since large amounts of money no longer need to be riskily carried upon each person who is on the move.

Thus, some elements can be physically or symbolically 'small' but highly significant (see Birtchnell, Urry 2016; and Chapter 7 below). They are often embodied – carried on, next to or close to the body – and acquire a kind of corporeality. They are almost like *organs* of the body. So large-scale and grand technologies presuppose small, intimate and embodied technologies, including keys, bags, make-up, pads, phones, cards, pens, knives, purses, screwdrivers, wallets, sprays, books, receipts, paper and so on. These are put to work, especially when people are on the go and depend upon multiple systems for enabling 'mobile lives' (Watts, Urry 2008).

Perrow points out the significance of such small technologies:

> When you get to your car you realize you have left your car keys (and the apartment keys) in the apartment. That's okay, because there is a spare apartment key hidden in the hallway for just such emergencies (This is a safety device, a *redundancy*, incidentally). But then you remember that you gave a friend the key the other night because he had some books to pick up, and, planning ahead, you knew you would not be home when he came. (Perrow 1999: 8)

Such small, intimate and embodied technologies have to be remembered and not lost or discarded, such as these keys. Losing an old-fashioned house key only involves a key, since in complexity terms they are modular and there are no implications for other technologies (except perhaps for the other keys on a single key ring).

Everyday taken-for-granted small objects can be high-risk. Their loss may mean exclusion from many systems; the convenience of the digital is transformed into hyper-inconvenience. There are techniques by which people try to remember these small technologies, sometimes through mnemonics to make sure they are 'ready-to-hand', which is what combinations of these everyday objects need to be, as Heidegger argued (1962). They are intrinsic to many social practices and people may use memory practices of checks, routines, reminders and interventions to ensure the small element is 'ready-to-hand' at the right time, in the right place and condition. If not, then it is only 'present-to-hand', as Heidegger characterizes a broken hammer (1962).

Thus, many routines cannot be enacted without small technologies that ensure security, communication, identification and entertainment. One small item is the disc called the 'biscuit' that contains the US's nuclear missile launch codes; it is one of the most important technologies of military power. And yet Colonel Robert Patterson revealed how former US President Bill Clinton twice lost this disc as he carelessly sent his trousers for dry-cleaning and forgot to remove the biscuit (2003: 56). Everyone is thus fallible when it comes to keeping their small technologies safe, secure and ready-to-hand. One way of dealing with such problems is redundancy, such as extra keys, spare spectacles, alternative credit cards, multiple digital devices or a Vice-President able to provide back-up if the biscuit goes AWOL. But such redundancy may in turn generate complacency in the performance of remembering and lead to the small element being more likely to be lost, mislaid or stolen.

This dependency upon small technologies shows the power of mundane objects in future system change. For example, the potential growth of a worldwide system of electric vehicles partly depends on the small technology of universal plugs that fit charging points in every country and which cannot be vandalized (Royal Academy of Engineering 2010). Without this small technology, an innovation within the 'electricity industry', there is little prospect of fleets of electric vehicles replacing petrol-driven cars in the near future.

I now consider how the discourse of progress enables certain futures to develop as an apparently necessary new system.

Progress and the future

Explicit or implicit within anticipations of the future is the idea of progress, which presumes that it is possible to envisage the future and this future will represent improvement upon the present. There are many versions of the notion of progress, but most involve the idea that there is and should be a process of infinite expansion (Foster 2015: 51–2). It is believed that humankind has 'advanced', is advancing and should continue to advance. Few limitations should be placed on what lies in the future.

This discourse of 'progress' is used to justify many economic, social and political transformations, as in the well-used phrase 'we cannot stand in the way of progress'. Much development is conceived of as a kind of unambiguous progress. It is often argued that the interests of powerful fossil fuel companies or digital companies or medical technology should be strongly supported so a future of continued, smooth progress can be realized.

One discursive weapon used by those advocating 'progress' is the concept of the Luddite named after the late eighteenth-century Englishman Ned Ludd. Accusing someone of being a 'Luddite' is used to denigrate those seeking to resist the supposedly inexorable 'march of progress'. A person or organization can be stigmatized as Luddite, as holding back forward movement and improvements in people's livelihoods (www.newstatesman.com/sci-tech/2014/08/new-luddites-why-former-digital-prophets-are-turning-against-tech). Politics often is thus constructed as a battle between two groups, believers in progress and those Luddites striving to 'hold up' its forward march.

This discourse of Luddism can be seen in dilemmas expressed by the main character in Ian McEwan's climate change novel *Solar* (2010: 149–50; Foster 2015: 60–1). The Nobel prize-winning physicist Michael Beard maintains that societies must keep progressing and this will only be achieved through switching from the old energy of fossil fuels to the new energy of solar power. Beard argues that climate science is fully established, showing that global warming is happening and caused by burning fossil fuels. The key issue for the character Beard is to keep progress on the go and especially to find new sources of affordable clean energy. Since solar energy 'solves' the problem of climate change, opposing it is regarded by Beard as Luddite.

Much of the novel describes Beard's increasingly desperate attempts, as his personal life self-destructs, to get significant global investment to fund solar power, to ensure progress moves onwards and upwards. Beard tries to engender support for solar energy by referring to how there are many examples in the past where innovations were resisted by 'Luddites', but in fact progress won out, as with the industrial revolution, the internal combustion engine or the internet. In such cases, the forces of progress overcame Luddism. Beard argues for solar energy as a new dynamic force for progress – the only way to overcome the huge problems caused by the scientific reality of climate change.

So this is one way of bringing about the future, of making it seem necessary and inevitable, through framing opponents of the innovation in question as Luddites. However, the idea of progress can be differently conceptualized. Martin Luther King, for example, argued: 'Human progress is neither automatic nor inevitable... Every step toward the goal of justice requires sacrifice, suffering, and struggle; the tireless exertions and passionate concern of dedicated individuals' (www.thekingcenter.org/blog/mlk-quote-week-time-vigorous-and-positive-action). This powerfully expressed view shows that progress, and futures more generally, do not develop automatically but involve suffering, struggle and conflict. There is no simple progress, since one social group's progress is potentially another social group's loss. Indeed, the idea here of social futures highlights that most apparent 'progress' involves social struggle and conflict, with winners and losers (and sometimes just losers).

Conclusion

This chapter has documented the significance of system change and how there is often a long and contingent process of assembling systems that turn into a future innovation. And in those systems, a small element can be crucial, as being the final piece in the jigsaw of innovation. It has also been shown that social practices are key to which technology comes to develop and remake the world. I referred to the business *and* sociological models of innovation.

Also, we have seen how the notion of 'progress' and the concept of Luddism are central in many discourses and struggles that are seeking to produce a specific future. Various reasons were also put forward for why anticipating the future is very hard, it being neither empty and open nor fixed and given. Futures are multiple, contested and complex. In the next chapter, some of the 'methods' used for anticipating these broad social futures are briefly described and assessed, methods that have to deal with the complex systems involved here and that seek to deal with the sheer difficulty of future anticipation.

6

Methods for Making Futures

Introduction

We have seen in Part 2 many reasons why the future is mysterious, so hard to figure out and to plan for. There is really no science of the future. However, many attempts have been made to develop futures and this chapter examines some of these 'methods', ranging from the 'artistic' to the 'scientific'. It should be noted that some methods of 'thinking futures' have been turned into commodities that are bought, sold and circulated. The future is partly a set of commodities which have become key to the strategies of many organizations. There is a major commercial market for 'good futures'.

Learning from past visions of the future

The first method of anticipation is learning from the past and in particular examining how new technologies or ideas in a former period came to be developed, implemented and taken for granted. A good example of this learning from the past is Marvin's analysis of *When Old Technologies Were New* (1988). Another example of this learning from past futures is developed in Chapter 8, which examines the history of the many innovations which in the end were assembled together as the 'car system'.

Another way of looking backwards is to examine previous attempts made to anticipate the future. Nigel Calder's *The World in 1984* was an effort to foretell various technology futures and whether they would constitute progress (1964; see Armytage 1968, on *Yesterday's Tomorrows*). In 1964, leading technological experts were invited to present their expectations of what the world would be like twenty years later in 1984 (drawing the date from Orwell). Dr Arthur Samuel from IBM predicted that not only would telephones be portable but libraries for books would have disappeared. He thought that most of the world's recorded knowledge would be in machine-readable form with remote terminals providing access to all films, information and books (Calder 1964: 142–7).

Dr Wilkes from Cambridge described the likely importance of networking computers. He thought that computers would be talking to each other across international boundaries and thus be able to transmit messages between them (Calder 1964: 148). Wilkes also warned against the way that computers would be able to keep 'much closer tabs on what people are doing', thus anticipating what is now critically termed the surveillance society (Calder 1964: 149).

However, none of these computer specialists in 1964 successfully anticipated the transforming effects of silicon, which subsequently became the basic material used in computer chips. Its atomic structure makes it ideal as a semiconductor. Because of the use of silicon, Intel founder Gordon Moore stated in 1965 that the number of electronic devices placed upon a microprocessor would double every two years, leading to Moore's law (see Chapter 1). Originally this was a casual prediction, but it was subsequently transformed into a clear expectation and target for the rapidly growing industry organized around future exponential change in computing (and see Turner 2006).

One reason why expectations of the future can be broadly right, but often wrong with regard to timing, is because futures are nonlinear. Futures stem from distinct combinations of social and technological processes, as elaborated in Arthur's analysis of the making of new technologies (2009). Their development at any moment depends upon other 'events' some of which also lie 'in the future', such as, in the case of computing, the black swan of silicon. Anticipating futures, while essential for social science, is the most difficult of tasks because of the many interdependent contingencies involved in initiating what can turn out to be a new system of beliefs, or practices, or technologies.

Studying 'failed' futures

A second method of thinking futures is to examine 'failed' futures, where what was anticipated as a momentous change did not develop and transform the world as anticipated. The relative failure of the supersonic jet Concorde is interesting here, indicating that the 'fastest' and the 'most advanced' is often not necessarily the most successful. Another failed future is the prediction often made during the final decades of the last century that by now all homes would contain domestic robots serving people's household needs. And the classic failed future is the prediction proposed in 1943 by Thomas Watson, President of IBM, who confidently stated: 'I think there is a world market for maybe five computers' (www.techhive.com/article/155984/worst_tech_predictions.html).

A related exercise in anticipating the future assessed fifty predictions made in *Scientific American* in 2005 (http://gizmodo.com/why-scientific-americans-predictions-from-10-years-ago-1701106456). Overall, many of the 'predictions' made had not yet occurred after a decade, with work still ongoing, artificial intelligence being the clearest example. Many of the hyped-up innovations took much longer to find uses and were more uncertain. Thus, carbon nanotubes had not had their predicted effects and have been overtaken for some uses by the new material of graphene. Some predicted futures, especially in medical science, turned out to be blind alleys, with companies having gone bankrupt or key scientists identified as fraudulent. Other predictions, such as the widespread development of Airbus's A380 aircraft, were found wanting, with such planes being much less commercially successful than anticipated. Also some innovations are not necessarily predicted but actually developed rapidly and secretly, such as the emergence of radar during and after World War II.

Thus there are some interesting interconnections between technologies and futures, as elaborated by Geels and Smit (2000). First, expectations of the future are heavily influenced by changing sociocultural expectations at the time and not just the technological possibilities. Second, technological developments in one sphere can lead to shifts in what may emerge in others; there are many potential cross-overs. Third, it is usual to imagine that the new technology will in some dramatic way replace the old but often there is a long period of co-existence between the two; so, less the paperless office and more the printing office made up of paper *and* computers. Fourth, it is often presumed that the pool of social practices remains unchanged, but this is not usually the case. A new technology can have both substitution and generative effects. New social practices emerge that no one knew they would be part of, or indeed need. The growth of SMS texting is a good example of this unplanned-for transformative technology that led to many new social practices that people had not known they wanted to be part of, let alone 'needed'.

Moreover, much thinking of the future is too functional, ignoring the social–emotional bases of changing social practices. Just because some potential new technology is functionally superior does not mean that it will be widely adopted, fashionable or emotionally rewarding. This may be true, for example, of driverless cars, around which there is currently enormous excitement being generated by their developers but no clear sense of just what social practices they will enable.

Further, the embedding of new technologies often takes longer and is more contested than technology optimists expect. Indeed, the 'benefits' of a new technology are often more ambivalent than anticipated. Geels and Smit term such new technological niches as 'hopeful monstrosities' (2000: 879–80). Technology innovators often hype the possibilities of the new as representing unambiguous 'progress' in order to attract attention, and especially funding, for what is often a rather limited system in the initial stage. The performative dimension of the visual and other images of an attractive future can be crucial in innovating new systems. The future may present a promissory note that helps to transform the present in the direction of progress and is especially directed against those stigmatized as Luddites.

Developing dystopic thought

The third method for anticipating the future is to develop dystopic visions that act as a warning to those living in the present.

Dystopias reveal just how difficult it is to move societies into a desired future. Various lock-ins, path-dependencies and unintended effects mean that dystopic futures are often the outcome, even if what is planned for is totally different. They make it difficult to avoid dark futures (Beck 2009). Many dystopic futures have been developed within literature providing future visions that many wish to avoid (see the recent art installation, Dismaland: https://en.wikipedia.org/wiki/Dismaland). The following are some of the most persuasive dystopias.

The first is the general *collapse of a society* (see Dunn, Cureton, Pollastri 2014; Kumar 1987). A good filmic example is *Mad Max 2* made following OPEC's 1973 oil price rise (film released in 1979). During this period, corporations and states energetically tried to lessen their dependence upon 'foreign' oil. People took desperate measures to access oil and ensure their continued motorized movement (www.couriermail.com.au/business/scientists-warnings-unheeded/story-e6freqmx-1111112631991). *Mad Max 2* presents a vision of a bleak, dystopian, impoverished society facing the breakdown of civil order, with collapse caused by inhabiting 'a world without gasoline'. There are bloody wars over energy resources. Power in this collapsed society partly rests with those able to improvise new mobilities, including short-term flight (and see *Mad Max – Fury Road*, 2015).

The second future is a world of greatly *increased surveillance*, often drawing upon Orwell's account of Big Brother and Newspeak. Jean-Luc Godard's 1965 film *Alphaville* presents a futuristic soulless society where free thought and individualist concepts, such as love, conscience and emotion, are outlawed. It is said that people should not ask 'why', but only say 'because'. Citizens showing signs of emotion are seen as illogical and are gathered up, interrogated and often executed. Rather reminiscent of Newspeak, dictionaries are placed in each hotel room and continuously updated as words evoking emotions are banned. The city of Alphaville is represented as an inhuman, alienated dystopia where life is controlled by the omnipotent computer Alpha 60. There have been many subsequent representations of surveillance societies, often showing sites of escape from surveillance that are typically located far away from the centres of power in society.

The third dystopia is one where people experience life as *atomized*, as described in E. M. Forster's account of the all-powerful

Machine. This can be seen in the 1996 film *Twelve Monkeys*, set in a post-apocalyptic Philadelphia of 2035. Because of a deadly man-made virus, everyone is forced to live separately underground. There is almost no movement on the surface of the city. A form of time travel has developed and much of the film concerns a convicted criminal sent on a dangerous mission to a previous time to collect information on the virus so that it can be overcome. The film also shows how technology diminishes people's efforts to communicate with each other. Somewhat similarly, Houellebecq's novel *Atomised* presents the bleak day-to-day lives of two half-brothers devoid of love (2000). The novel suggests that humans are, in the end, separate particles, the novel also being entitled *The Elementary Particles*.

The fourth presents societies that are *over-regulated* by rules and laws, so leading to the loss of wealth. This is developed in Ayn Rand's vast *Atlas Shrugged*, a key text in American neo-liberalism (2007[1957]). The book depicts a dystopian US where many prominent and successful industrialists abandon their fortunes and the nation in response to aggressive new regulations. Vital industries collapse. *Atlas Shrugged* advocates reason, individualism and capitalism, critiquing failures of government intervention. Rand sees 'man' as a heroic being, with his own happiness posited as the moral purpose of life. A key distinction is drawn between looters and the non-looters, the looters being proponents of high taxation, big labour, government ownership and spending, government planning, regulation and redistribution.

The fifth dystopia is where the earth is taken over by *engineered cyborgs* operating within a post-apocalyptic derelict urban landscape. In the film *Blade Runner* (1982), set in 2019 (not long off!), genetically engineered replicants, visually indistinguishable from humans, are manufactured by powerful mega-corporations. These replicants are banned on earth and used for dangerous work in off-world colonies. But those replicants returning to earth are forced to 'retire' by the Blade Runners. The plot focuses on a desperate group of four recently escaped replicants hiding in Los Angeles and being pursued by the expert Blade Runner. The film is famous for its many scenes of a dystopic dark, futuristic landscape with high-density living, constant drizzle, neon lighting and flying cars (Dunn, Cureton, Pollastri 2014: 41). There are no longer suburbs, the earth is decayed and millions of people have colonized other planets. Those remaining on earth live in huge 'vertical cities' with new buildings 400 storeys high and set alongside the dilapidated remains of earlier periods.

Sixth, there is the dramatic *emptying out of earth*, with streets or the countryside more or less deserted and derelict. The shock involves seeing familiar places normally teeming with people as empty. Such a population collapse is often caused by a deadly plant or virus, normally one produced by scientists in their own laboratories. This modern version of the Frankenstein story is seen in John Wyndham's novel and TV series *The Day of the Triffids* (Wyndham 2008[1951]), and Danny Boyle's film *28 Days Later* (2002). A different example is *Waterworld*, set in 2500 (1995). Human-induced climate change has melted polar ice caps, the sea level has risen hundreds of feet, most of the earth is covered by oceans, and civilization is under water. Here humans have to deal with living upon a watery world. A further version of the emptying out of earth is where life on earth is so unbearable that many view space as the final solution. Marge Piercy's *Woman on the Edge of Time* describes how the wealthy elite live on space platforms and subdue most of the population with psychotropic drugs and surgical control of moods (1976). There are various versions of this escape into 'space' which possesses possibilities for life exhausted on earth, normally because human activities have destroyed such possibilities. In the 2013 movie *Elysium*, the poor remain on earth while the rich live perfect lives on the planet Elysium (see *Interstellar*, 2014).

Most dystopias are versions of one or other of these visions that should be avoided. They can provide a terrible warning to those in the present to change direction, to reject business as usual, to take a different path.

Utopias

We already noted aspects of the history of utopia, beginning with More's *Utopia* (Kumar 1987; Levitas 2013). Many efforts have been made to establish utopian visions of what future societies should be like. Bauman maintains that the capacity to think futures is emancipatory, enabling people to break with the dominance of the currently routine and normal (1976). Specifically, 'utopia as method' relativizes what is in the present. Bauman argues that the 'presence of a utopia, the ability to think of alternative solutions to the festering problems of the present, may be seen therefore as a necessary condition of historical change' (1976: 13; Levitas 2013). Bauman terms this process the 'active utopia', a utopia never fully achieved but one which exists on the limits of what is possible. According to Raymond Williams, utopias thus 'form desire. It is an imaginative encouragement to feel and relate differently' (1983: 13; Bauman 1976; Pinder 2015).

In his major social scientific study of a range of existing utopias, Erik Olin Wright maintains that people should: 'not only envision real utopias, but contribute to making utopias real' (2010: 373). Lefebvre argues something similar in the emphasis he places upon experimentation and invention in the context of urban change that was occurring during the 1960s and 1970s. Later chapters examine various real utopias where the objective of 'making possible tomorrow what is impossible today' is a key move for social science and social policy (Lefebvre 1976: 36). According to Pinder, utopian thought has the important task of 'reconstituting the possible' (2015: 32); such a reconstitution of the possible is applied to developing the utopia of a carfree city in Chapter 8 below.

A recent example of utopia as method is Richard Llewellyn's *News from Gardenia* (2013), a novel inspired by Morris' *News from Nowhere*. This novel is subtitled *A World Where We Have Finally Got Things Right* and is set in 2211, to which the hero Gavin inadvertently travels in time. Gavin arrives in a utopian future with many people living in small-scale communities. In this utopia people live to a considerable age eating exceptionally high-quality fruit and vegetables. There is no industry, no large cities and no government. Each community appears to produce what it needs for its own purposes. There is almost no inequality, crime or prisons. The population is significantly smaller than today. People principally think of themselves as 'gardeners', with Gavin arriving in an area called Gardenia. How did this utopia of Gardenia emerge?

Llewellyn's novel highlights how during the mid-2050s there were many wars, a dark period in which systems collapsed, including those supplying oil and those which organized industrial production. Three hyper-powerful large corporations went to war with each other (Gazprom, Saudi Aramco, Google?) and generated many years of conflict and dysfunction, including what he calls the Russian–Chinese energy wars. During this period sea levels rose and London was turned into a large depopulated lake.

In consequence, many small-scale communities emerged. These were off-grid, producing their own energy which was now more or less free and no longer based upon fossil fuels. And this energy was given away in a system termed the 'nonecon', as opposed to an 'economy': 'We garden the whole country, we look after it, we waste nothing, we hoard nothing, we take nothing from people less well off than ourselves' (Llewellyn 2013: 63). This society is dependent upon new technologies. Interestingly, its older members criticized younger people for not gaining the skills and competence that would be necessary to develop new sources of energy to replace those in decline.

One criticism of these utopian visions is that they often do not specify how to get from existing societies to such a utopian future. So, although *News from Gardenia* details the future world, there is little analysis of the constellation of social forces that would have been necessary to bring about this dramatic transition. The use of a period of the 'dark ages' in Llewellyn's book is a rather limited analysis of the events and processes that would happen so that contemporary societies could move from now to this utopia.

Other utopias have been developed in literature, TV and film, as well as in some of the futuristic visions in Disneyworld and other theme parks. The 2015 Disney movie *Tomorrowland* is a recent filmic utopia partly drawing upon areas of Disney theme parks with the same name. Disney actually built the utopian town of Celebration in Florida, although this has been critiqued as being more dystopic than utopian (www.theguardian.com/film/2015/may/21/tomorrowland-disney-strange-utopia-shaped-world-tomorrow).

We return to various utopias in Part 3, where we will see the powerful role that they can play in helping to imagine, anticipate and bring about that which seems in the present so difficult to realize.

Extrapolating

A fifth method for anticipating futures is to extrapolate from elements of the present. Earlier sociological examples of this included Max Weber's account of the increasing 'iron cage' of bureaucracy,

Durkheim's anticipation of the future spreading of anomie or normlessness within modern social life, and Simmel's expectations regarding how life within the metropolis will increasingly entail growing systems of punctuality *and* the spreading of a blasé attitude.

A later example of social science extrapolation developed during the 1960s and 1970s was modernization theory. This theory imagined a single trajectory for modern societies. If societies adopted western education, free markets, western values and political forms, then they would move along the route to modernity, this being seen as the best form society has yet taken. This had major impacts, as the World Bank and the IMF adopted and implemented versions of 'modernization'. Appadurai, however, documents the many empirical inadequacies of such extrapolations from the present to a single future, linking them to modernization theory's conceptual weakness (2013: 218–20).

More recent extrapolations have become far more technical, often drawn from time series data from the recent past which are then used to develop 'foresight' into the future (Son 2015: 128). Much future-making here normally involves the assumption of 'business as usual'; and the main issue is the new 'technology' that might develop and what it might do to the future. Such forecasting involves seeing some feature of the present as the key mechanism in how people's lives will predictably unfold in the future.

But many such extrapolations do not get the future right – as, for example, many of those made around 1970 (https://www.aei.org/publication/18-spectacularly-wrong-apocalyptic-predictions-made-around-the-time-of-the-first-earth-day-in-1970-expect-more-this-year). Especially significant in generating difficulties in this kind of extrapolation are two problems with what are often termed the 'drivers' of change. First, such extrapolations are often based on a limited understanding of long-term path-dependent relationships from the past, which can be enormously difficult to dislodge. This significance of the past is well demonstrated in Tilly's *Coercion, Capital and European States* (1992; and see Morris 2011). This book examines 1,000 years of history and shows just how multiple pasts are inextricably intertwined with developing possible futures. The conclusion is that drivers of change in the future must be located in understanding the influence of the long-term past. Or, as pithily expressed by

Keynes in 1936, 'The difficulty lies, not in the new ideas, but in escaping from the old ones' (1936: viii).

Second, such extrapolations may ignore crucial changes in the relations between the elements or components in the near future, and how these disrupt linear extrapolations. Thus, extrapolations under-emphasize possibly dramatic non-linear changes, and especially those brought about through the occurrence of unpredicted extreme events. These extreme events can provoke reversals or sharp breaks or tipping points in how societal processes develop, as was examined in Chapter 4.

Scenarios

The final – and in a way the most significant – method is that of scenario building. This technique is employed by many of the world's leading companies following its development by Rand and Shell in the late 1960s and early 1970s (Hiltunen 2013; Son 2015: 127; Turner 2006: 186–9). Scenario development involves establishing a characterization of the economy or society for a future year in the light of known trends, the main sources of change and the likely patterns of economic and social life. Such a scenario is often described in detail, with visual images and vignettes to assist those trying to imagine its characteristics and potentialities. The scenario builder will specify the events and processes that would have to occur in order for the scenario as described to materialize by the time chosen. Through backcasting, often conducted within 'scenario workshops', a sustained effort is made to determine the conditions and events that need to occur so that the scenario in question will be realized.

Sometimes, a number of scenarios are specified (see Atherton 2005, on eight scenarios of small business development). Often these are derived from a two by two table (see, on climate change futures, Hunt et al. 2012). In a study described in detail in Chapter 7, four scenarios were developed for workshop examination, relating to the possible future of 3D printing. Analysts determined, through backcasting, the probabilities of various events occurring related to each scenario, and hence which future would be more probable. If those events are likely then that makes the scenario probable rather than possible. Certain policies can be advocated in order to help bring about that future, or alternatively to prevent a less desirable future from occurring.

An interesting example of scenario construction is Jonathon Porritt's *The World We Made* (2013). This is a detailed and informed analysis of key events and changes that would have to happen for the dynamic scenario for 2050 to be achieved. The backcasting is said to be written in 2050, detailing what happened over the previous few decades, told through the eyes of male history teacher Alex who had been born in 2000. The text is an interesting mix of fact and fiction, describing fifty snapshots from previous decades. The book is well illustrated, with photos from the future as well as illustrative drawings. It presents a kind of rallying call for energetically developing a sustainable world. Alex describes how, by 2050, 90 per cent of energy derives from renewables, especially solar; manufacturing industry has been transformed by nanotechnology, biomimicry and 3D printing; personal genomics allow everyone to manage their own health and to live longer; and happiness, not wealth, is key to people's lives, with much-reduced social inequality. It thus shares various features also examined in chapters below.

The book begins with an interesting timeline documenting many events that lay on the path to the world everyone has 'made' in 2050, and in particular the 'technologies' realized by then. Porritt presents a utopian vision in which 'we already have everything we need, technologically, to get the job done – just about' (2013: 275). He argues for a 'vibrant, dynamic, risky, innovation-driven transition' based upon a series of step-changes (Porritt 2013: 276). Crucially significant is the growth of what he calls global empathy, rather than a war of all against all. This empathy is facilitated by two technologies, the internet and solar energy, which is much less likely to be owned by corporations (on global empathy, see Rifkin 2009). Solar is described as the 'greatest ever technological leveller in the history of humankind' and is seen as becoming almost ubiquitous as its cost plummets over the course of the twenty-first century (Porritt 2013: 269).

According to Porritt, this world of 2050 was not arrived at in a smooth manner. His backcasting is notable for how the book documents many potential reversals and catastrophic events that occurred on the way. At different periods these events included water riots in the Middle East, peaking of oil, cyber-terrorism especially directed against nuclear power stations, hurricanes and massive water inundations, the great famine, climate change disasters, peaking supplies of meat, and massive protests such as the *Enough! Manifesto for Tomorrow* movement.

However, Porritt describes how many of these events were framed as reasons to move the society on technologically and to deal with crisis through innovation, these being well-described and illustrated. Porritt sees crisis as the basis for innovation, especially as organized through the 'global cooperative movement' in relationship to finance and capital markets. Such innovations involve retrofitting old cities, building new eco-cities, developing co-housing, establishing community farming and initiating 'virtual travel experiences' (on urban design, Porritt 2013: 128–9).

Porritt provides a detailed analysis of the next few decades as well as a broad-brush account of how people managed to get the world 'back from the brink of collapse'. It involves a complex backcasting from a better world and shows how there would be many kinds of events, some of which other writers would describe as catastrophic. For Porritt and his alter ego Alex McKay, the world can indeed be a better, fairer and more content place, but only through a social movement of a vast army of 'young people, NGOs, business leaders, entrepreneurs and academics who had already called time on the old world view' (Porritt 2013: 6).

This book is the single most detailed account of backcasting from a reasonably well-specified desirable future; it details the system changes that would need to happen in order to arrive in *The World We Made* by 2050. In later chapters, I establish a number of parallel scenarios with regard to global manufacturing industry, urban mobility and climate change.

Conclusion

Six methods of futures research have been elaborated in the light of the complexity thinking outlined in this part of the book. The methods that were briefly set out in this chapter were learning from the past, studying 'failed' futures, developing dystopias, envisaging utopias, extrapolation and scenario-building/backcasting.

These futures especially draw upon utopic and scenario-building methods as elaborated in this chapter. These both seek to make futures in the light of the complex systems thinking that has been developed in Part 2. The chapters in Part 3 examine different forms of future-making deploying these various methods of the future. Chapter 7 deals with the future of manufacturing industry and the transformed systems in which manufactured objects or data may be 'moved' physically or digitally from producers to consumers. Chapter 8 examines cities and the degree to which the system of automobility may be replaced by alternative post-car systems of movement within future urban centres. Chapter 9 explores the 'futures' of changing climates and some of their methodological complexities. It shows that potential changes of climate are the most significant topic for contemporary futures thinking, and especially about low-carbon systems, which need to be rapidly developed.

PART 3

FUTURE SCENARIOS

7

Manufacturing Future Worlds

Manufacturing objects

This chapter examines a possible future transformation of how over the next few decades goods will be 'manufactured'. In conventional manufacturing, materials have to be worked on by humans using tools, machines and designs. There is a co-present relationship between humans and the objects manufactured deploying designs located within a person's mind, books, drawings and computer software. The objects, once 'made', are often transported elsewhere to be sold and used. There are increasingly vast distances travelled by many such objects once they have obtained their objectness. But the key notion here is what can be called 'co-present manufacturing', involving producers, materials and what Marx termed the 'forces of production'.

Until the eighteenth century, most manufactured objects were directly produced by male craft specialists working in a local area and using materials and energy found nearby. Such workers included ironmongers (iron goods), blacksmiths (metalwork), cobblers (shoes) and so on. Raw materials, energy and final products were not moved far, and there was relatively little division of labour, apart from between these predominantly male-based craft trades (as well as women's work within childcare).

But, beginning in late eighteenth-century England, the momentous shift to industrial manufacturing meant that these craft trades became less significant. People moved considerable distances to work in 'dark satanic mills', workshops and factories powered by coal and later electricity. Industrial fabrication was performed by new combinations of workers and machines. Work became more complex, a process analysed in 1776 by political economist Adam Smith in describing the advantages of the division of labour in a pin-making factory (1979[1776]). Such a division of labour generated large economies of scale. Both the raw materials and final products were often moved great distances by steam railway, and later, during the twentieth century, by trucks. Many factories exploited raw materials that had been appropriated from colonial territories. Their 'resources' were turned into manufactured products, and then often sold back to the colonized populations (Urry 2014b).

More automated mass-production manufacturing by the 1960s meant that skilled labour was increasingly replaced by standardized and mechanized assembly-lines. Large American corporations (and similar entities in Europe) organized production, employment, promotion, welfare and savings. These corporations were staffed by 'corporation men' who worked for much of their career within such vertically integrated organizations. Large, relatively stable organizations producing low-cost manufactured goods were central to 'organized capitalism', or Fordism (Lash, Urry 1987, 1994).

But with the 'disorganization' of western capitalism from the late 1970s, commencing first in the US, the industrial corporation became increasingly fragmented. Ownership was vested in financial institutions that were principally concerned with short-term 'shareholder value' (short-term can be less than a second). The large corporation and its long-term commitments to workers and place became outdated, with a halving in the number of American corporations since the turn of the twenty-first century (Davis 2009; Sennett 1998). Corporate cultures providing reasonably generous benefits for 'corporation men' became less common. Many US industries and towns in the rustbelt experienced astonishing reductions of income and employment. Similar shifts occurred in other developed economies, with production moving away from previous centres of manufacturing industry that had been based around large vertically integrated corporations.

Relatedly, much manufacturing work was relocated to countries offering low wages and weaker unionization and regulation of assembly-line work. This offshoring of manufacturing was key to the growth of the BRICS (Brazil, Russia, India, China, South Africa). Blinder examined how the offshoring of production was 'the next industrial revolution' (2006). Much labour was relocated within regulation- and tax-reduced zones where labour was cheaper, less unionized, deregulated and more pliable (see Urry 2014a, on offshoring). It became common to describe products as being 'designed' in the global North, but actually manufactured/ assembled in the global South, especially within various Asian countries (Saunders 2010; a British example of this pattern is the much-applauded firm Dyson).

The development of container ships was key to this emerging pattern, sometimes known as the Walmart model. Sekula writes how the 'cargo container, an American innovation of the mid-1950s, transforms the space and time of port cities...The container is the very coffin of remote labour power, bearing the hidden evidence of exploitation in the far reaches of the world' (2001: 147; Cudahy 2006). The average 20-foot equivalent unit (TEU) cargo container is crucial within the wider sociomaterial system based upon global production, distribution, consumption, investment and transportation. As a protective shell surrounding artefacts largely produced in the global South, container ships dominate world trade and global manufacturing production. Such ships are growing ever-larger, with some transporting an astonishing 18,000 containers. The scale of these ships is leading to the redesign of port cities and to the transformation of the overall geography of world trade (Birtchnell, Savitzky, Urry 2015).

The container is thus a vital component within the 'assemblage' of economies based upon cheap unskilled labour, low energy costs, limited pollution standards and increasing 'free trade'. This sociomaterial system has remade global production, especially since China became the new 'workshop of the world' following the reform movement beginning in 1978. This system seems to have much forward momentum, and it is difficult to envisage that it could ever go into reverse. The issue to be discussed in this chapter is whether this current system of global manufacturing, transportation and consumption is locked in and irreversible, or it is possible to anticipate new niches that could turn into a different sociomaterial system of manufacturing over the next few decades.

What is 3D printing?

In particular, I examine the future of the sociomaterial niche popularly known as 3D printing. 3D printers enable the 'printing' of three-dimensional shapes and not just two-dimensional text and pictures with which we have grown so familiar over the last quarter-century. There has been an exponential increase since about 2010, as recorded on Google, in references to 3D printing. This rise is striking since the basic patents used in 3D printing actually date back to the 1980s and 1990s (Birtchnell, Urry 2013a; Birtchnell, Viry, Urry 2013: 64).

3D printing involves transforming digital bits into physical atoms, blurring the line between ideas and objects. Virtual bits of data are fabricated (or fabbed) into atoms and this can in theory happen anywhere (Gershenfeld 2007). Commentators writing in *The Economist* describe 3D as a possible 'third industrial revolution', involving the assembling together of smart materials, 3D printers and network technologies (see Anderson 2012). Digital files could be shared and sold online, with objects being printed at the touch of a button.

In this potential revolution, manufacturing could become more localized. Key here is how objects will be printed near to or by the user from standardized material resources, much like a photocopier or paper printer combines feeds of ink and paper to generate images and texts. And just as the key indicators of the second industrial revolution, of PCs, software and the internet, involved social networks of garage innovators, entrepreneurs, venture capitalists, scientists and policy makers, so too does 3D printing (see UK government: https://www.gov.uk/government/publications/future-of-manufacturing).

There is a range of 3D printers, but in each case feedstocks are transformed into three-dimensional 'objects'. The main differences lie in how the layers are built up as they are laid on top of the other in micromillimetres of detail. As they are laid down, so 3D objects are printed or manufactured, such as very tough bespoke

3D-printed cycle racing helmets. Each layer is in effect a digital slice generated through a computer-aided design. After each layer, the next layer is added by a fraction of a millimetre until the object is fully printed or 'manufactured'. Low-cost printers use plastic which is heated into a liquid and then extruded. More expensive printers use binding agents and powders, lasers and electron beams and more diverse materials including resin, nylon, plastic, glass, carbon, titanium and stainless steel. Recently developed machines can mix together a number of materials within the same 'print'.

Printing 3D objects was initially developed for rapid prototyping, to produce prototypes of an object before tooling up a factory to manufacture 'real' objects in large numbers. As the system developed, it was realized that a much wider range and larger numbers of shapes and materials could be manufactured (Kross 2011). Some objects that can now be 'printed' include medical implants, car parts, jewellery, chocolate, football boots designed for individual feet, as well as bespoke objects, toys, replicas, models, prosthetic limbs, musical instruments, clothes, bicycles, furniture, lampshades, Formula 1 car parts, aircraft parts, stainless steel gloves, bike helmets, dental crowns and customized mobile phone covers. Researchers envisage 'printing' the entire wings of an aircraft, electric vehicles or whole buildings, as a result of the planned up-scaling of 'printers'. Many 3D designs possess an organic appearance with, in certain cases, the direct digital copying of shapes from 'nature'.

Future innovations may include machines that routinely print various mixed materials at the same time; the printing of active systems such as batteries, circuits, actuators and assembled machines; infrastructure printing of buildings, large structures and vehicles; and *in-situ* printing inside the body, in space, in deep oceans, or whilst in motion. 3D printing enables printing models of organs and prosthetic limbs, and eventually there may be printing of organic material such as teeth and blood vessels using stem cells and other organic matter (Clarke 2011; Gore 2013: 241–3; Moskvitch 2011). There are thus rapid increases in the materials that can now be 3D printed (Silverman 2012). Moreover, 3D printing enables the producing of complex geometric designs that would be impossible with other forms of manufacturing. Various software packages, some open source, enable complex and custom designs to be 3D printed.

These 3D printing technologies are sometimes known as 'additive' manufacturing. This contrasts with most previous 'subtractive' manufacturing processes involving cutting, drilling or bashing wood, metal or other materials. Such subtractive manufacturing has many disadvantages, including generating much 'waste'. Instead of subtracting or removing quantities of material through machining or cutting, or forming objects by moulding or stamping, additive manufacturing involves making three-dimensional solid objects from a digital file, building up the product layer by layer (Hopkinson, Hague, Dickens 2006).

This potential revolution in making has many implications for a future economy-and-society. Such 3D printers could become as ubiquitous as networked computers. This would generate huge reductions in the scale of transportation of objects worldwide. Such 'printing', or 'additive manufacturing', would enable objects to be produced near to, or in some cases by, consumers. This chapter examines the implications of what may be a new manufacturing system that could emerge 'after the factory' (Fox 2010).

A new system?

I describe below some emerging features of 3D printing, drawing upon a range of innovators and analysts. In *Fab*, Neil Gershenfeld describes personal manufacturing using pervasive, ubiquitous home computing, open source software and a possible merging of digital and material worlds (2007; Day 2011). Personal fabrication is a 'lead indicator' of how digital resources and techniques are moving into the physical environment. This is generated not only by large corporations but also by grassroots community enterprises, through the 'materialization of digital information' (Ratto, Ree 2010).

Web-based digital technologies would play a central role in global networks of digitally transferable and downloadable files containing designs and blueprints that portable computers could then build or print anywhere and out of anything. Objects would thus not be mass produced but individually produced from digital bits, transferable via online networks, translated into atoms by computers and computer-controlled interfaces. The agents in these networks include a range of suppliers of 3D printers, from small-scale start-ups such as Makerbot to large specialist producers such as Z Corporation. As well, existing printer companies such as HP are investing in research and development and selling products through tie-ups with smaller companies such as Stratasys, on a range of small-to-large consumer and industrial 3D printers (Shankland 2010).

We might also anticipate that people would not so much buy objects as pay for accessing or gaining a licence to produce or download the design of objects. This would be part of a growing 'access' rather than 'ownership' economy that seems to be developing with the digital 'internet of things' (on access, see Rifkin 2000). There is already a large online open source network of designs and blueprints available for download.

The open source community is especially involved here. The inventor of the original self-replicating printer RepRap, Adrian Bowyer, makes clear the importance of open source: 'it's designed to copy itself because that's the most efficient way of getting a large number of them out there' (quoted Stemp-Morlock 2010: 1). By self-replicating, the RepRap 'leapfrogs' the gradual development and adoption of a technology, disrupting incumbent and niche suppliers, and allowing small users, including schools, community groups and pioneer individuals, to adopt the technology without much effort beyond assembling the printer and purchasing feedstocks and other components. A major factor in the growth of home and office-based 3D printing are open source designs that come in kits assembled by the user and print, or self-replicate, the technology for others. Self-replication means that once a single unit is purchased, there is no limit to the number of printers that can be produced. A pioneer in open source 3D printing, Bowyer notes similarities with the early computer revolution, when enthusiasts built their own desktops from generic parts.

3D printing could lead to a decentralized, onshored manufacturing system based on shifts in consumer practices towards online browsing and shopping. Within a couple of decades, it may be that low-cost manufacturing centres would not possess the comparative advantage in manufacturing objects. 3D digital manufacturing could replace the transport of many manufactured objects, even eliminating the business of 'logistics' or turning it into a 'materials economy' based around standardized supply chains of material feedstocks for printers. Digital objects can travel almost for free – although, significantly, oil is the basis of many of the feedstocks used in 3D manufacturing.

One key disadvantage of current internet-based online stores and suppliers is that buyers have to wait for products to arrive, so they cannot try out or touch the product beforehand, usually relying on conventional mail systems. So, personal fabrication could replace or augment the production of many consumer objects, and this will increase with the innovation of very fine printing layers and units that offer mixed materials. Current high-end units print in steel and titanium and have produced finished parts for Formula 1 cars, motorbikes and aeroplanes.

No longer will products be bound to supply-chain forces: digital designs from anyone could be accessible and free to flourish, or die, depending on how well they have been designed. A dominant elite will not determine the range, and energy will not be wasted by forcing physical products through an expensive supply chain before they come to the market. Giving people control over what they can make means they can get what they want, and, through collective processes, designs should rapidly improve (Sells 2009: 173).

Regardless of which specific 3D technologies dominate, there remains the question of the raw materials and feedstocks for these printers, their production and transportation. Currently, tested feedstocks include nylon, plastic, resin, carbon, glass, stainless steel, sandstone and titanium. It is probable that many resources will still be required for feedstocks, and existing infrastructures now in place could be retrofitted for the purpose, although in many cases these resources could be managed via local 'refineries'. As retail supply chains and markets move from creating, storing and distributing a myriad of manufactured products to feedstocks, a materials 'rush' might occur where companies compete to produce and market feedstocks. Corporations could adopt business models in order to produce and control supply chains of resins, plastics, metals, nylons and even foods, which would be transported in standardized cartridges, perhaps similar to – if much larger than – those used in current inkjet printers.

One significant direction is that of closed-cycle processes, in which redundant, broken or unwanted 3D printed objects are recycled through an industrial process into further feedstock. Consultants McKinsey and Company and yachtswoman Ellen

MacArthur championed 3D printing in a report on the potential of the 'circular economy' presented to the 2012 World Economic Forum in Davos (Ellen MacArthur Foundation 2012). David Flanders, a technology enthusiast and blogger in London, makes clear: 'imagine I print you a shoe. Your child grows, as they do. You take that shoe, you throw it back in the shredder – the shredder then processes the plastic' (quoted *BBC News* 2010; Ricca-Smith 2011). As outlined already, there is potential for home recycling and print-to-use practices. Currently, powders and other composite feedstocks have been derived from recycled glass powders or other patent-protected resins: companies such as Z Corporation use their own 'non-hazardous, eco-friendly' powders. One solution that raises the possibility of a circular economy is a 'recyclebot' whereby plastic wastes, including old 3D 'prints', generate more feedstocks for new products in the home from a machine that accompanies or is built into the Makerbot 3D printer (Peels 2011).

As noted, the technologies and practices of personal fabrication would disrupt existing systems of consumption, manufacturing and transport, having cascading effects throughout the world's supply chains. Scott Summit, a co-founder of Californian company Bespoke which designs and 3D prints custom products, argues that 'There is nothing to be gained by going overseas except for higher shipping charges' (quoted Vance 2010: 2). Companies, for a long time, have been looking at the cost of freight and the possibilities of reducing costs by using fewer materials. Some see this progression emerging from the convergence of open source software, increasing home bandwidths and internet access, widespread printer ownership and online shopping practices.

In a major BBC report, one expert argues: 'entire businesses that are built around managing huge numbers of the exact same part and shipping them all over the world and creating them and distributing them all of a sudden need to change because that role is not as critical to the economy' (Sieberg 2010). It is less clear why a company would airfreight an urgently needed spare part from abroad when it could print one when and where required.

Crucial here is that objects can be manufactured next to, or even by, consumers with their own 'printer'. Also, local 3D printing shops could develop on the high street, or in warehouses, or shopping centres. More generally, there is for some products the capacity to scan an object and make many copies, which would produce large cost savings. According to Autodesk's Jeff Kowalski: 'Manufacturing is probably going to be more localized than it has been. We won't be shipping as many raw materials around the world, producing things in lower-cost labor areas then sending it back. If manufacturing the actual production of something is effectively free, and more importantly, complexity is free, that can be performed locally' (quoted Karlgaard 2011: 1).

This would enable printing on demand, and even print-to-need, rather than conventional patterns of order, stock, supply and procure. As well, currently popular practices in fashion, hobbies and craft of personalization, repair and customization may increase and become mainstreamed within retail and leisure. With infinite bandwidth and zero latency in online networks, the conventional trading pattern could be 'turned on its head' with artisans in the developing world 'crafting products for 3D printing' in the developed world, in the process reengineering current craft value chains (Bell, Walker 2011: 532).

We can thus see 3D printing as an aspect of a wider technology movement in which digital information becomes materialized and empowers users through 'future craft'. Part of this process is the creation of new designs that are self-assembled and modular, that users can put together rather like IKEA furniture (www.itproportal.com/2011/7/25/objet-demonstrates-ready-use-3d-printing).

New or altered practices emerging from home, or local, 3D printing can also be imagined as aspects of self-sustainability alternatives, and indeed transition. 'Transition towns', such as Totnes in the UK, imagine communities supported by local manufacturing, small-scale subsistence and craft, as well as alternative forms of exchange, including bartering (Hopkins 2011). The desire for locally accountable skills and products envisaged in transition towns is driven by a rejection of the long supply chains of the current sociomaterial system. 3D printing can generate more local manufacturing, sustainability and renewable energy.

Finally, however, it is important to note that 3D printing generates many copyright and ownership issues (see Weinberg 2013). Some critics have drawn analogies between 3D printing and

Napster, the peer-to-peer filesharing network which enables the often illegal downloading of copyrighted music files. Indeed, an information economy built on the trade and sales of digital designs rather than products faces many challenges. It is also unclear how Digital Rights Management technologies, currently used in music files, might apply to designs that could be readily and easily re-engineered.

There are also problematic consequences of printing objects that may enable criminal activity. Keys can be printed from a photograph that enable access to locked premises (www.independent.co.uk/life-style/gadgets-and-tech/news/the-3dprinted-key-that-can-unlock-anything-9701203.html). 3D printers could be used by anyone, including children and teenagers, to print illegal artefacts such as weapons or counterfeit goods.

Also, 3D printing could undermine the authenticity of cultural artefacts through flawless replicas from 3D scanned originals or from the dissemination of original blueprints or designs. Easton describes the importance of the economy of trust – organizations and investors in valued objects may lose the trust of consumers if products are endlessly reproduced (2011).

In the next section, I elaborate just what might be the pattern of development here. There is, incidentally, very little social science analysis of the implications of 3D printing, although the possible development of 3D printing has many implications for social futures (Gore 2013).

Four possible futures

Futurist Brian Johnson from Intel proposed that science fiction (SF) should be a method for futures work. He argued that thinking about the future of current innovations is core to companies where final products appeared many years after patents were submitted and exhaustive testing and prototyping conducted (Johnson 2011: 31). He presents SF prototyping as an emergent tool within forecasting – a 'prototype' in this context is 'a story or a fictional depiction of a product' (Johnson 2011: 12). SF is not just a resource to draw upon for possible imaginings of future worlds, but also a technique for generating scenarios through developing characters, plots and narrative stories: 'stories are not about technology, megatrends or predictions' – rather, the 'future is about people' (Johnson 2011: 5).

The usefulness of SF within 'futures thinking' is shown elsewhere (see Birtchnell, Urry 2013b; Collie 2011). And there are significant examples of scientists themselves being influenced by SF. In many cases, the writer works in dialogue with scientific inquiry, extending the argument in ways that scientists are unable to do, as well as thinking through the social consequences of innovation (McCurdy 2011: 15; Verne 2005).

Four detailed scenarios of manufacturing futures are now set out, drawing upon media commentaries, twitter feeds, science fiction novels, expert presentations at conferences, reports, interviews and opinion pieces (these are drawn from Birtchnell, Urry 2013b). There are two axes: the first measures the affordability of 3D printing, and the capacity for users to learn and master everyday functions and develop social practices around 3D printing. The second axis concerns the degree to which large corporations dominate 3D development or whether there are many groups within civil society that are 3D printing. In plotting four distinct worlds, attention is paid to the systems and challenges emerging within societies up to 2030, including the impacts of climate change and energy scarcity. These four scenarios are now set out – each, illustrated by a brief vignette, drawing from a range of empirical materials. They were the basis of a scenario workshop held in London in 2013.

The first scenario is that of *Desktop Factories in the Home*. Here, people engage with 3D on an everyday basis. Corporate control over the innovation is reduced through open source sharing of designs and technologies, as well as piracy. In this scenario, 3D scanners and/or printers are common in people's homes. The character Ben highlights the role of education, childhood and family life (Barlex, Stevens 2012), since children would be likely to lead the adoption of 3D, especially via school projects and technical classes.

> *My name is Ben and I was born in 2020. I'm trying to finish my homework but my sister, Lucy, is using the printer again for the new bracelet she's been designing all weekend. Everyone at school has a 3D printer at home now (we finally got one last year) and the teachers regularly give us assignments to design and print out all sorts of things to bring to class.*

For ubiquitous 3D printing in unregulated settings (the home), there are many possible consequences for Intellectual Property (IP). Indeed, it was a similar home revolution in peer-to-peer (P2P) websites and transferrable digital music files that had major consequences for the global music industry. These challenges emerged not from the corporate sector, but from small start-ups founded by young users, sometimes at school. For 3D printing, the unregulated sharing of digital files printable as physical objects is a strong possibility:

Today we worked on a history project to imagine how medieval villagers built their towns. My job in the group was to print out what I thought the village smithy might look like. I cheated a little, going onto a peer-to-peer website with my dad and downloading a replica from an archaeological survey, then messing about with it to make it my own; I hope the teacher doesn't realize!

The wider world in the scenario is also introduced and the limitations of the technology are made clear, based on current trajectories of innovation. For instance, the laser sintering, or electron-beam melting, printers are unlikely to be found in the home any time soon, and this rules out metal products being manufactured by consumers. Thus, it is necessary to stress other forms of 3D printing alongside the desktop printers in the home:

My dad is a real expert: he works in one of the local factories where they have electron-beam printers. He designs and prints motorbike parts in steel. I wish I could come into his work and use one, but he says it's too dangerous and you need proper training.

The prototypes also played the role of introducing possible ideas about alternative business visions in this scenario. One idea raised in interviews with experts prior to the workshop was that manufacturers of complex products, such as white-goods, could make online repositories of parts. These databases would carry downloadable designs, which product-owners could browse via identification numbers, enabling them to replace modular non-critical parts themselves after printing them out at home (see Dean 2012, for scepticism as to this development). There are many issues with this vision, such as the relative strength of 3D printed objects, delamination due to the relatively weak layering process, and the limits of 3D printing as compared with injection moulding. Repositories would allow the diagnosis and addressing of issues, most likely under warranty, but more complex materials and electronics would require repair by specialists:

> *I only have an hour on the printer, as my mum also wants to use it to make a part for the dishwasher, which is broken. She will go onto the manufacturer's website, put in the part's identification number, and print out the new bit. Hopefully the part will just click into place although it's never that easy in real life and sometimes she complains to my dad that we should buy a new dishwasher.*

By using characters and plots, the vignettes created a space in which to imagine wider social practices. In this example, the notion of a 'circular economy' is involved, as a complementary 3D 'shredder' allows printed objects to be recycled. Ben also comments on the possible impacts of current business models – companies selling expensive printer cartridges compatible with only single models – and their development in future to similar technologies:

> *I think she would like one of the new shredders, which you just throw your old knives and forks into instead of washing them up. Mum says it's much cleaner and more convenient and scolds my dad for making us live in the dark ages! Last week I got into trouble because I printed out my little smithy nearly 20 times to see what it would look like as I made each modification. My dad says the printer cartridges are really expensive and that it's wasteful and bad for the environment to use so much material on things I don't need. You can get cartridges everywhere now, even in the local corner-store. The companies who produce the printers also make the cartridges.*

The vignette also introduced backcasting, outlining the future and working backwards to see how it would come about. In this case the logistics of a future distribution service for materials is prototyped:

> *A couple of years ago they changed the size of one of the most popular models and everyone had to go out and buy a new one! We have started to buy our cartridges online and they are delivered by the mail to our house. My dad says that this is how many of the objects we now print used to be delivered and it would be difficult because you'd never be at home when they arrived so you'd*

have to pick them up from the local post office instead. The cartridge designers cleverly made them the same size as the mail-slot on our door so the cartridges can be pushed through.

Finally, the vignette highlights some unintended consequences of this future, such as increased waste stemming from the taken-for-granted character of 3D printing and the copies made of many items:

Next year we will get a local recycling station so we can just take the unwanted objects down to them to get shredded into more printer stock. Our shed is full of all the old bits and bobs we are always printing out and breaking. I couldn't imagine life without a printer at home. Where else would I get all the toys, tools, clothes and things we use around the house and at school? I can't imagine how they managed before home printing.

The second scenario presents a vision of *Localized Manufacture*, a future of high-end printers that are available for use locally. These would operate in a corporate market, so competition between bureaus would be fierce. This would impact upon both retailers and customers, and, more significantly, upon global systems of production. The character Amran describes the shift:

My name is Amran and I was born in 2007. The shift seemed to just happen without anyone realizing. It was shopping-as-usual but behind the scenes everything was changing. In the back of the shopping centres the inventories, pallet jacks, shelf stackers all pretty much disappeared overnight. In their place appeared rows of complicated looking boxes with little screens showing off even more complex insides. The technology seemed second nature to staff already used to printing paper. But these printers now produce most of the things we all want to buy with the added bonus of offering custom designs. Hardly any products say Made in China anymore except ones you pick up in the charity store or on computers and those kinds of things.

Amran describes the experience of shopping for shoes. 3D allows customization but such manufacturing is not as 'rapid' as anticipated:

Today I am going to buy some new shoes for a job interview. You can model the shoe you want online and then go and pick it up from the nearest outlet. I've already paid for it online with my credit card, but instead of selecting home delivery, I chose to try it on in-store instead. They have a policy where if it doesn't fit perfectly according to the scan I submitted for my feet they'll print another one. They also scan your feet in-store as well if you don't have your own scans, although the shoes don't print out instantly (now that would be cool); instead, you have to come back the next day.

The wider system involves the aggregation of retail shops into single suppliers printing a range of products. As well as the production of alternative kinds of products derived from customization and demands for bespoke designs, new business visions were based upon mass-customization rather than mass production:

Many of the outlets print multiple products so you can collect toys for your kids as well as your shoes from the same place. I have an important meeting so I want some shoes that look good, but they've got to be comfortable too. I have brought along a piece of my Great Grandmother's old dress from the 1920s. The colour and design is just amazing. I'm hoping the store assistant will be able to scan it and print me some shoes to match.

People are peer producers in the design process, a part of a business vision rather than a self-led movement. Here, possible inspirations for involvement include comfort, convenience and aesthetic qualities. This might bring up some 'nostalgic' social practices, which supplant mass production:

Of course, the comfort is important too. A couple of months ago I had some shoes printed and they fitted like a glove – it's amazing to see the inner sole with the same curves and dimensions as my foot. My Grandfather used to say this is how they did it in the old days – everyone would have their own wooden 'last' carved to match their foot. He says it's surprising how long people tolerated ill-fitting shoes!

Business visioning through vignettes in this context allows normal situations, the trying on of a shoe, to be juxtaposed with more futuristic practices – laser scanning and sintering:

My friend Ruth buys her own personalized glasses. She orders the lenses then prints the frames to the exact measurements but with completely different frames. It's become part of her identity to try out a new colour or design of glasses every week and the lenses just slot in and out with a click! Sometimes the store manager will take people into the back room to see the shoe being printed. The little kids just love seeing the laser printing out their shoes layer by layer.

In addition, other relevant business interests can be flagged where innovation might take place, and overlaps will occur in the future between different visions. This is the case with medical 3D printing:

I work for a biotechnology firm and we use bio-printers to make organs and other transplants. Often I'm struck by how the processes are in many ways quite similar. I just wish they could print my shoes instantly instead of having to wait!

The third scenario is that of *Community Crafts*, and is drawn from already existing examples of co-production and collaboration happening within libraries, government buildings, collectives, public/private partnerships, museums, galleries, arts centres and so on. The use of 3D printing in not-for-profit community settings is already found (see http://theurbantechnologist.com/2013/11/12/the-sharing-economy-and-the-future-of-movement-in-smart-human-scale-cities/). Richard Sennett's advocacy of making things in *The Craftsman* would also apply to making things through craft-based 3D printing (2009). He argues that it is only through craft work – being curious, trying, failing and then repeating – that people gain effective understanding of the world. He talks of the value of experience 'as craft' (Sennett 2009: 288). In this vignette, Jill goes to her local library to participate in such craft work using 3D printers:

My name is Jill and I was born in 1997. Tonight after work I am looking forward to going to the local library for my weekly crafting group. A couple of years ago the council gave the library a big grant to purchase the new range of large multi-material 3D printers in a special centre designed for the community.

The power of vignettes lies in capturing current technological issues in society and transposing them into the future. In this case, issues arise from interaction with mediators, who engage with the new technology on behalf of users, and also in the use of a shared non-corporate community space:

> *At first, I was intimidated by the large machines (standing as tall as me against the wall) although they do look a lot like the centralized paper printer we had down the hall in my office, which always seemed to be going wrong and jamming! These printers all seem to work fine, except once when a young man tried to mix in his own materials; we found out he was trying to print using flour! From now on the technicians all watch the younger users really closely. I think they are also afraid of illegal and pirated items being printed. One of the printers still smells a little like burnt bread.*

In this scenario it was important to convey the axes of uncertainty behind its design. In order to show her relatively low engagement with the technology, Jill describes her interaction with the library personnel and equipment:

> *There is a digital information officer on-hand most days to assist with converting the files we bring in from home or, for those of us who are real beginners, getting us set up on the computers the library provides for people in the community who don't have software at home. The software in the library combines together all sorts of templates in an easy-to-use interface. You simply select the object you want to make from a list, which you can change as much as you like with the haptic controller. The software on these library computers is far simpler than my home program, but I prefer the convenience of designing in my own time, so I attended a special course that the library also offers once a month; I was so excited about what I learnt that I ran out and bought one of the small handheld 3D scanners! The first thing I scanned was my dog and the librarians all laughed when they saw the life-size replica emerging from the powder with its bemused expression.*

As in the other scenarios, the wider systemic attributes of the 'world' are a crucial feature to convey to the workshop participants, including materials and the transportation of resources for printing. The use of creative prototypes was instrumental in exploring these landscape features:

> *Once a week the library gets a big delivery of new cartridges for the printers and a special technician comes in to replace them and*

take away the empty ones. Our group meets the day after the delivery so we never have any problems with running out of materials. Apparently they come straight from a special oil refinery on the coast, which produces both petrol and feedstocks for the regional market. Seeing the oil company's logo on the side of the truck certainly raises some eyebrows about the environmental aspects of what we are doing.

Finally, Jill notes the sociabilities that are involved in such craft work:

The craft group is as much a social occasion as anything else. We all bring in homemade cakes and have many tea breaks while the printers are working. It is very much part of the sharing economy. We all help each other out and there are so many eclectic interests. My crafting friend Michael is running a small home business and sells his own range of model train accessories. We all marvel at the incredible detail of the houses and railway stations. He assures all his clients that the parts he sells are unique. Every month we have a local maker-fair where we all have stalls selling our items and other homemade things.

The final scenario is *Only Prototyping*. Here the character explains why the 3D world did not develop as many technology optimists envisaged. 3D printing never moved much beyond the prototyping stage (see Tita 2014, on 3D printing firms getting a 'reality check'). In the text *Sustainable Materials*, there is limited attention devoted to 3D printing, with many problems being identified, such as those involved in manufacturing steel (Allwood, Cullen 2012). A parallel example of a stalled technology future within communications is the limited uptake of video conferencing where the hype has not so far been realized, with problems of standardization, maintenance and consistency. This vignette from Juliet ends with the bursting of the 3D printing bubble rather similar to the bursting of the dot.com bubble in 2000:

My name is Juliet and I was born in 2004. I read about 3D printing in the news and that's why I got together a bunch of friends and an angel investor to put together a garage of industrial printers. We'd been tinkering around with Makerbots and other open source small footprint desktop printers for a while and we decided to start a niche bureau drawing on our IT and engineering experience. We were inspired by how the company 3D Systems had gone from a garage to a multinational company almost overnight. We wanted to be part of the next computer revolution, although at the time we'd forgotten about the dot.com bubble.

In this vignette, 3D printing is not seen as leading to the restructuring of global manufacturing, and it explores why this did not happen.

Our idea seemed risk-free. There would no inventories, no transport and importation costs and no difficult sub-contracts with factories in China. Our idea, we thought, was sound. Building companies always need to have complicated scaffolding and they often have to purchase small steel parts in bulk or at great expense individually. We promised to print small runs of unique steel parts with amazingly quick turnarounds and all done locally. Nothing shipped over from China. But once we'd actually bought the printer things started to go wrong. First, the company kept messing about with the cost of the materials. We'd been assured that the feedstocks would always be affordable, but hadn't realized just how much powder we'd go through. Then another company who we sourced materials from started changing the size of their orders. We had to source alternatives from elsewhere and have not been satisfied since then. It's not worked out well for us.

As in the other vignettes, inferences are drawn from the logic of paper printing. In a world of low engagement, the reliability and intuitiveness of the 3D technology play an important role in its limited scale of adoption. This is captured in Juliet's comment:

Then the printer completely broke. There was some issue with the warranty contract and we couldn't get consistent repairs. It just kept on breaking and this added delays to our orders. Then the technician the 3D printer supplier had trained, left to work for a competitor. We could barely turn the thing on, let alone refine and often re-engineer the custom objects supplied by customers. In some cases we'd have to cancel jobs because we couldn't get their file format to work with our machine.

In business visioning, careful attention needs to be paid to hype cycles, trends and fashions as well as technological pitfalls. And there are black swans, unforeseen events which have massive consequences for society:

> *We weren't alone in being disappointed in how 3D printing has panned out. The market was saturated with desktop prototypers, middle range machines and other start-up bureaus. Quite a few bureaus shut down for lack of consumer interest and difficulties with machines and a lack of common standards. And when it emerged that the aeroplane which broke up in mid-air over the US had been partly built with 3D printed parts the game was up. Consumer sentiment and investor support crashed. Who knows if in the future it'll take off driven by some demand we don't yet know about. But at the moment it appears that the bubble has burst and the momentum is with old style manufacturing and ever larger container ships moving goods manufactured in large factories around the world.*

Conclusion

So, four futures of a potentially emergent sociomaterial system have been detailed, setting out briefly new products and modes of experimentation (see recent examples at https://twitter.com/3DPrintGirl). These four scenarios illustrated by a brief vignette are Desktop Factories in the Home, Localized Manufacture, Community Crafts, and Only Prototyping.

We cannot predict whether any of the first three futures will be assembled with other elements into a major new system that over time would displace the mass-production/mass-consumption (Walmart) system of recent decades. Writing the history of the present is fraught with many dangers, especially avoiding the technology hyperbole of those innovating an apparently 'new' system.

One crucial issue with 3D printing is the lack of common standards for diverse printers. These standards need to be developed and implemented fast, rather like the standards developed for personal computers by Microsoft and Apple. If they were to develop, then there is potential for a major new system to emerge, with significant economies of scale. Another 'event' that would weaken the existing global system is a change in the relatively low cost and availability of oil that is currently used to power the container ships that transport almost all goods from one side of the globe to the other. If oil was indeed to be much less available and relatively expensive, then the current basis of the Walmart model of production, distribution and consumption would be undermined. I elaborated elsewhere the many complexities of how oil makes the world goes round, and this is explored in the next chapter (Urry 2013b).

So far, the rate of growth of 3D is not that large; by 2018, the global size of 3D printing will be around $3billion per annum (www.slashgear.com/3d-printing-market-to-hit-3-billion-by-2018–23239870). Thus, it seems unlikely that a 'new' future world of 3D fabrication will, in the near future, substitute for offshored manufacturing, long supply chains and containerization. But 3D printing will change the overall ecology of machines and technologies, and a combination of Localized Manufacture and Community Crafts 3D printing is the most likely. 3D will constitute an important niche, and the issue then is the extent to which that niche will turn into a whole system change.

8

Cities on the Move

Autopia?

By 2007, for the first time in human history, more than half the world's population lived in cities. And it is projected that this proportion will rise to two-thirds by 2050 when the world's urban population will exceed 6 billion (www.un.org/en/development/desa/news/population/world-urbanization-prospects-2014.html). This seems a plausible extrapolation, although it assumes an absence of catastrophic events such as global epidemics, climate change catastrophes, large water and food shortages, major global recessions and so on.

Such cities are characterized by an exceptional scale of connections, networks and flows (UN-Habitat 2013). They are places of intense, overlapping and resource-dependent movements of people, information and objects. Underlying that movement is energy: 'much of the city's existence is concerned with energy flows taking place on different levels: from water and sewage through to electricity and information, from people and animals, to machines and vegetables' (Amin, Thrift 2002: 82). Cities are places of high-intensity energy.

Central to movement within almost all contemporary cities is automobility. As J. G. Ballard writes: 'If I were asked to condense the whole of the present [twentieth] century into one mental picture I would pick a familiar everyday sight: a man in a motor car, driving along a concrete highway to some unknown destination' (quoted Platt 2000: 194). The sociomaterial system of automobility structures the spaces of the city, generating a distinct 'machine-space' based upon steel-and-petroleum cars and trucks monopolizing space (Horvath 1974: 174–5).

Virginia Woolf described this transformative power of the novel car system after she bought her first car in 1927: 'Yes, the motor car is turning out to be the joy of our lives, an additional life, free and mobile and airy... Soon we shall look back at our pre-motor days as we do now at our days in the caves' (quoted Morrison 2008). The car system was, for Woolf and others, a utopia, or what Wollen and Kerr term an 'autopia', which has successfully spread around the world over the past century (2002).

There are alternative interpretations of the car system. SF author Arthur C. Clarke wrote that contemporary civilization could not survive for ten minutes without cars, but while the car is incredible, it is not something a sane society should ever tolerate (2000: 33). Clarke describes how a casual observer on a Monday morning would conclude that they had entered a living hell produced by all these moving cars. Similarly, the British poet Heathcote Williams in *Autogeddon* noted how aliens observing life upon earth would think that its major life-form was not humans at all, but automobiles acting as hosts to its needy carbon-consuming occupants (1991; Schneider 2005[1971]).

The automobile symbolizes many aspects of human civilization. The car system developed over the last century, especially after the first appearance of an oil gusher in 1901 at Spindletop in Texas. Virtually free energy spurting out of the ground led many to believe that there really was (black) gold at the end of the rainbow. If people only drilled in the right place, then vast amounts of more or less free energy would spurt out. Upton Sinclair described this in *Oil!*: 'The inside of the earth seemed to burst through that hole; a roaring and rushing, as Niagara, and a black column shot up into the air, two hundred feet, two hundred and fifty – no one could say for sure – and came thundering down to earth as a mass of thick, black, slimy, slippery fluid' (2008[1926]: 25; Urry 2013b).

There was nothing natural about the way in which four-person cars powered by petroleum and made of steel took over the planet. At the end of the nineteenth century, there were in fact three main ways of propelling new 'horseless carriages': steam power, electric batteries and petroleum. The last of these came to dominate, but due to what were historically contingent 'small' causes (Dennis, Urry 2009; Urry 2013b). Public races were held in both Europe and the US for the new 'speed machines' and only a handful of vehicles finished these races. They were powered by petrol but the most impressive horseless carriage during this period was battery-powered, an electric roadster that set a new land-speed record near Paris in 1899. At that time over one-quarter of cars produced in the US were battery-powered, including many manufactured in Henry Ford's new factories (Miller 2000: 7).

However, following Spindletop and many other oil gushers, cheap American oil greatly increased the viability of petrol-driven horseless carriages. Supporters of them even claimed that 'their dirty, noisy, smoky machines were simply the latest obnoxious manifestation of progress...a progression of modern machines that were progressively more intrusive, noisome, filthy, and fouling' (Black 2006: 64–5). The petrol system was established and 'locked' in, with the first Model T Ford appearing as early as 1908, more or less simultaneous with the Futurist thinker Filippo Marinetti proclaiming the new 'beauty of speed'. Overall, the history of major technologies shows that the best new system is often not the system that happens to win out.

In Chapter 3, we saw that once a new path was established social institutions were crucial for the way that such a system developed over the long term (Franz 2005; North 1990). The steel-and-petroleum car system laid down a path-dependent pattern which meant that oil was central to 'western civilization'. Oil is energy-dense, storage-able, mobile, versatile, convenient, and was exceptionally cheap for most of the last century (see Owen 2011: 95). Burning oil provides almost all transportation energy in the modern world (at least 95 per cent), powering cars, trucks, planes, ships and some trains (Worldwide Fund for Nature 2008: 2). Almost all activities that presuppose movement rely upon oil; and there are few activities significant in modern cities that do not entail movement of some kind (Owen 2011; Urry 2013b).

Overall, cars made of steel and powered by petrol are the exemplary manufactured objects produced by the leading economic sectors and iconic firms of twentieth-century capitalism. Aside from the costs of housing, they are also the major item of personal consumption and, until recently, were more popular with each new generation of young adults. Sheller argues that cars provide status and emotional affect through speed, security, safety, sexual success, career achievement, freedom, family and, often, masculinity (Sheller 2004: 221–42). Cars are visual icons developed and reinforced through immensely powerful and seductive literary, filmic and advertising images (Wollen, Kerr 2002). They also enable making multiple trips and carrying and locking away objects that are needed while people are 'on the move', travelling from task to task, place to place.

Cars provide a sanctuary, a zone of protection between their inhabitants and the dangerous world of other cars moving towards and beside one at high speeds on the 'killing fields' of modern roads. The driver is car-cooned in an iron cage separated from many risks, strapped into a comfortable if constraining armchair and surrounded by micro-electronic informational resources, controls and sources of affect (see Bijsterveld, Cleophas, Krebs, Mom 2014, on the sounds of the car). The dangers of cars have been significantly externalized onto non-drivers: cyclists and pedestrians and especially children.

Early suburbs were made possible by public forms of transport, in north America known as 'streetcar suburbs' (Glaeser 2011: ch. 7; Ross 2014; streetcars are trams in Europe). Later, the spreading of suburbs worldwide was realized through car-based commuting along roads not built for cars (Reid 2015). Architect Richard Rogers summarized how 'it is the car which has played the critical role in undermining the cohesive social structure of the city ... they have eroded the quality of public spaces and have encouraged suburban sprawl ... the car has made viable the whole concept of dividing everyday activities into compartments, segregating offices, shops and homes' (1997: 35). Such zoning partly resulted from campaigning by homeowners seeking low-density housing and spread-out suburbs (see Ross 2014: ch. 7).

This car-based suburbanization is neither natural nor inevitable, and in the US partly stems from a 'conspiracy'. Between 1927 and 1955, General Motors, Mack Manufacturing (trucks), Standard Oil (now Exxon), Philips Petroleum, Firestone Tire & Rubber and Greyhound Lines conspired to share information, investments and 'activities' to eliminate streetcars from American cities. They established various front companies, especially National City

Lines, which during the 1930s bought up and then promptly closed at least forty-five electrified streetcar systems (Urry 2013b: ch. 5). These cities lost their streetcars and came to depend upon petrol-based cars, trucks and buses for moving about.

Indeed, the President of the manufacturer the Studebaker Corporation expressed outrage that some people who could own a car did not. He exclaimed in 1939 that 'Cities must be remade. The greatest automobile market today, the greatest untapped field of potential customers, is the large number of city people who refuse to own cars' (quoted Rutledge 2005: 13). But of course the number of people refusing to own a car dramatically fell in north America during the post-war period – and the rest was history, we might say.

The car's unrelenting expansion and domination over other systems of movement came to be viewed as natural and inevitable, as autopia spread, partly bolstered by vast New Deal roadbuilding programmes. Nothing was to stand in the way of the car's path to domination, which was viewed as central to American modernity. Sennett describes how 'Today... we take unrestricted motion of the individual to be an absolute right. The private motorcar is the logical instrument for exercising that right, and the effect... is that... space becomes meaningless or even maddening unless it can be subordinated to free movement' (1977: 14).

Thus, 'carbon capital' managed to get widely accepted the notion that roads are good for business, natural and necessary to a modern economy and society, although at the beginning cars had been viewed as interlopers. Early road improvement was promoted by organizations of cyclists (Reid 2015). But the car and oil lobby created the idea that such roads were 'needed' for cars, and that taxation and not the car manufacturers should pay for them. Over the twentieth century, cities and suburbs thus became monopolized by cars, which dominated most road space and city environments. Autopia was realized first within the US, especially linked with Robert Moses' roadbuilding schemes. It then spread worldwide. Nye described the high-energy utopia that this cluster of developments helped to conjure up: a 'future of miracle fabrics, inexpensive food, larger suburban houses, faster travel, cheaper fuels, climate control, and limitless growth' (Nye 1998: 215; Ross 2014: ch. 3). Mobility-systems within cities are mostly based upon a combination of cars-and-oil-and-suburbs.

What problems are caused for cities when cars and trucks dominate? First, extensive car-based movement, especially for commuting, reduces face-to-face socializing, volunteer work and philanthropy. Putnam argues, in *Bowling Alone*: 'mobility undermines civic engagement and community-based social capital' (2000: 205). Two-thirds of car trips involve driving alone, and each additional minute in daily commuting time, often along congested roads, reduces involvement in community affairs by both commuters and non-commuters. We get more transportation infrastructure, less efficient city services, increased pollution, greater vehicle expenses, more collisions and higher levels of illness (http://usa.streetsblog.org/2015/03/24/study-sprawl-costs-every-american-4500-a-year/; Owen 2011: 25). Many commentators advocate that people should spend less time travelling and more connecting with neighbours, generating 'happy cities' (Montgomery 2013; see Jacobs 1992[1961]).

Second, one consequence of high rates of commuting and car-dependence is that much of the physical space of the city comes to be devoted to cars. As Joni Mitchell famously sang in 1970: 'they paved paradise to put up a parking lot'. The many car parking spaces and roads can use up to one-third of the urban land area (see Ben-Joseph 2012). Each car has, in effect, access to very many parking spaces; this is said to be an astonishing thirty for each car in Houston. Cars are a kind of monocrop generating much dead space. Lewis Mumford pointed out half a century ago: 'The right to have access to every building in the city by private motorcar in an age when everyone possesses such a vehicle is the right to destroy the city' (www.nytimes.com/2012/01/08/arts/design/taking-parking-lots-seriously-as-public-spaces.html). Significantly, there are some major cities without rights of access to every building, including many of the world's so-called global cities, such as Hong Kong, London, Paris, New York and Singapore (Owen 2011: 205–7).

Third, cars transform everybody's urban movement and their sensescapes (see www.streetsblog.org/2011/06/15/the-art-and-science-of-designing-good-cities-for-walking). Pedestrians have low priority and face long waits at red lights, which are then followed by short green-light periods. Crossing the streets is not constructed as a basic human right but as something that pedestrians apply to do by pushing a button at intersections. Moreover, where there are lights, then pedestrians have to move in crowds to get across within their allotted period, and this assumes an 'able-bodied' walking speed. Many societies levy fines against so-called jaywalking, while one could propose that the default activity should be 'jaywalking', and 'jaydriving' should be made illegal.

Fourth, around one and a quarter million people die each year from road traffic crashes, this being the leading cause of death among young people across the world (see http://en.wikipedia.org/wiki/List_of_countries_by_traffic-related_death_rate). There are very significant variations in death rates per 100,000 inhabitants. The lowest figures are 3 (Norway, Sweden), the US figure is around 12, and the highest is in Libya at 40. Half of those dying on the world's roads are 'vulnerable road users': pedestrians, cyclists and motorcyclists. It is also calculated that 20–50 million people suffer non-fatal injuries each year. No wars or terrorist attacks currently cause anything like this toll of death, pain and injury.

Fifth, serious air pollution is caused by excessive levels of nitrogen dioxide. This results in major respiratory problems and leads to much premature death. City-dwellers living next to congested roads are particularly exposed. Poor air quality causes heart attacks, while children living near busy roads grow up with underdeveloped lungs and high rates of asthma. This pollution is the leading environmental cause of premature deaths and results in many billions in extra health costs. Air pollution, especially from diesel-powered vehicles, prematurely kills over 29,000 people in the UK each year, and millions worldwide (www.airqualitynews.com/2014/12/05/uk-nitrogen-dioxide-mortality-figures-due-next-year).

Sixth, the viability of cities depends upon the price and flows of oil; there have been spectacular increases in those prices at particular moments, and whenever this happens there is a global recession (most recently in the early to mid-2000s: Murray, King 2012). According to the International Energy Authority, oil supplies have peaked, since most 'easy oil' has been burnt (see Mitchell 2011; Urry 2013b). There has also been an exceptional financialization of oil markets, which increases uncertainties about oil prices and availability (Labban 2010). Recently, it is clearer that much of the fossil fuel under the ground must remain there and not be burnt – so ensuring that future global temperature rises will be kept within the 2 °C limit (Berners-Lee, Clark 2013; Carbon Tracker 2013). Over one-quarter of 'global warming' is thought to result from the oil-based movement of people, foodstuffs and objects (Banister, Schwanen, Anable 2012).

So, the car system, as it developed and spread into almost every society, generated various wicked problems (Ross 2014: 69). But here and there alternative utopian visions of cities and movement have been articulated. In Sweden there is a national vision of zero road deaths (see www.visionzeroinitiative.se/en/Concept/Does-the-vision-zero-work). Other societies and organizations articulate the utopia of a zero-carbon future. And, most recently, the notion of 'carfree cities' has developed as a distinct utopic vision for cities across the globe. It was proposed at the 2014 Davos Summit that $90 trillion should be spent redesigning and rebuilding cities so they could function without cars, and that this was crucial in dealing with climate change (http://uk.businessinsider.com/plan-to-spend-90-trillion-redesigning-cities-without-cars-2015-1?r=US). There is a world carfree network/institute (www.worldcarfree.net), with many cities starting to plan for a carfree future (see http://carfreechicago.com). An impressive Design Manual establishes design goals and relevant planning studies for developing carfree cities (Crawford 2009).

Finally, the conventional way of thinking about travel is to see it as a 'derived demand' affected by many external factors that are then statistically modelled. But the 'new mobilities paradigm' focuses instead on the array of social institutions and practices that form people's lives (Sheller, Urry 2006). While people may be 'on the move', this is contingent depending upon the significance of movement and meetings within social institutions and practices. Also, there is a complex assembly of mobilities which together make possible different forms of social practice. And these various and interdependent mobilities are organized in and through socio-material systems. Moreover, practices can emerge from 'unintended consequences', shaped by and through the ways that people use, innovate and combine multiple different technologies. Thus, new or existing technologies should not be thought of as bounded and specific to certain sectors or 'domains'. Although one can talk of 'transport technologies', they do not develop in themselves; they operate within an environment, and components of that environment can be drawn into and become part of a new system, such as GPS, freezers, lithium ion batteries, motorway sensors, take-away coffee cups and so on.

After the car

We now consider whether an 'after the car' mobility-system will develop in the future and, if so, what it will look like. In Chapter 5, it was noted, following Buckminster Fuller, that a straightforward substitution of one system by another is unlikely. Rather, new systems may develop along with the old system, as with mobile communications growing up alongside landline phones but providing a partly different set of affordances. Over time, the new may drive out the old, but not through any simple substitution. The question here is whether a reworlding will happen soon that will make it difficult to remember our 'motoring days' of the past (as described by Virginia Woolf). Could they become like those far-off times in the past of mechanical typewriters, black-and-white TVs or computer-free houses?

We can begin by noting how experimentation is taking place around the world, seeking new ways of producing, using and organizing 'personal vehicles', as well as other innovations concerned with reorganizing the patterns and flows of mobilities more generally. There are many potential innovators, including not only large motor vehicle manufacturers, but other large and small corporations, NGOs, cooperatives, universities, software designers, science institutes, city councils, community-owned enterprises and 'consumers'. A 'new wave of environmental pioneers' is developing various low-carbon niches within many different contexts. This is a question not only of 'new technologies' but of 'wider forms of innovation, such as innovation in organizational forms and business models' (Willis, Webb, Wilsdon 2007: 4). Moreover, certain cities are concentrated spaces for developing low-carbon experimentation and implementation (Urry 2013a).

This social movement of 'environmental pioneers' around the world is not necessarily working towards a definite objective. But, over time, each innovative drum can come to beat to the same rhythm. There may be no conductor but the synchronization of innovation can happen behind the backs of the musicians and result in a regime or system change (Strogatz 2003). Thus, it is important to develop vanguardist policy which would engender 'a global low carbon commons'. Unexpected disruptive innovations may move, recombine and be taken up within unexpected locations. An emerging set of interlocking changes could constitute a new system comparable in scale and significance with twentieth-century automobility (see Dennis, Urry 2009; Geels, Kemp, Dudley, Lyons 2012; Mitchell, Borroni-Bird, Burns 2010; Sloman 2006).

The rest of this chapter is devoted to anticipating what might replace the car-based dominant system. If there are 'cracks in the car system', will these get larger and be wedged open or is the car system so robust it can 'drive' out competitors as happened over the past century or so? Central to imagining and developing a carfree utopia are many significant cracks in the car system that have developed over the past couple of decades:

- policy makers, transport planners and the car industry are becoming more aware of the car's health, environmental and energy problems, which seem impossible to 'solve' in any simple sense (Owen 2011);
- there is a weakening in the commitment of policy makers and car manufacturers to the business-as-usual of the current car system (Better Transport 2014; Böhm, Jones, Land, Paterson 2006);
- there is much experimentation by small and medium-sized enterprises, NGOs, city governments and large corporations in developing alternative charging systems, body shapes, batteries, fuel types and much lighter body materials (Barkenbus 2009; Royal Academy of Engineering 2010; Tyfield 2014);
- urban design is being developed towards car restraint, including parking restrictions and tariffs, traffic calming, pedestrianized city centres, bus lanes, bicycle tracks, public bike schemes, road pricing and so on (Nikitas, Karlsson 2015; Ross 2014: ch. 10);
- there is significant uncertainty about future supplies of oil (Murray, King 2012) and major campaigns that challenge the continued burning of fossil fuels (Carbon Tracker 2013);
- there is evidence that cities with less car-based movement and more city centre living display higher levels of wellbeing for residents and visitors (Montgomery 2013; Ross 2014);

- there has been some reduction in car use in car-dependent societies, including decreasing numbers of young people obtaining driving licences, as well as a growth in carfree times and spaces within cities (Lyons, Goodwin 2014; Millard-Ball, Schipper 2011; Sheller 2015a);
- there is evidence from some countries that younger generations prefer smartphones to cars, if given a choice, with two-thirds of young people stating they like spending money on 'new technology' rather than cars (Rosenthal 2013).

There are, however, formidable technological, economic, organizational and social problems in 'engineering' a new system. The first problem is the issue of power – both of power over others and of the capacity or power of social forces to orchestrate a new system (Tyfield 2014). Especially significant are the organized interests of 'carbon capital', which consists of the networked relationships between oil companies, auto companies, state oil corporations, and various states and governments protecting the interests of oil-based mobility and production systems (Paterson 2007; Mitchell 2011; Urry 2013b). Former Shell consultant Jeremy Leggett calls this complex the world's most important single 'interest' (2005: 12, 15; Oreskes, Conway 2010), while others document the complex tentacles of the 'carbon web' (www.carbonweb.org). The IMF estimates that this carbon web is the recipient of an astonishing annual global 'subsidy' of $5.3 trillion (*The Guardian*, 19 May 2015), equivalent to 6.5 per cent of global GDP.

No new system will develop without the power of this capital being either emasculated or somehow incorporated within the emerging system. It is noteworthy how major vehicle manufacturers are indeed 'rebranding' themselves as organizers of mobility more generally, rather than as mere automobility manufacturers (see http://audi-urban-future-initiative.com/facts/award-ceremony).

The second issue is that any future system that is 'after the car' must not eliminate its affordances or fail to innovate others which are in some sense 'as good'. Sheller writes: 'Car consumption is never simply about rational economic choices, but is as much about aesthetic, emotional and sensory responses to driving, as well as patterns of kinship, sociability, habitation and work'

(2004: 222). Any post-car system must become an object of consumer fashion and not only involve 'loss' and nostalgia for the previous regime. It may not involve all the affordances of the current car system but it will need to provide others: a new kinaesthetic intertwining of motion and emotion, as Sheller expresses it (2004: 227). The new system should be fashionable and faddish, and win hearts and minds by being more fun, which was the case with smartphones as opposed to landline phones. It is also necessary to avoid the 'rebound' problem: if energy savings are made in one sphere, then there must not be subsequently increased energy consumption in that or other spheres (Paterson 2007: 199).

The third issue concerns the scale of the public expenditure necessary for a new system, since much of the transformation will have to be infrastructural. In order to generate sufficient revenues, taxation should be raised roughly in proportion to the scale of activities characterizing each company's production within each society. This would presuppose some reversal of the scale of 'off-shoring' finance and tax that characterizes contemporary economies (see Urry 2014a). Moreover, systems of calculation need to be in place so that interventions with regard to mobility initiatives can be assessed alongside each other. This requires a common cost–benefit system, a clear method of attributing benefit to particular schemes and a way of de-siloing potential funding streams. Such systems of calculation should further the collective interests or 'commons' of a 'city' and not just those of individuals. The latter often prioritizes the interests of those with high incomes, whose time saved from new schemes will count for more, although in fact all benefit from effective mobility systems, as Montgomery brings out in determining what makes a 'happy city' (2013).

However, this is problematic since much infrastructural funding is generated from within the private sector where companies often use the notion of 'commercial confidentiality' to hide the costing/pricing calculations that are made. This lack of transparency makes it hard for democratic forces to assess alternatives and ensure that collective benefits are properly calculated and implemented. It is also difficult to innovate and fund systems that are of long-term benefit but whose benefits are not measurable, or stretch over decades or even centuries (as, apparently, with the new HS2 railway planned in the UK). This is one reason why mayors with a vision for their city can make a significant difference, as in Medellin and Curitiba, London and Paris (Montgomery 2013). But the broad question is: how can citizens vote for and fund different possible futures when the gains/losses are so hard to identify, being long-term and collective, frequently regarded as 'the commons'?

Also, in any assessment of infrastructures, it is necessary to examine the impacts of future benefits upon all social groups, and not to prioritize, say, the interests of air passengers, or supermarket users, or those with school-age children. Developments vary in their impacts upon social groups as they generate new losers and sometimes new winners. Some developments which are apparently 'public' are mostly beneficial for private-sector companies using or operating public-sector investment (such as train operating companies in much of Europe).

In order to examine these many problems and issues, I now set out and consider four future scenarios relating to mobilities within cities. In examining these potential city futures, it is salutary to remember what Geels and Smit term 'potholes in the road to the future', examined in Chapter 4 (see many examples in Geels, Smit 2000). There is no simple prediction possible, no smooth path to the future. Most anticipations of innovation have not turned out as predicted. Also, similar predictions have been made every decade or two, such as the anticipated growth of teleconferencing and teleworking, both first envisaged during the 1960s and regularly repeated, even though they have only developed to a very limited extent (Geels, Smit 2000: 874–6).

The following four scenarios anticipate different routes that could emerge, 'squeezing' through the cracks in the current car system. Each of them presents a broader view of a future world and not just a narrow vision of how people will (or will not) be physically mobile. I developed these anticipated futures through reviewing much social science literature relating to the future of mobilities within cities (including Costanza 1999; Forum for the Future 2010; Hickman, Banister 2007; Urry 2013b; Urry, Birtchnell, Caletrio, Pollastri 2014).

Fast-mobility city

First, then, this city involves people experiencing ever-more-speedy and extensive mobile lives (see Elliott, Urry 2010, on 'mobile lives'). People would be on the move within cities, and very rapidly between cities. The forms, scale and intensity of globalization are much enhanced. These are cities without significant limits on movement of their many citizens and, especially, visitors. Current futuristic cities emerging in developing societies, such as Shanghai, Dubai, Qatar, Hong Kong, Rio, Seoul and Singapore, provide exemplars of what might be seen as desirable mobility cities.

In this future, fast movement is central to each person's 'persona'. Social status is acquired through one's own travel and consumption, as well as that of children and friends. Average citizens travel for up to 4–5 hours a day, rather than the hour or so at present (known as the 'constant travel time' hypothesis). Astonishing new consumer experiences become globally available as the planet really does develop into a supermarket of goods, services and friendships. Much work, friendship and family life and many leisure activities occur 'on the move', with 'devices/apps' making most aspects of location almost irrelevant to daily experience. Education and work are globalized, with much on-line, but also with rapid frequent movement so 'talk' can happen. Cities 'hum with talk' and this will be pronounced in the high-tech mobile city (Amin, Thrift 2002: 86–7).

There will be extensive growth and further development of 'coffices' as sites for meetings and itinerant work (Garside 2014). Organizations are already facilitating informal 'unoffices', or 'jelly', where spontaneous meetings take place amongst casual (precarious?) co-workers. As people meet for face-to-face multi-sensory communication, very many carefully choreographed spaces – such as airport lounges or hotel foyers – enable brief exchanges within ever-more intense 'mobile lives' (we can note the design transformation of campuses into airport lounges).

Some meetings will occur within driverless (or 'digital') cars, with a greatly increased use of time while people are on the move (Laurier, Dant 2012). Driverless cars would reduce fatigue in long-haul commutes and at the same time enable commuters to make their travel time more productive and/or more fun (see the visionary Sharon 1983). In this future, driverless cars would develop into places for brief meetings as people are freed from operating the vehicle (www.bbc.co.uk/news/magazine-25861214). It could be that people will be much less frustrated by congested roads and slowed-down traffic since 'life' continues anyway, ever on the go.

In this future city, the space above the city's surface would be traversed by multiple vehicles, as envisioned in many architectural and filmic futures (Bridge 2013). Cities would be vertical and increasingly orbited by many kinds of manned and unmanned aerial vehicles. Already, helicopters are commonplace in contemporary Sao Paulo and some other cities, so that richer residents and visitors avoid the traffic and crime below (Budd 2013; Cwerner 2009). Many light personal airborne vehicles are legally permitted within some urban areas. Micro-light flying is a familiar sight on urban fringes as a form of extreme leisure (Laviolette 2012).

Space-scrapers will be so large that they would require aerial vehicles to access them, such as jet packs and other forms of vertical transport (Lehto 2013). The increasingly vertical city of Dubai and the world's tallest building, the Burj Khalifa at 2,717 feet, exemplify such a vertical future. It is also possible that vertical farms made up of high-rise towers could house animals and crops rather than only people, the first commercial vertical farm opening in Singapore in 2012 (Biel 2014: 194; see Despommier 2009). The push for verticality in urban planning and infrastructure design will be driven by elites, escaping the masses through unhindered aerial mobilities and high-rise living. Increasing social inequality will bolster development of the vertical high-mobility city, which rests upon astonishing advances in elevator technology, as Graham documents (www.slideshare.net/sdng1/supertallultradeep?related=1; see Birtchnell, Caletrio 2014). An SF version of this is J. G. Ballard's dystopian *High-Rise*, in which the forty-storey vertical city rapidly changes from civilization to hunter-gatherer savagery (2005[1975]; see the 2015 movie).

Relatedly, Amazon has been developing the possibilities of drones for distributing packages to customers. Freight could travel above the city, so reducing surface traffic. Overall, unmanned drones are getting smaller, while some are designed to mimic the flight characteristics of insects, such as hawk moths. These micro-drones have come out of the pages of science fiction and are getting up close and personal, even being able to land on a window sill. Drones will increasingly be able to swarm, and so this mobile city will involve airspace as much as road space (see *City of Drones*, https://www.youtube.com/watch?v=GF2s5r-trRQ).

Also, elites will make regular trips into space via the latest versions of Virgin Galactic spaceships. Space tourism will be familiar, with regular adverts and booking via websites (space travel insurance is already available at www.thelocal.de/national/20111118–38951.html).

But this fast-mobility city will only develop if a new post-carbon energy system is innovated and implemented around the world. Such a system will enable the mobilities of peoples and objects to be more extensive and frequent, at the same time as reducing CO_2 emissions. In this scenario, doomsday futures do not materialize and the problems of energy supply and climate change are fixed through a new low-emissions sociotechnical system (Geels 2014). The fast-city future requires a new system to emerge and spread rapidly on a global scale.

However, such a system that would move people and objects on the scale necessary to replace oil must already be present today in embryo form. It would be similar in scale and significance to what followed the world's first oil gusher at Spindletop in 1901. It will necessitate a cluster of reinforcing innovations (see Perez 2002, on clusters in innovation). And historically new clusters of systems take decades to go global. In order to develop a new system of mobility for cities, to impact within the next two decades, this system must already be being developed. The US National Intelligence Council summarizes the time-scale involved here: 'An energy transition from one type of fuel (fossil fuels) to another (alternative) is an event that historically has only happened once a century at most with momentous consequences' (http://news.bbc.co.uk/1/shared/bsp/hi/pdfs/21_11_08_2025_Global_Trends_Final_Report.pdf). Any new system likely to make possible such a future high-mobility city by 2050 has to be gaining global traction at the present time.

The only possible energy source that could substitute for oil is hydrogen power. A decade ago, it looked likely that hydrogen would indeed be the basis of an energy system providing a major alternative to oil, gas and coal. Hydrogen makes up 75 per cent of the universe and, in theory, could provide a virtually unlimited and CO_2-free source of transportation energy. Rifkin described the hydrogen economy as an 'energy elixir' producing zero emissions (2002). In the 1990s, many research programmes began exploring how hydrogen would provide this alternative energy system. Companies developed large hydrogen research teams and certain city governments set about becoming hydrogen-based (Chicago,

Hawaii). In 1999, Iceland announced that it was to be the first 'hydrogen society'. Significant research expertise was built up developing hydrogen power, which seemed to be 'the future'.

However, unlike fossil fuels, hydrogen is not a free-floating resource and is more of an energy carrier somewhat like electricity. It has to be produced, stored and distributed. At least half the hydrogen so far produced as energy has involved burning natural gas. There are non-carbon forms of hydrogen production, but so far these are many times more expensive and are rarely used (Ehret, Gignum 2012; Romm 2004).

Hydrogen can either be used directly as a gas or turned into a liquid and pumped into a fuel cell. If it is used directly, a whole new production and distribution infrastructure is required. The pipelines would need to be designed to allow for high leakage and the tendency for hydrogen to evaporate. At room temperature, hydrogen takes up more space than normal petrol fuel. Vehicle cylinders would thus contain a gas prone to leaking and would need to be able to withstand high-impact crashes. Another way to transport hydrogen is as a liquid in tankers, but because the liquefaction of hydrogen only occurs at the ultra-low temperature of –253 °C, refrigerating the gas is hugely expensive.

The best possibility for developing a system of hydrogen-based vehicles is a fuel cell, something Toyota is trialling with its Mirai car (this means 'Future' in Japanese: www.toyota.com/fuelcell/fcv.html). A fuel cell consists of a box that takes in hydrogen and oxygen and produces electricity and water vapour as outputs. Fuel cells convert energy through a chemical reaction and produce electricity in a similar way to how a battery functions. This promises near-zero emissions. Unlike batteries, fuel cells do not have to be recharged and they produce energy as long as fuel is provided. As well as Toyota, General Motors and Honda are planning joint developments of hydrogen fuel cell cars in the face of stricter CO_2 emissions targets that are now found in most vehicle markets.

The type of fuel cell suitable for transport is known as a proton exchange membrane fuel cell but this requires very pure hydrogen. Current models, however, supply the hydrogen from converted natural gas or oil with an energy efficiency of around 35–40 per cent, which is similar to the internal combustion engine. A hydrogen filling station costs around $1 million to build. The challenges of forming a low-carbon hydrogen-based mobility city are thus daunting.

We next consider a scenario for future cities which does not extend the physical movement of people and objects.

Digital City

In the Digital or smart city, there is widespread substitution of physical movement of objects and people by many modes of digital communication and experience. In Chapter 1, it was noted that by the middle of this century there may have been an exceptional 'intelligence explosion', the 'singularity', when the computing power of computers exceeds that of humans. Kurzweil maintains that humanity and technology will merge through parallel advances in computing, genetics, nanotechnology and robotics (2006). Even if there is not a literal singularity, there would be dramatic changes in the nature of humans as a species.

Currently, 'meetings' within cities are regarded as essential for human life. Crucial is face-to-face talk, along with food, drink, music and many shared spaces. Glaeser demonstrates how proximity, density and closeness are central to city life (2011: 6). Certain cities engender particular kinds of encounters between people, both planned and – especially – unplanned. These meetings enable 'tacit knowledge' to be developed, the kind of knowledge that is not easily codified and can often be lost. This co-presence and its role in coordinating businesses, professions, teams, families and friendships is central to city lives (Glaeser 2011; Storper 2013). Cities acquire a 'buzz' in part because of the scale of collegial, family and friendship encounters, encounters that depend upon travel, so enabling proximity, density and closeness. Establishing and maintaining meetings and tacit knowledge is costly in terms of money, time, emotional work and carbon resources (see details in Elliott, Urry 2010).

But in the Digital City, these 'physical meetings', or the sites for such meetings, would be less special. People would consider that they know someone although they had not 'met' them physically, never shaken their hand or kissed them on the cheek. Rather, the digital encounter would be seen to be as good as meeting others face-to-face. As in Forster's 'The Machine stops', everyone would depend upon connections brought about through the 'machine', or, as we would say, the web or the Cloud.

So, in this future city, 'digital lives' would develop into life instead, with little need for physically travelling elsewhere. Software would 'intelligently' work out the best means of undertaking tasks and experiences. Overall, digital worlds would be central to work, friendship and social life. Likewise, people would say that they had visited a particular place even though they only 'travelled' there digitally. People would consider the digital 'experience' as good as the 'real thing'. By the middle of this century, immersive environments will effectively simulate both co-present meetings and people's embodied experiences of other places (Montgomery 2013: 158–9).

Moreover, physical environments will themselves be 'smart'. Such a smart background senses, adapts to and transforms people's lives more interactively, as people move in and around urban and other environments (www.theguardian.com/smarter-cities/smarter-cities-new-technology-social-improvements; Shepard 2011). The New Zealand city of Christchurch was rebuilt after the earthquakes in 2010–11 and became a kind of living laboratory. It established a 'carpet of sensors' and made the resulting supplies of big data available through an open data store (see Condie, Cooper 2015).

'Encounters' will occur with often-distant participants, with the latter operating remote-controlled 'doubles' in real-time (Weiss 2012). The face of the controller would be projected onto a small tablet or display screen and they would use an onboard video camera to stream events live, with a microphone and outward video camera for two-way communications. The double moves about the physical space and interacts with other participants, virtually and physically. Ubiquitous wireless charging facilities will allow doubles to move around spaces, never being unpowered. Intangible, digital information will increasingly connect with the tangible world, allowing people to, for example, interact with this information via hand gestures.

Some forerunners of the digital-city model can be seen in the practices of young people in the global North. Central to growing car use in the past was the tendency for each new generation (especially young men) to hold more driving licences, and hence more likely to own a car. But motorized travel has levelled out (most European societies) or declined (US): 'travel activity has reached a plateau in all eight countries' (Millard-Ball, Schipper 2011: 364–5). Since 2006 in Britain, distances travelled by car have started to decline (D. Clark 2011). There has been a similar downturn in vehicle miles travelled in the US, after continuous increases for the previous fifteen years (Sheller 2015a, on 'peak car').

And, according to most surveys, digital experiences are now more significant to younger people (Geels, Kemp, Dudley, Lyons 2012: ch. 16). Obtaining a driving licence and owning a car is a less important signifier of 'distinction' and what determines a person's 'cultural capital' (Bourdieu 1984; Rosenthal 2013). Smartphones, rather than cars, now mark social distinction amongst young people seeking to be fashionable (Weissman 2012). Research in Germany shows that the car is no longer a 'must-have' status symbol (www.siemens.com/innovation/apps/pof_microsite/_pof-fall-2011/_html_en/networked-mobility.html). Half of young respondents in recent British research report that, amongst their friends, the car is losing its positon as a key status symbol (Lyons, Goodwin 2014).

We can anticipate that individual vehicles in digital cities would be more like 'networked computers' linked to many streams of data from other vehicles, sensors and servers. Sheller reports that there are now in the world close to 7 billion mobile phones and there will be 50 billion connected devices by 2020 (2015a). This hyper-connectivity would tip the individual car system, a series of cars, into a nexus system of 'connected cars' that orders, regulates, tracks and, in some cases, 'drives' each vehicle and monitors each driver/passenger. This connected car system depends upon a rich environment of information and messages that are mobile and increasingly part of the 'sentient city' (Shepard 2011). This would change the very nature of the 'car-driver' affective experience, making it connected, smart and swarm-like.

William Mitchell and collaborators have reimagined the automobile through the 'small technology' of the superfob (see Chapter 5 above). This integrates connectivity inside and outside the vehicle since it 'will dock into the vehicle's interior and provide all the navigation, music, radio, movie, and Internet content the driver needs' (Mitchell, Borroni-Bird, Burns 2010: 48). Small networked cars called EN-Vs depend on a small combined device like this that includes keyfob, music player, cell phone and access to big data and maps/satnav. 'Cars' in this future will be full of screens and connectivity, literally 'smartcars'.

It is calculated that the typical American already spends at least eight and a half hours a day viewing screens, often more than one at a time (Carr 2010: 87). Each screen can interrupt the others so there is little enduring linear thinking; digital cities will involve multiple interfaces, multitasking and overloading. Those in digital cities will be continuously 'on-line' even when in their 'car', and as screens are folded into furniture, clothing and much of the built environment.

Digital lives already seem to be altering what human brains are expected to do. Digital worlds involve non-linear reading, very fast browsing and little deferred gratification. This generates changed levels of understanding and recall, a state of 'distraction' or what Carr terms the 'shallowing of experience' (2010). He characterizes digital lives as hunting and gathering within an electronic data forest. Google has in effect outsourced memory and encourages forgetfulness, allowing each person to know less. But this will have long-term effects upon the very formation of brains and selves if selves become predominantly digital. Living digital lives flattens people's intelligence into 'artificial intelligence'.

More generally, in digital worlds, Greenfield asks how people can develop appropriate empathy with others, empathy being thought central to social capital and to the hidden wealth of nations (2011). Greenfield argues that real empathy is much more difficult 'if they conduct relationships via a medium which does not allow them the opportunity to gain full experience of eye contact, interpret voice tone or body language, and learn how and when to give and receive hugs' (2011). Studies seem to show that widespread use of social media does not increase trust and makes people lonelier, in ways similar to what happens in E. M. Forster's dystopic account of the Machine (Keen 2015: 68).

Digital cities would be characterized by ubiquitous computing, a 'sea of sensors' and much big data (as well as consuming much electric power). People will leave 'traces' of movements, purchases, communications and lives. And as databases are interdependent, so it will be possible to piece together separate digital traces, of which there will be thousands per day per person. Thus each person in the Digital City will be remade as a reintegrated 'digital' self across different databases stemming from billions of computers and sensors, some of which will be as small as smart dust. There could be a network of 1 trillion sensors covering the world and delivering data to anyone needing it (www.economist.com/node/17388368; Graham 2011). But with more devices, there are greater vulnerabilities of systems with fewer firewalls between them. There are major possibilities of cascading system breakdown (www.wired.com/opinion/2014/01/theres-no-good-way-to-patch-the-internet-of-things-and-thats-a-huge-problem).

With the Digital City, many people will no longer live in 'cities' as such, but intermittently visit them physically, whilst being there digitally all the time. We can expect 'counter-urbanization', with innovations enabling some people to live nowhere in particular. For example, the Bufalino is a single-person apartment on wheels powered by a three-wheel economic and fuel-efficient vehicle designed for digital nomads (www.designboom.com/design/cornelius-comanns-bufalino). Also, capsule hotels, first introduced in Japan for long-haul commuters, enable affordable, brief bursts of city living (Macdonald 2000). More widely available are apartment hotels for short visits to cities. People might live in a distributed fashion, commuting semi-regularly. People would rely on co-present digital technologies for communication, such as remote control doubles using camera and network technologies alongside telepresence and digital avatars so as to engender 'digital meetingness'. People may not commute daily or weekly, but instead dwell in personal mobile homes, as the city becomes a stop on a journey rather than a destination in its own right.

A further crucial element of the Digital City would be 3D printing, which involves replacing the physical movement of objects with the digital transportation of designs (see Chapter 7 above). 3D printing shops could proliferate on streets, high streets and shopping centres. 3D printing could transform the high street into more of a manufacturing street. Cities would once again hum to the sound of many kinds of manufacturing. At the same time, 3D printing, artificial intelligence and robotics could involve the elimination of many jobs and the drastic reduction of the working week as anticipated by Keynes in 1930 (1963[1930]). Much of this manufacturing would be automatically controlled from a distance, with the manufactured objects delivered to homes through the kind of AI systems prototyped in Amazon and similar 'warehouses'. There will be sentient robots undertaking much manufacturing and distribution work.

Liveable City

This third scenario involves developing social practices to replace other practices, increasingly based upon a powering down of the carbon intensity of cities. This future would draw upon innovation in thinking and practice currently undertaken by environmentalists, scientists, NGOs and thinktanks. In liveable cities, high-energy mobility-machines would be less significant. There would be a smaller-scale system of neighbourhoods, with cities fragmented into more self-sufficient neighbourhoods without rigid zoning. Cities based upon a 'centre-sprawl' model would become less significant and attractive (Ross 2014). Alongside bicycles, other personal vehicles would be electronically integrated through information, payment systems and physical access and connecting with collective forms of transport. Many 'vehicles' would be small, ultra-light, smart and deprivatized. Travelling would typically involve accessing such small, light mobile pods.

There would need to be policies and practices to ensure that, if the main power form were battery-driven electric vehicles (EVs), then these were not additional to petrol-driven vehicles, but formed a system with the capacity over time to make these obsolete. But even if EVs depend upon fossil fuel-generated electricity (especially in China), they can be four times more efficient per mile than petrol-based engines (Royal Academy of Engineering 2010).

Collective ownership would also be key. Car-sharing schemes are an example of a new 'access' economy incorporating wider systems of mobility. There are thought to be 1,000 cities worldwide with car-sharing schemes (Sheller 2015a). Smart 'cards' or 'superfobs' would regulate access and pay for people's uses of the many public and private forms of 'mobility service' being developed within Helsinki. These 'pay-as-you-go' schemes for EVs will attract younger users familiar with making 'access' payments for mobile phones and internet services (Owen 2011: ch. 3). The balance between 'roads for cars' and 'paths for cyclists/walkers' would be fundamentally transformed, with the latter allocated more space than that for cars. Roads would no longer be principally possessed by cars (Reid 2015).

Indeed, the carfree movement will have taken root and many cities will be partly or wholly free of 'cars'. It was noted above that at the 2014 Davos Summit it was strongly argued that fighting climate change means redesigning, or building anew, towns and cities without cars. This ambitious proposal came from former US Vice President Al Gore, former President of Mexico Felipe Calderon and their colleagues on the Global Commission on the Economy and Climate. There is already a world carfree network (www.worldcarfree.net). The Fast Company identifies various cities moving in a carfree direction, including Madrid, Paris, Hamburg, Helsinki, Milan, Oslo and Copenhagen (www.fastcoexist.com/3040634/7-cities-that-are-starting-to-go-car-free).

Liveable cities also involve redesigning places to foster higher-density living and shifting towards practices that are just much smaller in scale. Work would be found close to where people lived, and education would be provided within local schools and colleges. There would need to be a huge scaling-back of the numbers of 'international students' around the world (stemming from the 100-or-so offshore campuses in Dubai). In such cities, many goods and services would be simpler, produced, consumed and, especially, repaired nearby. There should be a systemic reduction in distances travelled by people, objects, goods and money.

Such a city would be one with reasonable levels of wellbeing, although in terms of normal economic measures most people would be 'poorer'. Liveable cities presuppose a cluster of elements reinforcing each other. Status would be re-localized and based upon contributions that people made locally. High status in a Liveable City would not stem from possessing extensive connections with others around the world (Peters, Fudge, Jackson 2010; Urry 2013a). Montgomery's *Happy City* details how, after a certain level of income has been reached, further goods, services and income, especially generated within unequal cities, produce more unhappiness and less capacity for 'flourishing' (2013; Sheller 2015b).

A Liveable City would involve much less energy use by enabling social practices on a smaller scale. This would provide more opportunity for face-to-face talk, and establishing and maintaining good relations with others (Latouche 2009: 70). Many studies here draw upon the classic Jane Jacobs, who shows the attractions of neighbours living close together, residences mixing with businesses, the lack of zoning, much use of slow modes of travel and an absence of extreme differences in income and wealth between those living near each other (1992[1961]; Owen 2011: ch. 1).

'Post-suburban' social lives will develop, systematically reversing the processes that generated 'sprawl' (Owen 2011: 25). Owen argues that the greenest city in the US is New York (or at least Manhattan) since it provides many local connections while making it almost impossible to own and use private cars. He advocates a threefold policy for promoting green metropolises: to live smaller, live closer and drive less. We have already noted that long commutes are bad for almost all aspects of social life and so the scale and impact of commuting will be reduced (Montgomery 2013: ch. 3; Owen 2011).

There are thus various examples around the world where some social practices at least have been downsized and localized as stages towards a Liveable City model. Bogotá has developed many innovations, including central areas of streets for bikes and pedestrians with cars on the margins. Curitiba started to develop the first extensive bus rapid transit system over fifty years ago (Nikitas, Karlsson 2015). Delft initiated the concept of shared-space (http://usa.streetsblog.org/2014/11/17/shared-space-the-case-for-a-little-healthy-chaos-on-city-streets). And Vancouver has the lowest carbon footprint of any major north American city achieved through high-density building, little sprawl, many journeys being by bike, on foot and by public transport, and the provision of green spaces and open views (Montgomery 2013).

There are thus various cracks emerging in the high-energy mobility system (Geels, Kemp, Dudley, Lyons 2012). Significant momentum is building up to develop a Liveable City future.

Fortress City

The final scenario involves the development of the Fortress City. Rich societies break away from the poorer into fortified enclaves. Those able to live in gated and armed encampments would do so, with much privatizing of what were, in many societies, public or collective functions (Davis 2000; Graham 2011; Leichenko, Thomas, Baines 2010: 142).

Outside the enclaves would be 'wild zones' which the powerful would pass through as fast as possible. Systems of long-range mobility would only be available for the super-rich. Bauman maintains that one key technique of power is: 'escape, slippage, elision and avoidance, the effective rejection of any territorial confinement' – to have the power to avoid being trapped by others, to escape into 'sheer inaccessibility' (2000: 11). There are many examples of such elites exiting from where obligations would be extracted. The elite, we can suggest, are increasingly 'absentee landlords' with potential for exit mobility, if and when the 'going gets tough' (Bauman 2000: 13; Urry 2014a).

This future involves 'fortressed' walled cities and an extensive 'security-ization' of populations, similar in some ways to cities in the medieval period which provided protection against raiders, invaders and diseases. Those outside the enclaves would be unable or unwilling to travel far. Long-distance travel would be risky and probably only undertaken if people or machines were armed. The rich would mainly travel in the air in armed helicopters or light aircraft, a pattern already prefigured in contemporary Sao Paulo, as noted above (Budd 2013; Cwerner 2009).

Futurists Gallopin, Hammond, Raskin and Swart thus argued: 'the elite retreat to protected enclaves, mostly in historically rich nations, but in favoured enclaves in poor nations, as well . . . Pollution is also exported outside the enclaves, contributing to the extreme environmental deterioration induced by the unsustainable practices of the desperately poor and by the extraction of resources for the wealthy' (1997: 34). Versions of this can be seen in the contemporary world with the 'offshoring' of waste and emissions to poorer, developing societies (Urry 2014a). We might say that significant parts of the Middle East and north Africa contain fortress cities, but with many wild zones.

In this 'barbaric' future, oil, gas and water shortages and intermittent wars would undermine production, mobility, energy and communication connections and critical infrastructures (Froggatt, Lahn 2010: ch. 4). Given energy shortages, many infrastructural systems would collapse, with increasing separation of production and consumption between different regions. There would be the increasingly localized recycling of bikes, cars, trucks, computers and phone systems. Much of the time these systems would not work, with little capacity within such cities to organize systems of 'repair'. The infrastructure would be left to rust away once it no longer worked. Dartnell argues that aspects of the collapsed world would need to be 'rebuilt' from scratch, redeveloping anew the multiple forms of knowledge necessary for a functioning society (2014).

Such an energy- and knowledge-starved city would entail falling standards of living, a greater focus upon the 'products' of the increasingly privatized security industry, probable re-localization of mobility patterns, towns and cities built for visitors deteriorating into ghost towns, and an increasing frequency of resource-related 'new wars' (Kaldor, Karl, Said 2007). These would involve private mercenaries as well as statist military forces; de-professionalized armies (sometimes made up of 'boys'); the use of cheap weapons bought through the market/internet; an asymmetry of military force with no fixed 'fronts' or treaties and peace processes; the military targeting of civilians through, *inter alia*, suicide bombing and drone attacks; the role of warlords combining entrepreneurial and military skills; and the tendency for such wars to last interminable periods of time. Lives in the Fortress City would be conducted with the continuous spectre of warfare, the militarization of young men and the raping of women and girls as constant threats to a decent life.

These new wars would develop in the context of failing states where there is no monopoly of physical coercion in the hands of legitimate national states, especially given the growth of 'private warlords' and much cheaper means of violence (Woodbridge 2005: 207). Such new wars are likely to be about energy and related resources, involving states, corporations, NGOs, terrorists and many other non-state networks. And, as noted above, new wars make states more likely to fail and render the conditions for extracting, transporting and refining resources exceptionally troublesome (this would reduce effective energy reserves even further). These new wars will generate much enforced migration.

This is a 'neo-Mediaevalist' vision of cities of the future. As in the Middle Ages, there would be little democracy, limited state power to govern legitimately, many non-state bodies with a mix of military and ideological powers, much illegal movement of peoples across borders, various empires, many new wars and intense conflict over scarce resources. City lives would be as in Hobbes' *Leviathan*: 'solitary, poor, nasty, brutish, and short'. Lovelock points to the 'peaking' of oil, gas and water, as well as 'western life' more generally. Shortages will make economic production and social lives more local than appeared likely during the increasingly mobile twentieth century (see Chapter 3 above).

Mad Max 2 depicted such a dystopian violent future. This movie was conceived of following the 1973 OPEC oil price rise when various doom-laden futures were envisaged for the 'west'. In it, power rested with those able to access oil or to improvise new mobilities such as being able to get airborne (see Budd 2013, on the increase in private air travel).

Some commentators argue that the spectacular history of Detroit, the 'Motor City', is a harbinger of such dystopian developments. In the early years of the last century, Detroit rose to become the third largest US city. It was the world's richest city per capita, with the greatest concentration of manufacturing industry and, in the Ford River Rouge plant, the most striking modern factory complex (Kerr 2002: 126–30). By the 1950s, its population was almost 2 million with very many working in this centre of the world's car industry, at the time the leading industry across the globe. But Detroit's population has now fallen to fewer than 700,000. It has been described as a forgotten place, with abandoned car plants, empty freeways, blackened corpses of houses, trees sprouting from deserted skyscrapers, half the children living below the poverty line, and many adults functionally illiterate (see the iconic *Detroit: The Last Days*: www.guardian.co.uk/film/2010/mar/10/detroit-motor-city-urban-decline).

This dystopia indicates what will unfold if fortresses are established in some places, while other cities such as Detroit are left to wither and die. Indeed, those places left to die may be 'rewilded' since cities are 'multinatural' (Lorimer 2012). Many dangerous 'invasive species' would spread through a rewilded 'urban jungle' (see Monbiot 2013). This future world would involve predators living outside the fortresses and generating the feral wildness of such zones, rather like the planned rewilding of contemporary Detroit, with one-quarter of the city to be returned to fields and forests (www.nbcnews.com/id/35767727/ns/us_news-life/t/detroit-wants-save-itself-shrinking/#.VTTe_v50yUk).

Moving around these wild zones will be various wild robots. These might be developed from Boston Dynamics' robotic 'mammal bionic quadruped' walkers, such as 'Bigdog' (www.bostondynamics.com/robot_bigdog.html). These four-limbed, battery-powered walker robots are modelled on animal movements and can, via sensors and artificial intelligence, self-correct their patterns of movement in response to the tough environments they move through. Able to carry heavy payloads, these bionic quadruped walkers could transport humans across varied terrains and be well suited to wild landscapes full of predators and de-domesticated animals living outside each Fortress City. We would also expect that there would be much 'algorithmic killing' in these wild zones, something currently campaigned against by the 'stop the killer robots' social movement (www.stopkillerrobots.org).

Assessing the scenarios

So, these are four city futures for 2050 in which personal vehicles play different future roles. None of these futures is simply preferable or probable. And there will be, of course, some variation in the likely urban form across different continents.

Overall, the first future is relatively unlikely. Romm argues that hydrogen fuel-cell technology is in fact a poor way of powering vehicles (2004). If hydrogen is produced using renewable energy, it would be easier to use such energy directly to charge the batteries of all-electric or plug-in hybrid vehicles. The most efficient way to convert energy to mobility is via electricity, since there already is an extensive worldwide infrastructure. Hydrogen fuel cells have not overcome the high cost of vehicles, high fuel cost, and the absence of a fuel-delivery infrastructure for hydrogen. Romm argues that it would take several miracles to occur to overcome simultaneously and speedily all these wicked problems within the next couple of decades (2004). Thus, there have so far been insufficient progress and support to build momentum for what would be a massive global change involving a major array of technologies that would need to come rapidly together to form a very complex system.

An alternative for a fast city future would be that fossil fuels were burnt and deployed even more rapidly for as long they were available. This might occur if the climate change denial movement won the global argument and, in the words of former US Vice-Presidential candidate Sarah Palin, the global orthodoxy became, or maybe remained, 'drill baby drill' (http://en.wikipedia.org/wiki/Drill,_baby,_drill). This would be a strong possibility if there was a prolonged global recession, although it will run up against the technical, political and financial limits upon extracting and burning increasing amounts of 'easy oil' (Urry 2013b).

The Digital City future stems from the power of large international computer companies, the 'server sirens'. We noted Lanier's argument that the future is increasingly owned by digital corporations, maybe less a 'world brain' as envisaged by H. G. Wells, and more a 'google brain' (Lanier 2013). In particular, Schulz powerfully elaborates, 'how silicon valley shapes our future' (www.spiegel.de/international/germany/spiegel-cover-story-how-silicon-valley-shapes-our-future-a-1021557.html). Keen describes how, although 'the internet is not the answer', there has been a transformation of the 'nonprofit Internet into a winner-take-all economy', especially that located in and around Silicon Valley (2015: 39). This new data factory economy changes almost everything. Silicon Valley technologists and corporations constructed the notion that 'the Internet was always the answer' – those raising objections were Luddites (Keen 2015: 140). There is a strong momentum here, what Keen calls a 'gift economy where the only profits are being made by a tiny group of increasingly monopolistic Internet companies' (2015: 142). These are likely to ensure the arrival of the Digital City future by 2050, if not well before. This may well develop, even though growing numbers of books and reports seem to demonstrate that digital lives are not necessarily good lives at all (Carr 2010; Keen 2015).

Since the liveable cities future involves a significant reversal of all current systems, there is relatively low probability of this city being realized across the world. The most likely condition under which liveable cities would so develop is a climate change catastrophe within the rich North that is unambiguously framed as 'caused' by climate change, by high-carbon lives and systems (see Chapter 9 for further analysis). Another possible precondition is the occurrence of a global recession somewhat akin to that of

2007–8, since when there has been a long period in which output and income have been lost. A global recession might make smaller-scale city lives seem desirable and appropriate if there were a powerful movement able to force through, via argument, exemplars and protest, a liveable cities future as being absolutely necessary.

Finally, if none of these three futures materializes, then the most likely future, the default, is Fortress City. Significant parts of the world are already, of course, 'fortress cities', and elements of this system are well established. Many catastrophist texts examined in Chapter 3 point to something akin to Fortress City as the most likely city of the future.

9

Climates

Does climate change change everything?

Central to many of the previous chapters has been the issue of future 'climate change'. A powerful discourse assembled across many sciences now projects how human life will be transformed in the near and distant future. This concluding chapter of Part 3 examines climate change futures drawing upon material from previous chapters. The question of how and why climates may change is crucial to thinking through many intractable issues discussed in this book.

First, the issue of climate change places the future as its very centre of attention. Analysing futures is utterly necessary because of the intense and unresolved controversies over how the global climate will develop and why. Climate change necessarily involves trying to understand and model long-term futures, especially the consequences of GHG emissions and their effects, as they remain in the atmosphere for hundreds of years (see www.theguardian.com/environment/2012/jan/16/greenhouse-gases-remain-air). Climate change leads to new methods and theories for anticipating multiple futures and hence potentially for intervening to avoid its dire consequences. Moreover, such futures will partly result from events and social practices that are yet to occur and lie in the 'near' future.

Second, identifying the 'causes' and 'consequences' of climate change necessarily entails multi-disciplinary research and theory.

This is not and could never be just an issue for one science, let alone one social science. The sociomaterial systems involved in generating a changing global climate are multiple, interdependent and operate on varied temporal and spatial scales. 'Climate change' is no simple problem to be fixed through adjustments within a specific system. Gore describes it as the 'issue from hell' because 'its complexity, scale and timeframe all make public discussion of the crisis, its causes and its solutions more difficult' (2013: 314). It is the paradigm case of system interdependence and wicked problems; and it has indeed fostered such notions (see Chapter 4 above). Especially significant has been the paradigmatic shift in thinking about climate, as it morphed from being an element of the 'environment' to conceptualizing the earth itself as a 'system', following Lovelock's original Gaia thesis and the subsequent development of earth systems science (2006, 2010; Stengers 2015).

Third, climate change necessarily concerns social and not just physical or technological futures. That 'human activities' are principally responsible for increased GHG emissions and hence for changing climates means that how societies have been, and will be, organized is critical for anticipating likely future emission patterns and temperatures. I discuss below the thesis of the anthropocene, this being an arguably new geological period that some maintain involves huge changes in the nature of 'human activities' and their significant transformation of the 'earth system'.

Fourth, this book has shown how the present is often a poor guide to the future and this is especially the case with climate change. Much climate science involves the necessity of looking back and examining multiple often distant pasts, including the records revealed in ice cores showing climate conditions over 800,000 years. Other climate science examines the width of tree rings which reveals past changes in temperatures and then projects future emissions and temperatures. And the past history of societies and how energy production and consumption were organized enable analysts to anticipate future patterns through examining sociomaterial lock-ins and path-dependencies. Many climate scientists and energy experts developed scenarios stretching into the future based upon analysis and evidence from various past records. Interesting scenarios have been developed by Arup, BP, the Centre for Alternative Technology, Chatham House, Forum for the Future, IPCC, the Pentagon, the Tyndall Centre, the United

Nations Environment Programme, the United States Environmental Protection Agency and so on (Hunt et al. 2012).

Finally, the discourse of climate change can transform the trajectory of high-carbon societies. If climate change is viewed as *the* major threat to the functioning of contemporary societies then this bolsters arguments that 'business as usual' should be no more. It would lead to collaboration between states through international agreements; support public infrastructures such as mass transit and affordable housing; help to revive local economies/societies; assist in reclaiming democracies from corporate power such as 'carbon capital'; develop resistance to free trade deals and the global division of labour; promote indigenous land rights and local forms of knowledge; recalibrate economies/societies, demonstrating that much fossil fuel should remain in the ground with its value written off; and reject the promise of endless economic growth and resulting inequalities (see Bond 2012; Klein 2014; Sayer 2015).

This powerful set of consequences follows from the need to reverse high-carbon societies, since according to Klein, climate change 'changes everything' (2014). Such a reversal is not something that, say, green growth does much to alter. Many calculate that future temperature increases should be limited to no more than 2 °C, with the implication that the US and EU would need to cut emissions by 80 per cent. Such a programme cannot be delivered by 'growth' – it does not mean business as usual. According to Klein, what is needed is the very opposite of growth: 'managed degrowth', reducing GHG emissions by 8–10 per cent per year (Klein 2014: 21). Moreover, according to the Chief Economist of the International Energy Authority, there is only a short gap before it will be too late to change and societies will be on the path to those catastrophist futures examined in Chapter 3 (Klein 2014: 23–4).

So the issue of climate change concerns multiple contested futures, system interdependence and wicked problems, anticipating future worlds which depend on events and processes still to occur, long-term and large-scale shifts in the nature of the 'human' species and 'human' societies, and seeking to turn around the oil tanker of endless growth and pointing it in the opposite direction of systematic de-growth. This chapter assesses these crucial issues that climate change poses for anticipating futures.

The next section documents the issue of 'rising temperatures' and some of the processes which appear to generate such an increase. The following sections consider whether it is possible to reverse those processes by examining various future climate scenarios and the possibility of 'developing' de-growth.

Rising temperatures

The idea of the greenhouse effect is that there are documented rises in GHG and especially CO_2 emissions and these remain in the earth's atmosphere for long periods. In turn, these emissions trap the sun's rays (Stern 2007; https://www.ipcc.ch/report/ar5). Such a 'greenhouse' effect raises land and sea temperatures. From 1880 to 2012, average global temperature increased by 0.85 °C. Further increases in GHG emissions will engender further temperature rises, generating cumulative processes of 'global warming' (see www.nasa.gov/topics/earth/features/climate_by_any_other_name.html).

That there is 'global climate change' is striking since what people experience and observe is, in fact, weather. But, gradually, 'weather' has been turned into 'climate', something more lawful, regular and mathematical (Szerszynski 2010). A science of measurement developed based upon concepts such as atmosphere, air pressure, humidity and so on. Normally, climate was thought to be given and fixed, certainly not changing and changeable. Each region was thought to have its 'climate' written into the geography and sociology of places. Humans and their activities were not much in evidence in the accounts typically provided of relatively fixed and given climates.

But over the past three to four decades, 'contemporary science' determined that climates are in fact changing, they will continue to change, and this is partly the product of human activities. This paradigm shift has required an exceptional set of discursive and material interventions. Partly through the organizing activities of the IPCC various 'climate sciences' were assembled and sustained, as global warming and other climate characteristics came to be viewed as the object of global policy events and intense worldwide diplomacy.

But it was not inevitable that climate change would become how the environment was framed and dominate global agendas.

Silent Spring, the founding text of modern environmentalism, had a different focus, critiquing the environmental and health effects of synthetic pesticides such as DDT (Carson 1962). And many contested and significantly threatened 'natures' vied for dominance over the last half-century, including the issue of nuclear energy implicated in the development of various cancers (Macnaghten, Urry 1998).

The clearest example of the emerging power of global science was the identification of the growing hole in the ozone layer, understood as being caused by the use of chlorofluorocarbons in aerosol sprays and refrigerators. Following the Montreal Protocol, CFC production was sharply limited from 1987 onwards, with production phased out by 1996. As a result of this impressive global collaboration and policy agreement, the depletion of the ozone layer was significantly slowed down, although final recovery will require several lifetimes.

By contrast, climate change is a wicked problem. Tyndall discovered in 1859 that CO_2 traps heat. At the start of the twentieth century, Arrhenius showed how there was a 'greenhouse' effect resulting from the burning of fossil fuels and this could alter the earth's climate. But it was only in 1979, when four distinguished scientists warned of the dangers of possible global warming, that human-induced or anthropogenic climate change began to be taken seriously and to enter 'science'. In 1988, a year of record temperatures, the United Nations Environment Programme established the IPCC with the result that thousands of scientists began examining links between GHG emissions and climate change. Leading climate scientist James Hansen announced in landmark US Congressional hearings that anthropogenic global warming had indeed started (Klein 2014: 73–4), while Margaret Thatcher's speech to the UK's Royal Society, also in 1988, added to a growing structure of feeling within policy and political circles that human activities were indeed transforming future climates. Thatcher argued that the system of the planet was being subjected to a massive 'experiment' (see Gore 2013: ch. 6).

The IPCC organized the actions of thousands of scientists across the globe, transforming academic, public and policy debates. This organized 'power of science' led to the worldwide mobilizing of actions and events focused upon the perceived world crisis of climate change, a crisis increasingly viewed as global, urgent and possibly soluble. But at the same time a group of energy companies and car manufacturers formed the Global Climate Coalition to counter these efforts to take action on climate change and to promulgate climate change scepticism within government, the media and, later, the new media. This opposition to the climate change thesis especially focused upon the promotion of 'free trade' and the increasingly international division of labour (see Demeritt 2006). Klein maintains that the issue of trade is key in understanding how potential climate interventions were rolled back from the late 1980s onwards. She writes of 'the disastrous climate impacts of the free trade era' and the parallel pursuit of indiscriminate economic growth (Klein 2014: 85–6).

There has subsequently been much dispute about climate change and potential futures. Three broad positions or discourses can be identified within climate change science and policy pronouncements (Dayrell, Urry 2015; Demeritt 2006; Hulme 2009).

The first of these discourses is *gradualism*, as clearly represented by IPCC Reports. These show that climates are changing, human activities are significantly responsible for these changes, changes are relatively slow, and individuals and societies can be induced to transform future behaviour through appropriate incentives (Stern 2007). Gradualism also presupposes developing new technologies that will somehow fix the problem through providing novel ways of generating lower-carbon energy. Alongside the IPCC, there developed a huge climate politics and policy, within science, within the media – including Nobel prize-winning movies – and within much policy, with many major global institutions signing up to the notion of 'sustainability' and large-scale international collaboration. It is believed that the problem of future changing climates can be fixed at relatively modest cost, especially if changes begin now rather than being left for later decades when possible options will be many fewer (Centre for Alternative Technology 2013).

The second main position is that of *scepticism* (see Moran 2015). This involves challenging the sciences of climate change, especially because of the uncertainties involved in predicting temperature changes over future decades. It is said that there are too many 'unknown unknowns'. Also, since climates altered in the past, this would have resulted from 'natural' processes such as sun spot activity and not from human activities. Scepticism critiques the social sciences playing any role here. Some sceptics explain arguments for climate change as driven by the vested interests of research scientists and the media (Montford 2010; see Demeritt 2006). Other sceptics suggest that there will actually be benefits from changing climates, while some migration of populations happens anyway without that engendered by climate change. Overall neo-liberal thought maintains that competitive markets will fix the environment; climate change interventions provide ways of smuggling in anti-competitive statist policies and politics (see Gore 2013: 318–28, for insider details). In a different argument, political scientist Lomborg maintains that the costs of dealing with climate change, as compared with the costs of other global challenges, make it hard to justify de-carbonization (2001).

The power of scepticism as a system of thought and action has grown, especially in the US over the past decade, since the peak levels of climate change concern occurred around 2007 (Klein 2014). This scepticism is engendered by climate sceptic 'merchants of doubt' particularly operating within the internet, the blogosphere and thinktanks keen to promote 'business as usual' (Oreskes, Conway 2010). Many organizations of climate sceptics maintain that there is much uncertainty amongst scientists about future climates, although actually around 97 per cent of climate scientists accept some version or other of the thesis of anthropogenic climate change (Klein 2014: 31).

Catastrophism critiques both these positions. It takes from the former the reality of climate change, and from the latter uncertainty and the limits of science. And it locates both within a 'complex systems' framework emphasizing non-linearity, thresholds and abrupt and sudden change. Rial and colleagues report that the earth's climate system 'is highly nonlinear: inputs and outputs are not proportional, change is often episodic and abrupt, rather than slow and gradual, and multiple equilibria are the norm' (2004: 11). So far, IPCC Reports do not build in all potential feedback effects. Thus, modest projections of sea level change, which ignore future uncertainties especially related to the melting of ice sheets, enables climate change sceptics to argue that such increases can be dealt with through adaptation and do not require wholesale reversal of systems, as catastrophists such as Hansen maintain (2011). Catastrophists dispute the view that green or sustainable practices can easily and cheaply fix the problem of climate. Only large-scale structural changes can deal with these issues in a remotely robust fashion (as Klein 2014 argues).

What, briefly, does the scientific evidence suggest? By 2007, the IPCC stated that the warming of the world's climate through increased GHG emissions was 'unequivocal'. IPCC Reports show that the concentration levels of CO_2 in particular now exceed the natural range that scientists identified over the past 650,000 years (IPCC 2007). Such science concludes that this high and accelerating level of emissions must result from 'non-natural' human-produced causes. This accelerating scale of emissions, shown in Figure 1, derives from the longest set of readings taken of such emissions, derived from the Mauna Loa observatory established on Hawaii in 1957. By April 2015 CO_2 emissions had passed 400 parts per million for the first time, reflecting an apparently inexorable upward trajectory (www.theguardian.com/environment/2015/may/06/global-carbon-dioxide-levels-break-400ppm-milestone). It is significant to note how China's CO_2 emissions are now higher than those of the US and EU combined, although just

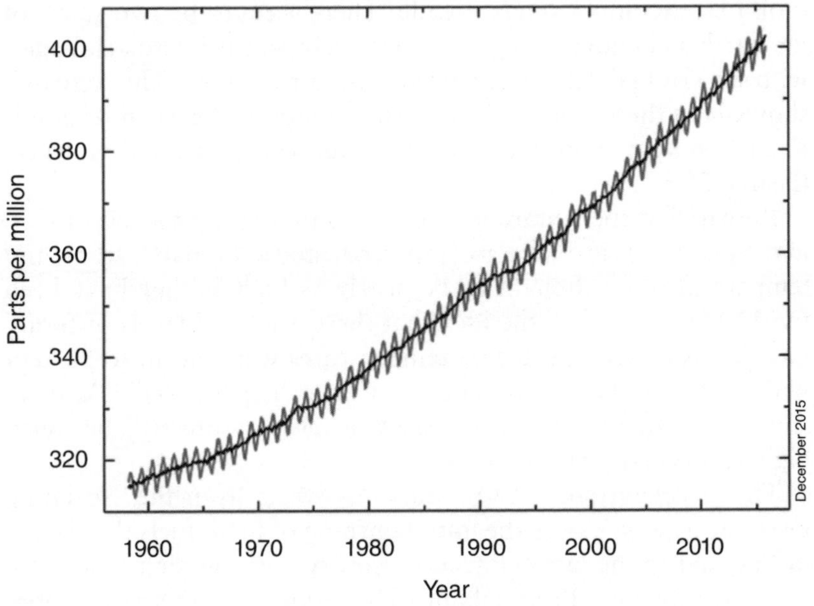

Figure 1 Atmospheric CO_2 at Mauna Loa Observatory

under one-sixth of these emissions is in fact generated by manufacturing goods consumed outside China, an offshoring of emissions as noted in Chapter 7 (www.exeter.ac.uk/news/research/title_412769_en.html).

Over the past 2–3 centuries, 2,000 billion tons of CO_2 have been spewed into the earth's atmosphere, and these emissions will remain there for hundreds of years (Berners-Lee, Clark 2013: 26). CO_2 emissions from 1850 to the present have increased exponentially (Berners-Lee, Clark 2013: 12). Climate systems are changing around the world and human activities appear to be significantly responsible for such changes.

Research also shows that CO_2 levels and temperatures have varied in tandem over thousands of years, indicating a robust relationship between them. And, rather than the thesis of relatively stable climates, Alley argues that there are sudden see-sawing shifts, a 'crazily jumping climate has been the rule, not the exception' (cited Clark 2010: 1). This pattern is derived from researching ice cores that are up to 2 miles in depth and has generated 'a full-blown paradigm shift' amongst climate scientists (Linden 2007: 227). Alley showed that half the warming between the last ice age and the subsequent postglacial world of around 9 degrees took place within a *single* decade. There seem to be two states of the earth's climate: ice ages, or relatively warm interglacial ages, with no gradual movement from one to the other. This research shows how there were sudden abrupt jumps as the earth responds to carbon shifts with what has been termed 'speed and violence' (Pearce 2007).

Research at the Antarctic also shows that current levels of CO_2 in the earth's atmosphere are unprecedented in human history, and temperatures are thought to be nearly as high as they have been for 420,000 years. So the idea that there are 'safe' levels of future CO_2 levels is wrong if future temperatures were meant to be kept within the limits of what humans have 'experienced'. Also, in some parts of the globe, increases in temperature will be much higher, especially at the poles.

This acceleration in CO_2 emissions stems from the escalating use of energy ever since the initial burning of fossil fuels that began in England in the late eighteenth century with the first 'manufactory' (at Soho near Birmingham). The resilience of this exponential upward curve indicates that the earth system moved beyond the natural variability exhibited over the last 11,700 years, during the relatively stable Holocene period. This stage commenced at the end of the last ice age and provided stable conditions for the human development of agriculture, towns, cities and industry.

But it is now proposed that the earth system has entered a new geological epoch, the Anthropocene, a term elaborated in 2000 by Nobel Prize-winner Paul Crutzen (N. Clark 2011; http://quaternary.stratigraphy.org/workinggroups/anthropocene). This new geological period began in the latter part of the eighteenth century as the global effects of human activities started to impact. Human activities are thought to constitute a 'great force of nature'. To hypothesize the Anthropocene is to argue against there being uniform or average processes upon earth.

The key process is that, from around 1900 when the first oil and gas were 'discovered' and started to be burnt alongside coal, there has been an exponential increase in burning fossil fuels (Berners-Lee, Clark 2013). According to McNeill: 'We have deployed more energy since 1900 than all of human history before 1900' (www.theglobalist.com/StoryId.aspx?StoryId=2018). And then, since around 1950, there has been a further rate of increase in this 'burning', an increase known as the Great Acceleration (of burning fossil fuels around the world). The exponential rate of increase of CO_2 emissions is shown in Figure 2.

Berners-Lee and Clark thus summarize how 'The unremittingly exponential nature of the carbon cycle fits perfectly with the idea that society's use of energy is driven by a powerful positive feedback mechanism' (2013: 13). It is difficult to overestimate the strength of the various feedback mechanisms generating this speed of change. A couple of generations after 1950, societies became transformed into a planetary-scale geological force. Major earth system changes were directly brought about by changes in global economic and social systems, as discussed below.

During this century, most scientists and analysts believe that large-scale undesirable consequences follow from this dramatic increase in burning fossil fuels occurring over the past three centuries, and especially since the Great Acceleration. It is anticipated that GHG emissions and world temperatures will significantly increase over the next few years through various positive feedbacks. Even as early as 1990 it was thought that there were sixteen feedbacks, of which thirteen were positive, taking systems away

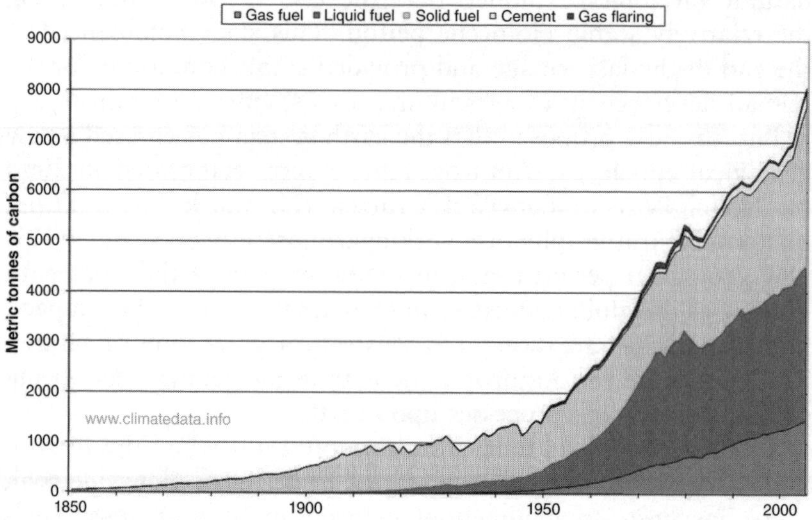

Figure 2 World CO_2 production by source

from equilibrium (Wynne 2010). Some of the most important of these concern the three great ice sheets, covering Greenland and different parts of the Antarctic. These are vast, with ice compressed up to 2 miles deep. Also there is the huge deposit of the most powerful greenhouse gas methane buried in permafrost in Siberia but which appears to be exploding and leaking; this has been characterized as the 'methane apocalypse' (www.newscientist.com/article/mg22630221.300-methane-apocalypse-defusing-the-arctics-time-bomb.html).

These four sources of potential runaway change mean that 'predictions' of future temperature increases vary widely, and explain why there has been such dispute over whether a global 2 °C increase of temperatures is the best (or perhaps the least worst) proxy for 'acceptable' climate change. This has been translated into a carbon budget that demands a full-scale reversal of what Anderson terms 'the dominant economic and growth paradigm' (see http://kevinanderson.info/blog/category/papers-reports). Anderson argues that, although the 2 °C limit is far from perfect, it is meaningful to scientists and understandable by policy makers, business and wider civil society (but see Anderson, Bows 2011).

One problem with regard to forming the right policy is that 'climate change' is not a single 'cause', nor a single set of 'effects'. As we have seen, there are many elements of changing climates, including increases in Arctic temperatures, reduced size of icebergs, melting of icecaps and glaciers, reduced permafrost, changes in rainfall, reduced bio-diversity, new wind patterns, more droughts, dust storms and heat waves, and greater intensity of tropical cyclones and other extreme weather events. Rockström and colleagues propose that there are nine planetary boundaries. Transgressing one or more of these boundaries may trigger non-linear, abrupt environmental change (www.stockholmresilience.org/21/research/research-news/1-15–2015-planetary-boundaries-2.0—new-and-improved.html). Rockström and colleagues estimate that contemporary societies have already transgressed four of these boundaries: climate change, loss of biosphere integrity, land-system change and altered biogeochemical cycles. Moreover, these planetary boundaries are interdependent so transgressing one has cascading impacts upon others.

Overall, the threshold now deemed to be a global 'safe' limit is likely to be breached if global CO_2 emissions exceed a further 1,200 billion tons. This is a future carbon budget that must be adhered to, thus ensuring a 66 per cent chance that average global warming can be kept within the 2 °C rise (see www.exeter.ac.uk/news/research/title_412769_en.html). But societies have already burnt through two-thirds of this global ration. At the current rate of generating CO_2 emissions through burning fossil fuels, this 1,200 billion ton 'quota' will be used up within about thirty years. Thus there is just one generation left before the safeguards to a 2 °C limit will be breached. To avoid this, it is argued that more than half of current fossil fuel reserves should remain unexploited and left under the ground (Carbon Tracker 2013). And there is the massive issue of equity in determining how this shrinking global carbon allowance can be shared between the world population of more than 7 billion, and especially in dealing with the large and apparently growing differences between rich and poor within contemporary societies (Piketty 2014; Sayer 2015).

Thus, with 'business as usual' and no significant reductions in high-carbon systems, the stock of GHG emissions could treble by the end of the century. It is thought that there is a 20 per cent risk of more than a 5 °C increase in temperatures by 2100 (Stern 2007:

3). The Pentagon maintains that climate change could result in a 'global catastrophe' costing millions of lives in wars and 'natural disasters' (US National Intelligence Council 2008). As early as 2000, the World Health Organization calculated that over 150,000 deaths were caused each year by climate change; and it anticipates this figure will rise to 250,000 in future decades (www.who.int/mediacentre/factsheets/fs266/en).

These climate change effects are global but their impacts are more concentrated in the 'global South'. They are also cross-generational; and women are more likely than men to be the victims of changing climates. Bangladesh, in the low-lying Ganges, is worst affected by climate change although it generates tiny levels of CO_2 emissions (0.3 per cent of the global total). Such global relationships are part of what has been termed 'climatic genocide', with millions forced to migrate away from global climate change risks mostly concentrated in the poor 'South' of the globe (Timmons Roberts, Parks 2007).

Especially significant are the effects within coastal waters, which are rising ten times faster than the global average. This results in dramatic increases in the level of the sea in areas where most people are forced to live upon land only a few feet above sea level (www.nytimes.com/2014/03/29/world/asia/facing-rising-seas-bangladesh-confronts-the-consequences-of-climate-change.html). It is thought that around half the world's population lives within 15 miles of the sea, with major infrastructures such as Schiphol Airport located below sea level and hence vulnerable to modest coastal sea level rises (Gore 2013: 297–8).

We have seen how the uneven effects of climate change work through food insecurity, water stress, rising sea levels, the loss of biodiversity, floods, droughts and heatwaves, new diseases and enforced 'climate change' migration. These processes especially affect those people living in societies located within what has been termed the 'tropic of chaos' that circles the earth. The effects of climate change generate a 'reserve army' of dispossessed labour which is forced to migrate and help to build new sites for ultra-high-carbon living (Parenti 2011). Many fleeing from the rising waters of the Ganges migrate to places like Dubai, which, as seen below, represents the ultra-high-carbon patterns of living that disproportionately generate climate change in places such as Bangladesh. So there is here a reinforcing circuit, with positive feedbacks linking together those places that cause, and those places that are affected by, climate change.

One sector of the global economy that understands the likely scale of these future climate-related developments is the global insurance industry. Its many reports document the rising scale, impact and cost of such climate events, such as the $65 billion cost of Hurricane Sandy in New York / New Jersey in 2012 (www.usatoday.com/story/weather/2013/01/24/global-disaster-report-sandy-drought/1862201). Insurance losses worldwide have seen sudden increases, with extreme weather being principally responsible. Since the 1970s, the number of extreme weather events increased by around 10 per cent per year. The insurer Swiss Re estimates that insurance losses from these weather events have risen fivefold since the 1980s (Klein 2014: 107). Oxfam reports that, while the numbers of earthquakes remained relatively stable, there has been an almost threefold increase in flooding and storm events. Munich Re (the world's largest reinsurance company) authoritatively concludes that 'the growing number of weather-related catastrophes can only be explained by climate change. The view that weather extremes are more frequent and intense due to global warming is in keeping with current scientific findings... And the risk is steadily growing, for climate change harbours the potential for torrential downpours while the risk of drought in certain regions is also on the rise' (www.munichre.com/en/group/focus/climate_change/ current/flooding_in_china/default.aspx). Flannery hypothesizes that such a rate of increase in climate-related insurance claims 'implies that by 2065 or soon thereafter, the damage bill resulting from climate change may equal the total value of everything that humanity produced in the course of a year' (2007: 235).

There are various climate change worlds but which is more likely by, say, 2050 is hugely difficult to estimate (see scenarios in Urry 2011). This is partly because different outcomes depend upon what indeed happens also in the future, what occurs elsewhere and what the likely interactions are between these, across space and time. It is necessary to establish what unexpected 'events' are likely to occur 'in the future', such as those described in Porritt's *The World We Made* (2013). Events elaborated in his fictional account included water riots, peaking of oil, cyber-terrorism, hurricanes, massive water inundations, the great famine, peaking of meat production and massive protests. Some of these events are unknown unknowns. Others involve knowing that certain kinds of events may occur, but not when or where, or how such an event will interconnect with others over time.

Finance and consumerism

The preceding section set out an array of wicked problems resulting from how rising emissions seem to be generating increasing temperatures that make unlikely the continuation of patterns of human, animal and plant life contingently established during the Holocene period. Stern maintains that 'Climate change...is the greatest and widest-ranging market failure' (2007: i). Global capitalism based on fossil fuel-based energy generated enormous 'external diseconomies', with the adaptive and evolving relationships between powerful systems being a 'juggernaut' careering at full pace to the edge of the cliff, as Giddens once put it (1990, 2009; Klein 2014). The earth is in a different state, especially since 1950, with significant earth system processes now driven by structures of human production and consumption (see Urry 2011). As energy use grew and there was less of an energy ceiling, so greater inequality and more divisions of interest between social groups developed. This has been taken to the extreme in many oil-producing states. Untold riches and ostentatious display sit side-by-side with impoverished migrant workers often fleeing from the consequences of rising temperatures 'back home'.

To illustrate this relationship and the nature of contemporary capitalism, I describe some features of the city that especially speeded up to the future over the past half-century or so, a place with its own Great Acceleration to ultra-high-carbon living (drawing on Urry 2013b). Dubai was, until around 1960, one of the poorest places on earth. It was a series of small mud villages located by the seaside and sitting on the edge of a vast inhospitable desert with more or less no rivers. It only became independent in 1971 as part of the United Arab Emirates but since then has grown exponentially. By the 2000s, it was the world's largest building site and the eighth most visited city on the earth. The rise of this City of Gold located in the most desolate corner of a desolate land illustrates an astonishing acceleration to a different future. It is a major hub where global flows of capital, money, people, culture and information land and intersect.

Pumping oil in this British Protectorate commenced in 1966 during the peak global period of oil discovery. But, unlike in much of the surrounding area, Dubai's oil supply peaked in 1991 (Krane 2010; Urry 2013b). Oil from elsewhere is used to build islands, hotels and exceptional attractions; to transport – especially via its modern airport (the world's largest international airport, with another being built) and leading airline (Emirates) – very large numbers of visitors, conference delegates, construction workers and sex workers; to import, especially via the world's largest man-made harbour, vast quantities of food and goods sold in the seventy shopping malls, including the world's largest (www.thedubaimall.com/en/Index.aspx); to facilitate a centre for transportation with one of the world's ten largest container ports; to generate the highest water consumption rate in the world through carbon-based desalination plants; and to use much energy, providing thermal monotony through climate control where average temperatures are 40 °C.

Dubai endeavoured to create a technologically speeded-up future, even though the society is patriarchal, religious and authoritarian. This futurism is embodied in its built environment but not within its society. 'Futuristic' developments include a 'museum of the future' (https://www.youtube.com/watch?v=9Wx0Lfyjmf0); two palm islands extending the coastline by almost 75 miles; a string of new islands shaped like the countries of the world; a domed ski resort and many major sports venues; the world's tallest building – the astonishing Burj Khalifa at 2,717 feet; the world's largest hotel – the Asia-Asia with 6,500 rooms; the world's first 7-star hotel – the Burj Al Arab with 100-mile views; the site of the world's biggest party at the opening of the Atlantis hotel complex; and the largest residential development, the Jumeirah Beach Residence with forty towers accommodating about 15,000 people (www.burj-al-arab.com; Davidson 2008; Krane 2010; Schmid 2009).

Dubai strives for visual and environmental excess, a place of and for accelerated consuming, shopping, eating, gambling and prostitution. Krane summarizes the paradox of Dubai: 'It's the earth's most barren landscape, a land with nothing in the way of historic sights, and big spending visitors fly half way around the world to see it' (2010: 117). It is a place of pure acceleration, an 'oasis' of free enterprise without income or corporation taxes, trade unions, planning laws, opposition parties or elections. Its residents, its companies and its visitors borrow huge sums of finance in order to make possible the exceptional scale of building and consuming the future. The future of Dubai is built on sand and debt.

Central to Dubai and much of the world economy over the past few decades has been a growing imbalance between 'financialization' and the 'real economy'. This is a further impediment to developing effective climate change policies. It is a huge problem for building momentum for a low-carbon future when almost all of the world economy is 'financialized'. By 2010, the total annual value of foreign currency transactions was US$955 trillion, more than fifteen times the value of world GDP (US$63 trillion: www.spiegel.de/international/business/out-of-control-the-destructive-power-of-the-financial-markets-a-781590.html). These circulations of finance generated a 'dictatorship of financial markets', as income and rights were redistributed away from the 'real economy' to so-called 'casino capitalism' (Latouche 2009; Sayer 2015). Economies were restructured from organizations producing goods and services towards organizations principally involved in financial circulation or intermediation.

A sense of a disappearing future results from computerized high-frequency trading. Actions happen beyond the speed of thought and involve movements of money and information that cannot be grasped by human minds (Lewis 2015). In such an accelerating world, financial futures arrive before they have been understood by the relevant actors (Gore 2013: 16–17). Much of this intermediation is directed by financial elites (Savage, Williams 2008). It runs counter to the interests of developing an economy made up of smaller companies that innovate and produce new products and services, and especially those developing the products and services of a lower-carbon economy-and-society.

Also financial intermediation (and related computer networks) hollows out large industrial corporations with ownership vested in financial institutions concerned with short-term 'shareholder value'; the short term here may extend to less than one second. We noted above how the large 'industrial' corporation became outdated, their numbers in the US halving since the mid-1990s

(Davis 2012). Sennett and others have lamented the resulting decline in people's long-term commitment to their workplaces that this new short-termism engenders and generalizes (1998). This is taken to the extreme where contracts do not have any hours attached – so-called zero hours contracts, in the UK. Here there is no commitment by either side, a paradox since many employees within this rapidly growing 'precariat' are in the front-line of services, delivering the 'brand' to customers.

Guy Standing describes the short-term futures of those working in the precariat, a greatly increased proportion of the workforce worldwide (2014). The networked model of work increasingly throws everyone into a precariousness with a lack of long-term skills and commitment, and this includes even those designing and implementing the digital systems that are the bedrock of intermediation and the web/App economy. Turner describes how the digital utopia that emerged as part of the counterculture has turned into its opposite, a dystopic world of temporary and precarious work and life (2006: 258–62; Srnicek, Williams 2015).

Contemporary capitalism is transformed into a significantly untaxed, ungovernable and out-of-control financial capitalism. The scale of finance is enormous and works more like gambling. Its growth and domination of the industrial economy, as well as of the physical environment, has magnified economic, social and property inequalities in most countries (Floyd, Slaughter 2014). Especially significant here are the multiple processes of offshoring (Urry 2014a): the moving of resources, practices, peoples and monies from territory to territory and hiding them. It involves evading rules, laws, taxes, regulations or norms. The offshoring world is dynamic, reorganizing economic, social, political and material relations between societies and within them, as resources, practices, peoples and monies are made or kept secret (Urry 2014a: 1). In particular, there has been an astonishing growth in the movement of finance and wealth through the world's sixty to seventy tax havens, representing close to one-third of all contemporary societies (Shaxson 2012). Tax havens are places of low taxes, wealth management, deregulation and secrecy, and became absolutely core to the world economy, as exchange and related controls were removed from the late 1970s onwards.

Almost all major companies possess offshore accounts/subsidiaries; more than half of world trade passes through them;

almost all high net worth individuals possess offshore accounts enabling tax 'planning'; and 99 of Europe's 100 largest companies use offshore subsidiaries. A sum equivalent to one-quarter to one-third of all global wealth is held 'offshore' (Urry 2014a: ch. 4). Centrally important in the power of finance, circulation and debt are private equity buy-outs (Appelbaum, Batt 2014). These involve a private equity firm putting up a small proportion of the purchase cost of a company or part of a company. The rest comes from institutional investors or is borrowed using the future company's assets as collateral. Once the public company has been bought, it will be made 'private' and mostly hidden out of sight. There are far fewer restrictions on what activities private equity firms can undertake, partly because those owning them are regarded as investors rather than employers. Most private equity funds avoid much regulatory oversight. And yet these firms are more likely to reduce employment levels, to grow more slowly, to go bankrupt, and to be less likely to sign up to the pursuit of low carbonism.

Thus, offshore is how the world of power now works and this runs counter to the interests of low-carbon companies and NGOs. Money staying onshore is almost the exception, suitable only for 'little people' still paying tax. Most big money is offshored. The annual loss of taxation is hundreds of billions of US dollars. Overall, offshore has been generated by and favours large corporations deploying complex computer systems. The offshore world makes it hard for 'innovative minnows' to compete and, even if they prosper, then they will become parts of large multinational corporate bureaucracies whose income flows will be in part offshored. The world of offshore systemically weakens local, smaller companies, which experience nothing like a level playing field when they compete with large offshored companies and their many offshore accounts (Goldman Sachs has over 4,000; Urry 2014a: 1–2).

Offshoring thus makes de-carbonizing society more difficult to realize (see Sayer 2015: part 5, for one of the few analyses of this). Powering down to a low-carbon future requires a strong mutual indebtedness of people around the globe and especially of current generations towards future generations, including those yet to be born. The need for this public or social indebtedness is expressed in many global documents, such as the *UNESCO Declaration on the Responsibilities of the Present Generations Towards Future Generations* (12 November 1997).

We should also consider here Lankford's analysis of the para-commons (2013). He asks who receives the benefits if there is a really significant improved use of resources through low-carbon initiatives. Is it possible to ensure that, if populations reduce their fuel consumption or increase their material efficiency or lessen their waste, then the benefits somehow return, in the present or future, to those communities where that improved efficiency took place? Realizing this is a massive challenge. Such paracommons or social indebtedness between people has been overwhelmed in much of the world through financial indebtedness. It is this which ties people, states and corporations into obligations. Financial indebtedness and the large-scale offshoring of potential taxation revenue make it hard for social indebtedness to gain traction. Public expenditure and a strong notion of public interest are necessary to plan and orchestrate improved resource-efficient low carbonism. And this is rendered especially difficult because of how leisure, work, taxation, waste, CO_2 emissions, torture and finance have been financialized and hence offshored (Urry 2014a).

As Klein notes, climate change changes everything and so, rather than more growth, an alternative cluster of sociomaterial systems must develop to effect 'de-growth'. The earth system would appear to be moving towards unstoppable global climate change unless there is such a dramatic change of direction, to rapidly find reverse gear. And this is not only a question of specific 'systems' and their clustering, but a longer-term and broader shift in the structure of feeling within societies (see Chapter 3 above). Such shifts may make the world different, although no institutions necessarily planned or envisaged such a shift or even noticed the shift at the time.

One long-term structure of feeling was engendered during and after the world's Great Depression during the 1930s. Keynes was crucial in arguing across much of Europe and north America that economic systems will not themselves rectify unemployment and economic depression (1936). Economies do not automatically restore equilibrium. He argued for the virtues of counter-cyclical tax-funded state expenditures, systems of national planning and the idea of a collective national interest to be seen as separate from the specific interests of individuals and companies. From the 1930s to the 1970s, the dominant Keynesian structure of feeling was that states had the capacity to rectify market deficiencies and they must do so. There was a *longue durée* centred on this powerful discourse and set of practices, involving the claim that states should intervene in the pursuit of the societal or national interest.

But, as early as 1947, a senior Swiss bank official brought various scholars together to a secret meeting at Mont Pèlerin, near Geneva, under the direction of Friedrich Hayek (see *The Road to Serfdom*, 1944). This Mont Pèlerin Society, funded by Swiss banks, was central in a global fightback against Keynesian support for state interventionism. This struggle to reverse Keynesianism was organized through many further secret meetings (Stedman Jones 2012: ch. 2). One person at these meetings was Milton Friedman, key in developing so-called neo-liberalism, which from the late 1970s, gained traction around the world (Klein 2007).

Various transnational organizations were involved in – often secretly – developing the economic, social and political conditions for neo-liberalism (Carroll 2010; Klein 2007; Stedman Jones 2012). These discussions reasserted the importance of private entrepreneurship, private property rights, free markets and the freeing of trade, such objectives being realized from around 1980. Partly because of iconic figures such as Reagan and Thatcher, neo-liberalism became the dominant global orthodoxy of economic and social policy and practice, a new structure of feeling that presumed that the 'free market' should indeed rule. And in the last few decades, this 'structure of feeling' became heavily reinforced through print media, TV, internet and social media. This 'freeing up' of capitalism and consumer demand for goods and services helped reinforce the exponential Great Acceleration of CO_2 emissions discussed above and made it hard to resist the discursive power of 'economic growth' brought about through policies of 'business as usual'.

A pervasive consumerism or 'consumer culture' is key in the contemporary world. People form their social identities through purchasing, using and making symbolic capital out of consumer goods and services produced by others within large energy-intensive factories, offices, shops and places of pleasure. What are important are people's habitual purchases, their material and symbolic uses of these goods and services, and especially the ways that consumed items are organized into relatively stable brands (Elliott,

Urry 2010; Klein 2000). Moreover, these consumer goods and services are put to work by people especially to produce and re-produce the self. TV programmes involve the 'makeover' of goods, services, homes, cars, self, relationships and the body (see Elliott 2013, on 'reinvention'). These forms of work are carried out with, and through, consumer goods and services involving various kinds of 'practice'. It is these social practices, of dining, shopping at supermarkets, showering daily, playing tennis or holidaymaking which organize and sustain life. They are ongoing and dynamic, and in them both the habit and the practitioners develop together. Often these practices get to be assembled within particular high-energy places, such as Dubai. Indeed, central to many such practices is extensive fast movement between key nodes within the consumerist global order.

De-growth

Challenging these sedimented economic and social patterns is exceptionally hard. While the early part of this new century saw widespread concern about 'climate change', there has been little effective policy to reverse high carbonism on anything like the required scale (Berners-Lee, Clark 2013; see Dayrell, Urry 2015 on such 'concern'). The story of Dubai shows how financialized bubbles help to generate vast increases in burning fossil fuels through providing widespread and seductive models of high-carbon living.

But it is possible that there are seeds of a new mode of capitalism, a new structure of feeling beyond both statism *and* neo-liberal or disorganized capitalism. Silver and Arrighi argue for 'an alternative path to the resource-intensive western model of capitalism development', warning that if this is not achieved then there may be a 'long period of systemic chaos' (2011: 68; see Chapter 3 above).

This alternative future is increasingly known as de-growth and involves developing and embedding social practices that presuppose a substantial powering down of carbon intensity on a global scale (Latouche 2009). The main innovation here is in changing 'demand' for fossil fuel energy rather than replacing fossil fuels with other energy forms (see www.demand.ac.uk). Such a possible future draws upon innovation in thinking and practice by environmentalists, scientists, NGOs and thinktanks. Much of this innovation is 'interstitial', occurring within the spaces and cracks of the dominant system of power, especially carbon capitalism (Wright 2010: 322; see Kirby 2013).

This alternative capitalism does not exist as such, being more like an archipelago of tiny islands scattered around the world in often unlikely and improbable locations. In most societies there are some such islands above the surface, but so far there are relatively few connections between them. These islands constitute an emergent 'low-carbon civil society' that is being formed out of tens of thousands of experiments, groups, networks, prototypes, laboratories, scientists, universities, designers and activists (see Thackara 2015). This involves new connections being made between post-carbon practices around the globe, many made possible through new digital worlds including the App economy. This low-carbon civil society is a social movement trying both to limit current processes of emissions generation and to prepare and prototype various post-carbon alternatives.

Central to this is the thesis of 'natural capitalism'. This involves a critique of how capitalism fails to assign value to the largest stock of capital it employs: both natural resources and living systems (Hawken, Lovins, Lovins 1999). Twentieth-century capitalism externalized the costs of using up nature, and especially its energy sources. It thus burnt fossil fuels without regard to their real costs for 'nature'. The IMF's estimate of an annual global 'subsidy' of $5.3 trillion to the fossil fuel industries was noted above (www.scientificamerican.com/article/fossil-fuel-subsidies-cost-5-trillion-annually-and-worsen-pollution).

Underlying the notion of de-growth is the idea that there should be an economy-plus-society which would value all forms of capital. What if the economy were organized not around economic and financial abstractions but around nature, which was not regarded as separate from the economy and available for transformation through short-term profit maximization (Urry 2011)?

With de-growth, local, national and international states would harbour resources over the long term. This requires an 'ensuring state', as well as appropriate and fair tax revenues. Future generations would be seen to be as significant as the present ones with no discounting the future, at least over the next few decades.

Within such overall resources, energy is viewed as preeminent, and short-term maximization would never be the central basis of policy. Finance would be based upon utility and not upon speculation, especially against futures. Regulations would be central to states taking a long-term view of their resources, energy and emissions.

Moreover, we know that there can be market failures, and it may be that there will be failures of 'resources' and the generation of global crises. Crises are significant since they make *global* actions by states or state-like organizations necessary in order to deal with them on an appropriate scale. Moreover, solutions to crises are as much societal as economic, involving the real economy as much as the money economy, long-term investment as much as short-term profit maximization. Given that there are tipping points in financial markets, so there can be tipping points elsewhere, as with the earth's climate or the price of oil.

So what then would de-growth involve? First, it involves generating and protecting many kinds of 'hidden wealth', such as good social interactions, wellbeing and low-carbon lives. These forms of hidden wealth are not effectively captured by figures recording the growth or decline of the usual measure of an economy, namely GDP (Gore 2013: 142–3, 184–5; Halpern 2010; Rifkin 2009: 548–9). This measure of GDP, first developed in 1937, quantifies the sum of measurable market transactions in an economy. One major problem with it is that the GDP can increase even though some of what gets counted is unproductive of individual wellbeing, and especially for the environment. GDP now includes measuring market transactions related to gambling, prostitution and illegal drugs! As a result of such problems with measurement, efforts have been made to develop alternative assessments of what makes a liveable society. A good example is the New Economics Foundation's Happy Planet Index, in which Costa Rica is the leading society, based on a measure including subjective wellbeing, long life expectancy and limited ecological footprint (www.happyplanetindex.org/data; see the video on the 'good life': www.youtube.com/watch?v=oGab38pKscw).

Highly unequal societies come out badly in these alternative measurement systems. If there are high levels of inequality, many extra goods and services are in effect 'wasted', including 'unnecessary' material products, unrewarding conferences that require air travel, multiple holidays abroad no more entertaining than those at home, building temperatures kept too high and so on (Offner 2006; Shove, Chappells, Lutzenhiser 2009). Moreover, these extra visible goods and services can engender resentment on the part of those unable to access them and may make everyone feel worse off, with lower wellbeing. More goods and services which most people cannot acquire produces less overall wellbeing within a society. More can generate less, and thus less can generate greater wellbeing (Sayer 2015; Wilkinson, Pickett 2009).

And there are interesting examples of how such a powering down can be achieved, albeit in unusual circumstances. In periods of war, 'everyone' can be seen as being in the same boat, inequality is reduced and, paradoxically, wellbeing may be higher. For example, during World War II, Britain almost ceased leisure driving, public transport use doubled in the US, there was a marked growth in biking and car sharing in most Allied countries, two-fifths of fresh vegetables in the US were grown in 'victory gardens', there was a big emphasis upon recycling and mending, and the American car industry was overnight turned into a producer of tanks and light vehicles and less 'locked in' to the individualist car culture (Klein 2014: 16–17, 90). But as energy use and consumption processes became organized on a larger scale after World War II, greater divisions of interest arose between social groups through the Great Acceleration. Klein argues that, in the future, 'we would need to return to a lifestyle similar to the one we had in the 1970s, before consumption levels went crazy in the 1980s' (2014: 90). In this previous period, there was a perfectly good standard of living for most – indeed, in most societies in the rich North, inequalities were lower and wellbeing seemed to have been higher (Piketty 2014).

The transition towns programme, as set out in *The Transition Companion* and elsewhere, documents the necessary stages of an 'energy descent' within towns and cities. Such innovation should be viral, open source, self-organizing, iterative and fun according to Rob Hopkins, the 'founder' of the transition movement (2011; www.social-life.co). The transition towns/city movement was initiated in Totnes, a movement that is now global (see https://www.transitionnetwork.org/initiatives/map). De-growth would generalize the notion of 'transition', with a smaller-scale system of neighbourhoods and cities fragmented into more self-sufficient neighbourhoods without rigid zoning. Powering down thus involves redesigning places in both physical and social engineering terms. This would foster higher-density living, heighten the possibilities of using slow travel alternatives, and shift towards practices that are smaller and more modest in scale (see *Ephemera* 15, 2015, for examples of low-budget organizing within cities).

There would also need to be a massive growth in local off-grid energy sources of wind, solar and water power, and this would be more likely if energy was state-owned, or at least state-regulated, rather than owned by corporations which are often offshored (Klein 2014: ch. 3). We have seen how big energy is a 'great divider', Illich arguing in the 1970s that it is only 'a ceiling on energy use [that] can lead to social relations that are characterized by high levels of equity' (1974: 27).

'Localization' of social practices would be key, with friends chosen from neighbouring streets, families not moving away at times of new household composition, and distant family members not being regularly visited. Families would often not live so far apart. As noted above, status would need to be re-localized and based upon contributions that people made locally. Re-engineering the nature of 'success' in societies involves emphasizing the achievements of 'local lives' (Peters, Fudge, Jackson 2010; Urry 2013a). There would have to be many transformations across systems, enhancing 'capabilities for flourishing' rather than 'income' (Jackson 2009). De-growth would involve designing places that enable social practices on a smaller scale.

Roads would no longer be just for cars (Reid 2015). Cities that were based upon a 'centre-sprawl' model would decline (Ross 2014). In such places many goods and services would be produced, consumed and – especially – repaired nearby. There should be a reduction in the distances travelled by people, objects, goods and money. The empowerment and repositioning of certain economic hubs, such as wholesale markets and other local small-scale businesses, would increase local ownership of economies as well as providing more equitable access to local resources and services.

John Thackara's *How to Thrive in the Next Economy* documents many local, smaller-scale and reduced-ownership prototypes, models and exemplars. They draw upon and release what he calls 'social energy' (Thackara 2015: 76). They include shifting from 'land use' to 'land stewardship', developing 'water sensitive urban design', the depaving movement in American suburbs, rewilding cities, urban farming, collaborative distribution systems, the carfree city movement, e-bikes fifty times cheaper than a car, and a general drawing upon and enhancement of the commons handed down and acquired from previous generations (Thackara 2015: 146). There are many other examples of social practices being downsized and localized – some described in the Liveable City scenario in the previous chapter – including Bogotá, Copenhagen, Curitiba, Delft, Freiburg, Totnes, Vancouver and Växjö. Växjö is developing a 'fossil fuel free future' in the context of the utopian plan of 'Making Sweden an oil-free Society' by 2020. It is halfway to such a future without, it is said, sacrificing lifestyle, comfort or growth.

The significance of this emissions reduction is hard to assess, especially because many developments consist of prototypes that are not yet widespread. However, the EU shows that CO_2 emissions do not need to increase inexorably, there being a recent small decline in 2013–14 (www.exeter.ac.uk/news/research/title_412769_en.html). This parallels the longer-term decline in UK resource use reported by Goodall, who argues that material consumption reached a peak around 2001–3 and since then has declined both absolutely and per head (Goodall 2011; D. Clark 2011). Strikingly, this decline in the rate of material consumption commenced before the onset of the 2007–8 economic and financial collapse. Interpreting data of this sort is complex, especially given the offshoring of CO_2 emissions to China over this period. Nevertheless, the main point here is that the relationship between 'western economies' and CO_2 emissions potentially varies, and it is *possible* for some de-growth to occur.

George Monbiot speculates whether this peaking of material consumption partially resulted from effective environmental campaigning (www.monbiot.com/2011/11/03/peak-stuff). In countless small ways the effects of NGO activities, environmental journalism, government campaigns, the developing discourses of sustainability, local government recycling and so on have made a difference to carbon intensity. The reduction in emissions in some specific countries may reflect at least the green shoots of a low-carbon civil society. If true, then this would be very significant for the possibilities of developing a de-growth future through consolidating a low-carbon civil society.

Climate futures

I now set out four possible climate futures; in each case, the potential 'social base' that would support each future needs examination. The first future is *Business as Usual*, as analysed and advocated by many orthodox commentators (see critiques in Centre for Alternative Technology 2013; Klein 2014). In this future, the goal of 'economic growth' trumps all other objectives. The objectives of state policy are to increase GDP and ensure the ever-greater availability of goods and services, whether these commodities are 'needed' or not, and without regard to their 'carbon footprint' (see Berners-Lee 2010).

In this future, avoiding climate change would only be a subsidiary goal of economic and public policy, to be implemented after economic growth was assured. Whatever their climate change rhetoric, most states adopt this 'economic growth first' model, with the majority of businesses lobbying for it and making it seem 'natural'. The electoral cycle within societies adds to the pressure to ensure short-term economic growth in order that governments get re-elected, while opposition parties also have to promise economic growth first.

Moreover, this growth-first model is often also the consequence of the internal structure of different ministries of state. A recent headline in the UK maintained: 'How Treasury obsessed with growth leaves climate action out in the cold' (Jowit 2015). The planned Transatlantic Trade and Investment Partnership between the EU and the US will further prioritize this economic growth model. What Keynes called the Treasury view dominates British decision-making, sometimes against the objectives of other ministries. Deregulated economic growth is the primary objective of government policy and nothing is allowed to touch that; this is broadly the case throughout the world.

This policy of 'economic growth first' means that many climate scientists believe that they are aware of a terrible future but it is one they can do nothing about: a 'Cassandra syndrome' (see

Chapter 2 above). Leading scientists such as Lovelock or Hansen are convinced that they know the climate future and, although they warn about what is going to happen, most people will not change their behaviour. The climate change catastrophe will necessarily unfold (on Lovelock, see http://richardfalk.wordpress.com/tag/james-lovelock). The tragedy of being unable to divert humans from the path of such a climate catastrophe is elaborated in *The Collapse of Western Civilization* (Oreskes, Conway 2014).

De-growth is the second possible climate future. I noted above the emergent 'low-carbon civil society' made up of a huge number of experiments and activists. This civil society is helping to realize preparedness in a context of ignorance and uncertainty about what will work. The crucial question here is whether such a 'low-carbon civil society' can generate sufficient new practices, habits and goods and services to power down societies on a global scale and so offset contending powerful forces especially those of carbon, financial and digital capital.

This possibility parallels E. P. Thompson's historical analysis of *The Making of the English Working Class* (1968). He showed how, during the nineteenth century, the newly forming working class was involved in its own 'making'. For Thompson, such a social class was fundamentally historical, involved in its making and transforming over time. And in making itself, it remade English society. We can think of low-carbon civil society analogously. As this civil society makes itself and gains traction, in transforming its own future, so it in effect remakes societies worldwide, just as the English working class remade nineteenth-century England, through making itself.

But it may well be that this can only result within the context of a large-scale catastrophe which is unambiguously framed as the result of climate change. Empirical research seems to show that concern for climate change developments is higher if people have directly experienced weather-related events within their locality (Spence, Poortinga, Butler, Pidgeon 2011). Many forces would thus cohere together, promoting and eventually implementing a global strategy of powering down. And, at the same time, other forces would find it impossible to sustain business as usual since those policies had got the world into that climate change catastrophe in the first place and this was evidenced in multiple ways locally.

The third future focuses upon economic growth but develops a different route: of *ecological modernization*. The claim is that a major new period of economic growth should be brought about through developing and implementing a range of eco-technologies, especially around renewable energies, new transportation and novel technologies of recycling (Mol, Sonnenfeld, Spaargaren 2009). This necessitates structural change focused on eco-innovations; ecological modernizers examine the processes which foster or hamper such a cluster of innovations like these developing global traction.

Sometimes advocates of 'ecological modernization' draw upon the arguments of early twentieth-century Russian economist Kondratiev and his followers (www.globalresearch.ca/nikolai-kondratiev-s-long-wave-the-mirror-of-the-global-economic-crisis/11161). They identified a series of technological booms in capitalism: the steam engine and textiles; the railways; chemicals and electrical engineering; the rise of the car system; and the internet and digital technologies. Each of these breakthroughs spurred a long boom of rising prosperity, then a turning point, and finally a crisis. Overall, such long waves have stretched over a roughly sixty-year period. Some economists argue that we may be on the cusp of 'the sixth Kondratieff' based around clusters of eco-innovations combined with biotech, nanotech and health. There is certainly a wave of innovation currently occurring, although it would take a monumental breakthrough for these developments to substitute for the power of carbon capital and fossil-fuel dependence, as we have seen.

The final future follows on from a large-scale series of catastrophic events, occurring across societies and unambiguously seen as being 'caused' by climate change. As a consequence, many governmental and corporate forces come together, promoting and eventually implementing a vast scheme for *geo-engineering* the future. Such a global social experiment could come to be viewed as the only way of keeping the fossil-fuel fires burning. Or, as neo-liberalism asserts, 'never let a crisis go to waste' (Klein 2007, 2014: 261–5).

The most likely form of such a major geo-engineering scheme is solar radiation management (SRM) – this would necessitate vast financial, organizational and scientific collaboration around the world (www.srmgi.org). Powerful interests would mobilize to develop this planetary technological fix. As a 'Plan B', such geoengineering is a Faustian bargain trumping democratic politics and dependent upon a globalist imaginary bypassing national processes. Szerszynski and colleagues argue that SRM interventions would produce novel climate configurations, with new winners and losers, and would generate complex issues of justice and redistribution (2013). Moreover, the indeterminacy that is endemic to climatic phenomena would mean that the attribution of cause and effect, and liability and accountability, would be impossible to resolve. This kind of 'global social experiment' would thus almost certainly engender a whole new scale of geopolitical conflict, or what Stengers refers to as the choice between 'barbarism' and 'barbarism' (2015).

So, we have seen there are many intractable issues related to climate futures. These include wicked problems, futures which depend on events and processes still to occur, potential shifts in the nature of the 'human' species, and the huge problem of turning around the logic of growth. This chapter thus shows that climate change does indeed 'change everything' (Klein 2014; also see Stengers 2015).

10

Conclusion: The Future of Futures

Adam and Groves end their interesting book on futures with the plea: 'Wanted: 21st Century Experts on the Future' (2007: 191). This book takes up this challenge, to develop expertise on the future, and especially social futures. But we have seen many ways in which this expertise is not straightforward to mobilize. Kaushik Basu, Chief Economist of the World Bank, summarizes: 'Very long-run forecasting is a hazardous activity because the uncertainties and imponderables of life have plenty of time to intrude, and bend and buck the charted path. At the same time, to craft policy that is rooted in reason and reality, we need to peer into the future with the best information, statistics, and models that we have' (http://econ.worldbank.org/WBSITE/EXTERNAL/EXTDEC/EXTDECPROSPECTS/0,,contentMDK:23413150~pagePK:64165401~piPK:64165026~theSitePK:476883,00.html).

This book has explored this paradox. In order to operate in the world and develop policy, we must peer into the future – there is no choice. We noted above that John F. Kennedy maintained that we must not miss the future. There is no doubting its importance for companies, environmental organizations, government bodies, military organizations and others. But forecasting what that future might be is hazardous and uncertain. There are many known and unknown unknowns, many intended and unintended outcomes. We have to do our best, but it will often throw up wicked and uncertain futures, the opposite of what we want and anticipate.

I have demonstrated that thinking futures involves imagining various kinds of social futures, that futures must be embedded within analyses of multiple social institutions, practices and movements. We also saw how anticipating futures makes one understand better that things could be otherwise, that outcomes are not necessarily determined, that a certain future is not inevitable (see Tutton 2016; Watson 2008).

Specifically, Part 1 documented the range of many of the anticipated futures that were developed in the past, which established some of the main terms of future thinking. A significant recent trend of writing, policy interventions, and filmic and literary thinking is the 'new catastrophism' that became widespread discourse during this new century. Such analyses show how there are many unintended, perverse and wicked problems arising in a world of contested futures including possibly the 'collapse of societies'.

A key notion developed in this book has been examination of the implications of 'complex systems' thinking for analysing varied, contested and uncertain social futures (see ESPAS 2015, for related analysis). This complexity thinking is set out in Part 2, and was used to examine futures made up of unstable, complex and interdependent adaptive systems. Powerful physical and social systems stretch over time–space, and are often locked in to distant futures. Yet these powerful systems are also fragile and often characterized by innovation, unpredictability and possible reversal. Futures involve cascading interdependencies and wicked problems with multiple 'causes' and 'solutions'. Efforts at solving one problem often reveal or produce others, and possible solutions depend on how issues are framed. Many problems are not solved but return, albeit in different ways within different places. The resources needed to solve a 'problem' can change over time. And many problems are not solved as such, but keep occurring and recurring in different forms and guises.

Such systems thinking was thus deployed in Part 3 to interrogate three substantive domains: the implications of 3D printing for global manufacturing and transportation; the nature of urban mobility and the possibilities of a post-car system; and multiple high-carbon systems and the possibility of societal de-growth. There are, of course, many other hugely significant futures beyond manufacturing, cities and climate; these include future ways of dematerializing commodities (Attali 1985[1976], on music, and 2011), global inequalities (Piketty 2014), the future of the 'west' within a polycentric system of power (Morris 2011), the rise and rise of China (Jacques 2012), the trajectory of the European Union (ESPAS 2015), the future of violence (Walby 2009), the divergent futures of world religions (www.pewforum.org/2015/04/02/religious-projections-2010-2050/) and the future character of humans as a species (these varied 'futures' roughly cover the agenda of Lancaster's new Institute for Social Futures: www.lancaster.ac.uk/social-futures).

Through exploring varied futures, it has been shown that they are indelibly bound up with the power of social actors to shape futures or even to 'have' a future. People, places and organizations that do not have a future are physically or metaphorically pushed into the slow lane (Srnicek, Williams 2015). It was also noted how enhanced computing and technological power is engendering exponential rates of future change. Financialized futures, especially, seem to be emerging ever more quickly. Actions happening beyond the speed of thought involve movements of finance which cannot be grasped by the human 'mind' and which problematize governance and resilience.

Overall, it has been seen that futures are contested and saturated with varied interests. Generations possess conflicting 'interests' within different futures, but current generations within a society normally ensure their visions come to dominate, especially through characterizing those opposed to their future as 'Luddite'. Apparently standing in the way of progress can make it difficult for social forces to organize to effect resistance against some new policy or technology or reform.

Indeed, we have seen how 'powerful futures' are almost literally 'owned' by private interests, rather than shared across members of a society. Certain futures are embedded within contemporary societies which bring them into being, being performative. Actors seek to perform or produce a future, and this can be realized as a self-fulfilling prophecy. Thinking through futures highlights something not articulated in much social science, which is that power should be viewed as significantly a matter of uneven future-making.

This book thus reclaims the terrain of future studies, both for social science and for progressive forces. It aims to 'mainstream' the future into social science since it is too important to be left to states, corporations or technologists. Analyses of 'social movements, institutions, practices and lives' are central to examining potential futures, to developing relevant theories and methods of the future. Moreover, future visions have powerful social consequences. The aim here has been to develop analyses of 'social futures', especially as contrasted with the more economistic or technological futures common elsewhere.

We have also seen that there is no single future as such, but many relating to different time regimes. There is a whole realm of social science issues concerned with how futures are embedded within energy, economic, social and cultural processes stretching from varied pasts to uncertain futures. The future is never a simple prediction or smooth extrapolation from what is happening in the present. There is no empty future just waiting to be filled.

One specific implication is that knowing the future means that it is necessary to know various pasts and their system-dependent trajectories. As noted, Marx argued how the tradition of dead generations weighs like a nightmare on the brains of the living. Even in revolutionary change, the spirits of the past are brought into service. Futures are thus never wholly open, although there are moments of greater openness when the die seems less cast, such as around 1970 across much of the world.

In particular, innovations normally involve partly unpredicted combinations of past elements, as Arthur shows in the case of innovating 'new technologies'. Such systems are in 'process' and not pre-determined in their organization or effects. We have seen how one source of unpredictability stems from how technologies 'move' around and exert intended and unintended consequences as synchronization contingently occurs with other elements, so constituting a new system.

It has also been shown that distinctions need to be made between various futures – the probable, the possible and the preferable. It was seen that what is preferable may turn out to be the least probable. That a particular future is preferred is no guarantee that it will be the one most likely to emerge. Futures are often the opposite of what are planned and imagined. We have seen various instances of how, once the genie has been let out of the bottle, it cannot be returned, and the stage can be set for a path-dependent pattern developing to an unpreferred future.

We also saw that there are various methods for envisaging futures. We examined many efforts made to anticipate, visualize, imagine, elaborate and document the future(s) across domains of human activity. It was shown that the powerful weight of history and embedded relations of power strongly bear upon those possibilities for future-making. Various future visions were examined. Especially significant has been developing utopias that show that things could be different and suggest what should happen to move towards that desired utopia. We especially examined the conditions under which the utopias of carfree cities and of a powering down to a low-carbon world might materialize.

Finally, thinking futures is a way of bringing back planning for the future, but under a new framing. Issues are now so big and wicked that individuals, local communities, corporations, states and international organizations have to coordinate futures. There seems no choice, since, as we have seen, markets can generate the most terrible of 'failures' of the future. But the discourse of planning derives from the post-war period, the period of social democracy, or at least national government. Such planning notions have been critiqued from left and right.

But, given long-term processes in much of social life, anticipating futures is absolutely essential. And once one is undertaking futures thinking, then public bodies are central to that process. Indeed, they are often the key coordinator of the future-making process. So I suggest that futures thinking is a major way of bringing the state and civil society back in from the cold, especially if the focus is upon social and not just technological futures.

Social futures problematize both the autonomous market and the endogenous development of technologies. Futures thinking authorizes many relevant actors as being centrally implicated in developing futures. Social futures thinking then enables forms of coordination in an era of civil society, global change, wicked problems, the limits of markets, unknown unknowns and so on. Thinking and practice must go beyond the market, minimal states and new technologies that are seen as more or less inevitable. A planned future may not be possible, but a coordinated one may be the best show in town. This requires mobilizing social futures thinking of the sort developed in this book. A key issue is how a productive way of developing 'democratic' futures thinking and practice can emerge and become embedded.

Futures are hugely significant for societies. It is essential to reclaim the terrain of future studies for social science and for social actors, since much theory and research is pertinent. In this book I tried to 'mainstream' and to 'democratize' the future. Future visions have powerful consequences and social science, via complex systems thinking, needs to be present in disentangling, debating and delivering social futures, in a way from within. The futures world may be a murky world but it is one that we have to enter, interrogate and hopefully reshape. It should be a direction of travel for fateful analyses of social life within this new century.

References

Abbott, A. (2001) *Time Matters*. Chicago: University of Chicago Press.

Abbott, C. (2008) *An Uncertain Future: Law Enforcement, National Security and Climate Change*. Oxford: Oxford Research Group.

Adam, B. (1990) *Time and Social Theory*. Cambridge: Polity.

Adam, B. (1995) *Timewatch: The Social Analysis of Time*. Cambridge: Polity.

Adam, B. (2010) 'History of the future: paradoxes and challenges', *Rethinking History*, 14: 361–78.

Adam, B., Groves, C. (2007) *Future Matters: Action, Knowledge, Ethics*. Leiden: Brill.

Albert, R., Barabási, A.-L. (2000) 'Topology of evolving networks: local events and universality', *Physical Review Letters*, 85: 5234–7.

Allwood, J., Cullen, J. (2012) *Sustainable Materials*. Cambridge: UIT Press.

Amin, A., Thrift, N. (2002) *Cities: Reimagining the Urban*. Cambridge: Polity.

Anderson, B. (1991) *Imagined Communities*. London: Verso.

Anderson, C. (2012) *Makers: The New Industrial Revolution*. New York: Crown Business.

Anderson, K., Bows, A. (2011) 'Beyond "dangerous" climate change: emission scenarios for a new world', *Philosophical Transactions of the Royal Society A*, 369: 20–44.

Andrews, C. (1901) *Famous Utopias*. New York: Tudor Publishing.

Appadurai, A. (2013) *The Future as Cultural Fact*. London: Verso.

Appelbaum, E., Batt, R. (2014) *Private Equity at Work: When Wall Street Manages Main Street*, https://www.russellsage.org/publications/private-equity-work.

Armytage, W. (1968) *Yesterday's Tomorrows: A Historical Survey of Future Societies*. London: Routledge and Kegan Paul.

Arthur, B. (1994) *Increasing Returns and Path Dependence in the Economy*. Ann Arbor: University of Michigan Press.

Arthur, B. (2009) *The Nature of Technology*. New York: Free Press.

Arthur, B. (2013) *Complexity Economics: A Different Framework for Economic Thought*. Working Paper. Santa Fe: Sante Fe Institute.

Atherton, A. (2005) 'A future for small business? Prospective scenarios for the development of the economy based on current policy thinking and counterfactual reasoning', *Futures*, 37: 777–94.

Attali, J. (1985[1976]) *Noise: The Political Economy of Music*. Manchester: Manchester University Press.

Attali, J. (2011) *A Brief History of the Future*. New York: Skyhorse.

Atwood, M. (2010) *The Year of the Flood*. New York: Anchor.

Axelrod, R., Cohen, M. (1999) *Harnessing Complexity*. New York: Free Press.

Ball, P. (2004) *Critical Mass*. London: William Heinemann.

Ballard, J. G. (2005[1975]) *High-Rise*. London: Harper.

Banister, D., Schwanen, T., Anable, J. (eds.) (2012) 'Special section on theoretical perspectives on climate change mitigation in transport', *Journal of Transport Geography*, 24: 467–535.

Barabási, A.-L. (2002) *Linked: The New Science of Networks*. Cambridge, Mass.: Perseus.

Barkenbus, J. (2009) 'Our electric automotive future: CO_2 savings through a disruptive technology', *Policy and Society*, 27: 399–410.

Barlex, D., Stevens, M. (2012) *Making by Printing – Disruption Inside and Outside School?*, www.ep.liu.se/ecp/073/007/ecp12073007.pdf.

Bauman, Z. (1976) *Socialism: The Active Utopia*. London: George Allen and Unwin.

Bauman, Z. (2000) *Liquid Modernity*. Cambridge: Polity.

BBC News (2010) '3D printing offers ability to print physical objects', www.bbc.co.uk/news/technology-11834044.

Beck, U. (2009) *World at Risk*. Cambridge: Polity.

Beckett, A. (2011) 'The economy's bust, the climate's on the brink and even the arts are full of gloom', *The Guardian G2*, 19 December.

Beinhocker, E. (2006) *The Origin of Wealth: Evolution, Complexity, and the Radical Remaking of Economics*. London: Random House.

Bell, S., Walker, S. (2011) 'Futurescaping infinite bandwidth, zero latency', *Futures*, 43: 525–39.

Bell, W., Wau, J. (eds.) (1971) *Sociology of the Future: Theory, Cases and Annotated Bibliography*. New York: Russell Sage.

Ben-Joseph, E. (2012) *Re-thinking a Lot: The Design and Culture of Parking*. Cambridge, Mass.: MIT Press.

Benkler, Y. (2007) *The Wealth of Networks*. New Haven: Yale University Press.
Berman, M. (1983) *All That Is Solid Melts into Air*. London: Verso.
Berners-Lee, M. (2010) *How Bad are Bananas?* London: Profile.
Berners-Lee, M., Clark, D. (2013) *The Burning Question: We can't Burn Half the World's Oil, Coal and Gas. So How Do we Quit?* London: Profile.
Better Transport (2014) *Car Dependency Scorecard*. London: Better Transport.
Biel, R. (2014) 'Visioning a sustainable energy future', *Theory, Culture and Society*, 31: 183–202.
Bijsterveld, K., Cleophas, E., Krebs, S., Mom, G. (2014) *Sound and Safe: A History of Listening Behind the Wheel*. New York: Oxford University Press.
Birtchnell, T., Büscher, M. (2011) 'Stranded: an eruption of disruption', *Mobilities*, 6: 1–9.
Birtchnell, T., Caletrio, J. (eds.) (2014) *Elite Mobilities*. London: Routledge.
Birtchnell, T., Savitzky, S., Urry, J. (eds.) (2015) *Cargomobilities*. London: Routledge.
Birtchnell, T., Urry, J. (2013a) 'Fabricating futures and the movement of objects', *Mobilities*, 8: 388–405.
Birtchnell, T., Urry, J. (2013b) '3D, SF and the future', *Futures*, 50: 25–34.
Birtchnell, T., Urry, J. (2016) 'Small technologies and big systems', in Endres, M., Manderscheid, K., Mincke, C. (eds.) *Discourses and Ideologies of Mobility*. London: Routledge.
Birtchnell, T., Viry, G., Urry, J. (2013) 'Elite formation in the third industrial revolution', in Birtchnell, T., Caletrio, J. (eds.) *Elite Mobilities*. London: Routledge.
Black, E. (2006) *Internal Combustion*. New York: St Martin's Press.
Blinder, A. (2006) 'Offshoring: the next industrial revolution', *Foreign Affairs*, 85: 113–28.
Böhm, S., Jones, C., Land, C., Paterson, M. (eds.) (2006) *Against Automobility*. Oxford: Blackwell Sociological Review Monograph.
Boltanski, L., Chiapello, E. (2007) *The New Spirit of Capitalism*. London: Verso.
Bond, P. (2012) *Politics of Climate Justice*. Scottsville: University of KwaZulu-Natal Press.
Bourdieu, P. (1984) *Distinction: A Social Critique of the Judgement of Taste*. London: Routledge and Kegan Paul.
Braudel, F. (1972) *The Mediterranean and the Mediterranean World in the Age of Phillip II*. Vol. I. New York: Harper and Row.

Bridge, G. (2013) 'Territory, now in 3D!' *Political Geography*, 34: 55–7.

Brown, V., Harris, J., Russell, J. (eds.) (2010) *Tackling Wicked Problems*. London: Earthscan.

Brundtland Report (1987) *Our Common Future*. New York: World Commission on Environment and Development.

Buchanan, M. (2002) *Small World: Uncovering Nature's Hidden Networks*. London: Weidenfeld.

Budd, L. (2013) 'Aeromobile elites: private business aviation and the global economy', in Birtchnell, T., Caletrio, J. (eds.) *Elite Mobilities*. London: Routledge.

Bunders, J., Bunders, A., Zweekhorst, M. (2015) 'Challenges for interdisciplinary research', in Werlen, B. (ed.) *Global Sustainability*. Switzerland: Springer.

Burt, R. (1992) *Structural Holes*. Cambridge, Mass.: Harvard University Press.

Butler, S. (2005[1872]) *Erewhon*, www.gutenberg.org/files/1906/1906-h/1906-h.htm.

Calder, N. (1964) *The World in 1984: The Complete New Scientist Series*. Harmondsworth: Penguin (see http://calderup.wordpress.com/2010/05/04/Internet-64).

Campbell, K. (ed.) (2008) *Climatic Cataclysm: The Foreign Policy and National Security Implications of Climate Change*. Washington: Brookings.

Canales, J. (2009) *A Tenth of a Second*. Chicago: University of Chicago Press.

Capra, F. (1996) *The Web of Life*. London: HarperCollins.

Carbon Tracker (2013) *Unburnable Carbon 2013: Wasted Capital and Stranded Assets*. London: Grantham Research Institute on Climate Change and the Environment.

Carr, N. (2010) *The Shallows*. New York: W. W. Norton.

Carroll, R. (2008) 'The temples of doom', *The Guardian G2*, 28 October.

Carroll, W. (2010) *The Making of a Transnational Capitalist Class: Corporate Power in the 21st Century*. London: Zed.

Carson, R. (1962) *Silent Spring*. Boston: Houghton Mifflin.

Castells, M. (1996) *The Rise of the Network Society*. Oxford: Blackwell.

Castells, M. (2001) *The Internet Galaxy*. Oxford: Oxford University Press.

Centre for Alternative Technology (2013) *Zero Carbon Britain: Rethinking the Future*. Machynlleth: Centre for Alternative Technology.

Clark, D. (2011) 'The only way is down', *The Guardian G2*, 1 November.

Clark, N. (2010) 'Violent worlds, vulnerable bodies: confronting abrupt climate change', *Theory, Culture and Society*, 27: 31–53.

Clark, N. (2011) *Inhuman Nature: Sociable Life on a Dynamic Planet*. London: Sage.

Clarke, A. C. (2000) *Profiles of the Future* (2nd rev. edn.). London: Indigo.

Clarke, T. (2011) 'How printing in 3D could save lives', www.channel4.com/news/how-printing-in-3-d-could-save-lives.

Collectif Argos (2010) *Climate Refugees*. Boston: MIT Press.

Collie, N. (2011) 'Cities of the imagination: science fiction, urban space, and community engagement in urban planning', *Futures*, 43: 424–31.

Condie, J. M., Cooper, A. M. (2015). *Dialogues of Sustainable Urbanisation: Social Science Research and Transitions to Urban Contexts*. Penrith, NSW: University of Western Sydney.

Costanza, R. (1999) 'Four visions of the century ahead', *The Futurist*, February: 23–8.

Coveney, P., Highfield, R. (1990) *The Arrow of Time*. London: Flamingo.

Crawford, J. (2009) *Carfree Design Manual*. Utrecht: International Books.

Cudahy, B. J. (2006) *Box Boats: How Container Ships Changed the World*. New York: Fordham University Press.

Cwerner, S. (2009) 'Helipads, heliports and urban air space: governing the contested infrastructure of helicopter travel', in Cwerner, S., Kesselring, S., Urry, J. (eds.) *Aeromobilities*. London: Routledge.

Dartnell, L. (2014) *The Knowledge: How to Rebuild our World from Scratch*. London: Bodley Head.

Davidson, C. (2008) *Dubai: The Vulnerability of Success*. London: Hurst.

Davis, G. (2009) *Managed by the Markets*. New York: Oxford University Press.

Davis, G. (2012) 'Re-imagining the corporation'. Paper presented to American Sociological Association, Denver, Colorado, 17–20 August.

Davis, M. (2000) *Ecology of Fear*. London: Picador.

Davis, M. (2010) 'Who will build the ark?', *New Left Review*, 61: 29–46.

Day, P. (2011) 'Will 3D printing revolutionise manufacturing?', *BBC News*, www.bbc.co.uk/news/business-14282091.

Dayrell, C., Urry, J. (2015) 'Mediating climate politics: the surprising case of Brazil', *European Journal of Social Theory*, 18: 257–73.

Dean, A. (2012) '3D printing in the home: reality check', www.develop3d.com/features/3d-printing-in-the-home-reality-check.

Demeritt, D. (2006) 'Science studies, climate change and the prospects for constructivist critique', *Economy and Society*, 35: 453–79.

Dennis, K., Urry, J. (2009) *After the Car*. Cambridge: Polity.

Despommier, D. (2009) 'The rise of vertical farms', *Scientific American*, 301: 80–7.

Diamond, J. (2005) *Collapse: How Societies Choose to Fail or Succeed*. London: Allen Lane.

Druce-McFadden, C. (2013) 'Driverless cars to invade England by 2015', *DVICE*, 4 November, www.dvice.com/2013–11–4/driverless-cars-invade-england-2015.

Dunn, N., Cureton, P., Pollastri, S. (2014) *A Visual History of the Future*. Foresight Paper from the 'The Future of Cities' Foresight Programme. London: Department for Business, Innovation and Skills.

Easton, T. (2011) 'A recession in the economy of trust', in Ricci, G. (ed.) *Values and Technology: Religion and Public Life*. New Brunswick, N.J.: Transaction.

Edgerton, D. (2006) *The Shock of the Old: Technology and Global History since 1900*. London: Profile.

Ehret, O., Gignum, M. (2012) 'Introducing hydrogen and fuel cell vehicles in Germany', in Geels, F., Kemp, R., Dudley, G., Lyons, G. (eds.) *Automobility in Transition? A Socio-Technical Analysis of Sustainable Transport*. London: Routledge.

Elias, N. (2007[1984]) *An Essay on Time*. Dublin: UCD Press.

Elias, N. (2012[1939]) *On the Process of Civilisation*. Dublin: UCD Press.

Ellen MacArthur Foundation (2012) *Towards the Circular Economy: Economic and Business Rationale for an Accelerated Transition*, www.thecirculareconomy.org/uploads/files/012012/4f26c6959d31c63107000018/original/120130_EMF_CE_Full%20report_final.pdf?1327941269.

Elliott, A. (2013) *Reinvention*. London: Routledge.

Elliott, A., Urry, J. (2010) *Mobile Lives*. London: Routledge.

Emmott, S. (2013) 'Humans: the real threat to life on earth', www.theguardian.com/environment/2013/jun/30/stephen-emmott-ten-billion.

ESPAS (2015) *Global Trends to 2030: Can the EU Meet the Challenges Ahead?* Brussels: ESPAS.

Farnish, K. (2009) *Time's Up! An Uncivilized Solution to a Global Crisis*. Totnes: Green Books.

Faye, G. (2012) *Convergence of Catastrophes*. London: Arktos Media.

Flannery, T. (2007) *The Weather Makers*. London: Penguin.

Floyd, J., Slaughter, R. (2014) 'Descent pathways', *Foresight*, 6: 485–95.

Forster, E. M. (1985[1909]) *The New Collected Short Stories*. London: Sidgwick and Jackson.

Forum for the Future (2010) *Megacities on the Move*. London: Forum for the Future.

Foster, J. (2015) *After Sustainability*. London: Routledge.

Fox, S. (2010) 'After the factory [post-industrial nations]', *Engineering and Technology*, 5: 59–61.

Franz, K. (2005) *Tinkering: Consumers Reinvent the Early Automobile*. Philadelphia: University of Pennsylvania Press.

Friedman, T. (2009) *Hot, Flat and Crowded*. London: Penguin.

Froggatt, A., Lahn, G. (2010) *Sustainable Energy Security: Strategic Risks and Opportunities for Business*. London: Lloyd's and Chatham House.

Gallopin, G., Hammond, A., Raskin, P., Swart, R. (1997) *Branch Points: Global Scenarios and Human Choice*. Polestar Series Report 7. Stockholm: Stockholm Environmental Institute.

Gamble, A. (2014) *Crisis Without End? The Unravelling of Western Prosperity*. London: Palgrave Macmillan.

Garside, J. (2014) 'Many more of us will work from home – or a cafe – says BT futurologist', *The Guardian*, 3 January.

Geels, F. (2006) 'Multi-level perspective on system innovation: relevance of industrial transformation', in Olsthoorn, X., Wieczorek, A. (eds.) *Understanding Industrial Transformation: Views from Different Disciplines*. The Netherlands: Springer.

Geels, F. (2010) 'Ontologies, socio-technical transitions (to sustainability) and the multi-level perspective', *Research Policy*, 39: 494–510.

Geels, F. (2014) 'Energy, societal transformation, and socio-technical transitions: expanding the multi-level perspective', *Theory, Culture and Society*, 31: 21–40.

Geels, F., Kemp, R., Dudley, G., Lyons, G. (2012) *Automobility in Transition? A Socio-Technical Analysis of Sustainable Transport*. London: Routledge.

Geels, F., Schot, J. (2007) 'Typology of sociotechnical transition pathways', *Research Policy*, 35: 399–417.

Geels, F., Smit, W. (2000) 'Failed technology futures: pitfalls and lessons from a historical survey', *Futures*, 32: 867–85.

Gell-Mann, M. (1995) 'What is complexity?' *Complexity*, 1: 16–19.

Gershenfeld, N. (2007) *Fab: The Coming Revolution on your Desktop – From Personal Computers to Personal Fabrication*. New York: Basic Books.

Giddens, A. (1990) *The Consequences of Modernity*. Cambridge: Polity.

Giddens, A. (2009) *The Politics of Climate Change*. Cambridge: Polity.
Gilding, P. (2012) *The Great Disruption: How the Climate Crisis Will Transform the Global Economy*. London: Bloomsbury.
Gladwell, M. (2002) *Tipping Points: How Little Things Can Make a Big Difference*. Boston: Little, Brown and Company.
Glaeser, E. (2011) *Triumph of the City: How Our Greatest Invention Makes Us Richer, Smarter, Greener, Healthier, and Happier*. London: Penguin.
Goodall, C. (2011) 'Peak stuff. Did the UK reach a maximum use of material resources in the early part of the last decade?', www.carboncommentary.com/s/Peak_Stuff_171011.pdf.
Gore, A. (2013) *The Future*. London: W. H. Allen.
Graham, S. (2011) *Cities under Siege*. London: Verso.
Granovetter, M. (1983) 'The strength of weak ties: a network theory revisited', *Sociological Theory*, 1: 201–33.
Granovetter, M. (1985) 'Economic action and social structure: the problem of embeddedness', *American Journal of Sociology*, 91: 481–510.
Greenfield, S. (2011) 'Computers may be altering our brains – we must ask how', *The Independent*, 12 August.
Greer, J. M. (2015) *After Progress*. Gabriola Island, BC: New Society Publishers.
Haldane, A., May, R. (2011) 'Systemic risk in banking ecosystems', *Nature*, 469: 351–5.
Hall, S. (2007) *The Carhullan Army*. London: Faber and Faber.
Hallam, T. (2005) *Catastrophes and Lesser Calamities: The Causes of Mass Extinctions*. Oxford: Oxford University Press.
Halpern, D. (2010) *The Hidden Wealth of Nations*. Cambridge: Polity.
Hamilton, C. (2010) *Requiem for a Species*. London: Earthscan.
Hansen, J. (2011) *Storms of my Grandchildren: The Truth about the Coming Climate Catastrophe and Our Last Chance to Save Humanity*. London: Bloomsbury.
Hardin, G. (1972) *Exploring New Ethics for Survival*. Baltimore: Penguin.
Hardt, M., Negri, A. (2006) *Multitude*. London: Penguin.
Harvey, M. (2014) 'The food–energy–climate change trilemma', *Theory, Culture and Society*, 31: 155–82.
Hawken, P., Lovins, A., Lovins, H. (1999) *Natural Capitalism*. London: Earthscan.
Hawking, S. (1988) *A Brief History of Time*. London: Bantam.
Hayek, F. (1944) *The Road to Serfdom*. London: Routledge.

Heidegger, M. (1962[1927]) *Being and Time*. New York: Harper & Row.

Heinberg, R. (2005) *The Party's Over: Oil, War and the Fate of Industrial Society*. New York: Clearview Books.

Heinberg, R., Lerch, D. (eds.) (2010) *The Post-Carbon Reader*. Healdsburg: California: Watershed Media.

Hickman, R., Banister, D. (2007) 'Looking over the horizon: transport and reduced CO_2 emissions in the UK by 2030', *Transport Policy*, 14: 377–87.

Hillman, M., Fawcett, T., Raja, S. (2007) *The Suicidal Planet: How to Prevent Global Climate Catastrophe*. New York: Thomas Dunne Books.

Hiltunen, E. (2013) *Foresight and Innovation – How Companies Are Coping with the Future*. London: Routledge.

Homer-Dixon, T. (2006) *The Upside of Down: Catastrophe, Creativity, and the Renewal of Civilization*. London: Souvenir.

Hopkins, R. (2011) *The Transition Companion*. Totnes: Green Books.

Hopkinson, N., Hague, R., Dickens, P. (2006) 'Introduction to rapid manufacturing', in Hopkinson, N., Hague, R. (eds.) *Rapid Manufacturing: An Industrial Revolution for the Digital Age*. Chichester: John Wiley and Sons.

Horvath, R. (1974) 'Machine space', *The Geographical Journal*, 64: 167–88.

Houellebecq, M. (2000) *Atomised*. London: Vintage.

Hughes, T. (1983) *Networks of Power: Electrification in Western Society, 1880–1930*. Baltimore: Johns Hopkins University Press.

Hulme, M. (2009) *Why We Disagree About Climate Change*. Cambridge: Cambridge University Press.

Hunt, D. V. L., Lombardi, D. R., Atkinson, S., et al. (2012) 'Scenario archetypes: converging rather than diverging themes', *Sustainability*, 4: 740–72.

Huxley, A. (1965[1958]) *Brave New World Revisited*. New York: Harper and Row.

Huxley, A. (1991[1932]) *Brave New World*. London: Longman.

Illich, I. (1974) *Energy and Equity*. London: Marion Boyars.

IPCC (2007) 'Summary for policymakers', in *Climate Change 2007: The Physical Science Basis. Contribution of Working Group I to the Fourth Assessment Report of the Intergovernmental Panel on Climate Change*. Cambridge: Cambridge University Press.

Jackson, T. (2009) *Prosperity Without Growth*. London: Earthscan.

Jacobs, J. (1992[1961]) *The Death and Life of Great American Cities*. New York: Vintage.

Jacques, M. (2012) *When China Rules the World*. London: Penguin.

Johnson, B. (2011) *Science Fiction Prototyping: Designing the Future with Science Fiction*. Synthesis Lectures on Computer Science, doi:10.2200/S00336ED1V01Y201102CSL003.

Jowit, J. (2015) 'How Treasury obsessed with growth leaves climate action out in the cold', *The Guardian*, 25 May.

Kaldor, M. (1999) *New and Old Wars: Organized Violence in a Global Era*. Cambridge: Polity.

Kaldor, M., Karl, T., Said, Y. (eds.) (2007) *Oil Wars*. London: Pluto.

Karlgaard, R. (2011) '3D printing will revive American manufacturing', *Forbes*, www.forbes.com/sites/richkarlgaard/2011/06/23/3d-printing-will-revive-american-manufacturing.

Kauffman, S. (1993) *The Origins of Order: Self-organization and Selection in Evolution*. New York: Oxford University Press.

Keen, A. (2015) *The Internet is Not the Answer*. London: Atlantic Books.

Kennedy Address (1963) 'Public papers of the Presidents: John F. Kennedy'. (Assembly Hall, Paulskirche, Frankfurt (266), 25 June.)

Kerr, J. (2002) 'Trouble in motor city', in Wollen, P., Kerr, J. (eds.) *Autopia. Cars and Culture*. London: Reaktion Books.

Keynes, J. M. (1936) *The General Theory of Employment, Interest and Money*. London: Macmillan.

Keynes, J. M. (1963[1930]) *Essays in Persuasion*. New York: W. W. Norton & Co.

Kicker, D. (2009) 'Wendell Bell and Oliver W. Markley: two Futurists' views of the preferable, the possible and the probable', *Journal of Futures Studies*, 13: 161–78.

Kirby, P. (2013) 'Transforming capitalism: the triple crisis', *Irish Journal of Sociology*, 21: 62–75.

Kirk, G. (1982) *Schumacher on Energy*. London: Jonathan Cape.

Klein, N. (2000) *No Logo*. London: Flamingo.

Klein, N. (2007) *The Shock Doctrine: The Rise of Disaster Capitalism*. New York: Metropolitan Books.

Klein, N. (2014) *This Changes Everything: Capitalism vs. the Climate*. London: Allen Lane.

Kloppenburg, S. (2013) *Tracing Mobilities Regimes*. Maastricht: University of Maastricht.

Kolbert, E. (2007) *Field Notes from a Catastrophe: A Frontline Report on Climate Change*. London: Bloomsbury.

Kolbert, E. (2015) *The Sixth Extinction: An Unnatural History*. London: Bloomsbury.

Krane, J. (2010) *City of Gold*. London: Picador.

Kross, R. (2011) 'How 3D printing will change absolutely everything it touches', *Forbes* www.forbes.com/sites/ciocentral/2011/08/17/how-3d-printing-willchange-absolutely-everything-it-touches.

Kumar, K. (1987) *Utopia and Anti-Utopia in Modern Times*. Oxford: Basil Blackwell.

Kumar, K. (1991) *Utopianism*. Milton Keynes: Open University Press.

Kunstler, J. (2006) *The Long Emergency: Surviving the Converging Catastrophes of the 21st Century*. London: Atlantic Books.

Kurzweil, R. (2006) *The Singularity is Near*. London: Gerard Duckworth.

Labban, M. (2010) 'Oil in parallax: scarcity, markets and the financialization of accumulation', *Geoforum*, 41: 541–52.

Lakatos, I., Musgrave, A. (eds.) (1970) *Criticism and the Growth of Knowledge*. Cambridge: Cambridge University Press.

Lanier, J. (2013) *Who Owns the Future?* New York: Simon and Schuster.

Lankford, B. (2013) *Resource Efficiency Complexity and the Commons: The Paracommons and Paradoxes of Natural Resource Losses, Wastes and Wastages*. Abingdon: Earthscan.

Lash, S., Urry, J. (1987) *The End of Organized Capitalism*. Cambridge: Polity.

Lash, S., Urry, J. (1994) *Economies of Signs and Space*. London: Sage.

Laszlo, E. (2006) *The Chaos Point*. London: Piatkus Books.

Latouche, S. (2009) *Farewell to Growth*. Cambridge: Polity.

Latour, B. (1993) *We Have Never Been Modern*. Hemel Hempstead: Harvester Wheatsheaf.

Latour, B. (1996) *Aramis or the Love of Technology*. Cambridge, Mass.: Harvard University Press.

Laurier, E., Dant, T. (2012) 'What we do whilst driving: towards the driverless car', in Grieco, M., Urry, J. (eds.) *Mobilities: New Perspectives on Transport and Society*. Farnham: Ashgate.

Laviolette, P. (2012) *Extreme Landscapes of Leisure: Not a Hap-Hazardous Sport*. Farnham: Ashgate Publishing.

Law, J., Urry, J. (2004) 'Enacting the social', *Economy and Society*, 33: 390–410.

Le Goff, J. (1980) *Time, Work and Culture in the Middle Ages*. Chicago: University of Chicago Press.

Lefebvre, H. (1976) *The Survival of Capitalism*. London: Allison and Busby.

Leggett, J. (2005) *Half Gone: Oil, Gas, Hot Air and the Global Energy Crisis*. London: Portobello Books.

Lehto, S. (2013) *The Great American Jet Pack: The Quest for the Ultimate Individual Lift Device*. Chicago: Chicago Review Press.

Leichenko, R., Thomas, A., Baines, M. (2010) 'Vulnerability and adaptation to climate change', in Lever-Tracy, C. (ed.) *Routledge Handbook on Climate Change and Society*. London: Routledge.
Levitas, R. (1990) *The Concept of Utopia*. London: Philip Allen.
Levitas, R. (2013) *Utopia as Method*. London: Palgrave Macmillan.
Lewis, M. (2015) *Flash Boys*. London: Penguin.
Linden, E. (2007) *Winds of Change: Climate, Weather and the Destruction of Civilizations*. New York: Simon and Schuster.
Llewellyn, R. (2013) *News from Gardenia*. London: Unbound.
Lomborg, B. (2001) *The Skeptical Environmentalist*. Cambridge: Cambridge University Press.
Lorimer, J. (2012) 'Multinatural geographies for the Anthropocene', *Progress in Human Geography*, 36: 593–612.
Lovelock, J. (2006) *The Revenge of Gaia*. London: Allen Lane.
Lovelock, J. (2010) *The Vanishing Face of Gaia: A Final Warning*. London: Penguin.
Lyons, G. (2015) 'The road investment strategy is a victory for "predict and provide" over transport planning', *Local Transport Today*, 663: 18.
Lyons, G., Goodwin, P. (2014) 'Grow, peak or plateau – the outlook for car travel'. Discussion Paper. New Zealand Ministry of Transport, http://eprints.uwe.ac.uk/23277.
Macdonald, R. (2000) 'Urban hotel: evolution of a hybrid typology', *Built Environment*, 26: 142–51.
Macnaghten, P., Owen, R., Stilgoe, J., et al. (2015) 'Responsible innovation across borders: tensions, paradoxes and possibilities', *Journal of Responsible Innovation*, 1: 91–9.
Macnaghten, P., Urry, J. (1998) *Contested Natures*. London: Sage.
Mahoney, J. (2000) 'Path dependence in historical sociology', *Theory and Society*, 29: 507–48.
Marvin, C. (1988) *When Old Technologies Were New*. New York: Oxford University Press.
Marx, K. (1962[1845]) *Eleventh Thesis on Feuerbach*, https://www.marxists.org/archive/marx/works/1845/theses.
Marx, K. (1973[1852]) *Surveys from Exile*. Harmondsworth: Penguin.
Marx, K., Engels, F. (1888[1848]). *The Manifesto of the Communist Party*. Moscow: Foreign Languages.
Marx, K., Engels, F. (1952[1848]) *Marx Engels: Selected Works*. Vol. II. Moscow: Foreign Languages.
May, R. (1974) *Stability and Complexity in Model Ecosystems*. Princeton: Princeton University Press.
Mazzucato, M. (2015) *The Entrepreneurial State – Debunking Public vs. Private Sector Myths*. New York: Public Affairs.
McCarthy, C. (2006) *The Road*. New York: Vintage.

McCurdy, H. (2011) *Space and the American Imagination*. Baltimore: Johns Hopkins University Press.

McEwan, I. (2010) *Solar*. London: Jonathan Cape.

McGuire, B. (2006) *Global Catastrophes: A Very Short Introduction*. Oxford: Oxford University Press.

McTaggart, J. (1927) *The Nature of Existence*. Vol. II, Book 5. Cambridge: Cambridge University Press.

Mead, G. H. (1959[1934]) *The Philosophy of the Present*. La Salle: Open Court.

Meadows, D. H., Meadows, D. L., Randers, J., Behrens, W. (1972) *The Limits to Growth*. New York: New American Library.

Millard-Ball, A., Schipper, L. (2011) 'Are we reaching peak travel? Trends in passenger transport in eight industrialized countries', *Transport Reviews*, 31: 357–78.

Miller, D. (ed.) (2000) *Car Cultures*. Oxford: Berg.

Miller, R. (2011) 'Futures literacy – embracing complexity and using the future', *Ethos*, 10: 23–8.

Mitchell, C. (2010) *The Political Economy of Sustainable Energy*. London: Palgrave Macmillan.

Mitchell, T. (2011) *Carbon Democracy*. London: Verso.

Mitchell, W., Borroni-Bird, C., Burns, L. (2010) *Reinventing the Automobile*. Cambridge: Mass.: MIT Press.

Mol, A., Sonnenfeld, D., Spaargaren, G. (eds.) (2009) *The Ecological Modernization Reader: Environmental Reform in Theory and Practice*. London: Routledge.

Monbiot, G. (2006) *Heat: How to Stop the Planet from Burning*. London: Allen Lane.

Monbiot, G. (2013) *Feral: Searching for Enchantment on the Frontiers of Rewilding*. London: Penguin.

Montford, A. (2010) *The Hockey Stick Illusion: Climategate and the Corruption of Science*. London: Stacey International.

Montgomery, C. (2013) *Happy City*. London: Penguin.

Montgomery, D. (2007) *Dirt: The Erosion of Civilizations*. Berkeley: University of California Press.

Moran, A. (ed.) (2015) *Climate Change: The Facts*, www.amazon.com/dp/B00S5L5Y0W/ref=cm_sw_su_dp.

Morris, I. (2011) *Why the West Rules – For Now*. London: Profile.

Morris, W. (1890) *News from Nowhere*, http://en.wikisource.org/wiki/News_from_Nowhere.

Morrison, B. (2008) 'It was the cathedral of modern times, but the car is now a menace', *The Guardian*, 26 July.

Morus, I. (2014) 'Future perfect: social progress, high-speed transport and electricity everywhere – how the Victorians invented the future', *Aeon*, http://aeon.co/magazine/society/how-the-victorians-imagined-and-invented-the-future.

Moskvitch, K. (2011) 'Blood vessels made on 3D printer', *BBC News*, www.bbc.co.uk/news/technology-14946808.

Motesharrei, S., Rivas, J., Kalnay, E. (2014) 'Human and nature dynamics (HANDY): modelling inequality and use of resources in the collapse or sustainability of societies', *Ecological Economics*, 101: 90–102.

Mumford, L. (1922) *The Story of Utopias*, www.sacred-texts.com/utopia/sou/sou04.htm.

Murray, J., King, D. (2012) 'Climate policy: oil's tipping point has passed', *Nature*, 481: 433–5.

Nancy, J.-L. (2014) *After Fukushima: The Equivalence of Catastrophes*. New York: Fordham University Press.

Nicolis, G. (1995) *Introduction to Non-Linear Science*. Cambridge: Cambridge University Press.

Nikitas, A., Karlsson, M. (2015) 'A worldwide state-of-the-art analysis for Bus Rapid Transit: looking for the Success Formula', *Journal of Public Transportation*, 18: 1–33.

North, D. (1990) *Institutions, Institutional Change and Economic Performance*. Cambridge: Cambridge University Press.

Nowotny, H. (1994) *Time: The Modern and the Postmodern Experience*. Cambridge: Polity.

Nye, D. (1998) *Consuming Power*. Cambridge, Mass.: MIT Press.

Nye, D. (2010) *When the Lights Went Out*. Cambridge, Mass.: MIT Press.

Nye, D. (2014) 'The United States and alternative energies: technological fix or regime change?' *Theory, Culture and Society*, 31: 103–25.

Offner, A. (2006) *The Challenge of Affluence*. Oxford: Oxford University Press.

Ohmae, K. (1990) *The Borderless World*. New York: McKinsey.

Oreskes, N., Conway E. (2010) *Merchants of Doubt*. New York: Bloomsbury Press.

Oreskes, N., Conway E. (2014) *The Collapse of Western Civilization: A View from the Future*. New York: Columbia University Press.

Orlov, D. (2008) *Reinventing Collapse: The Soviet Example and American Prospects*. Gabriola Island, BC: New Society Publishers.

Ormerod, P. (2012) *Positive Thinking*. London: Faber and Faber.

Orr, D. (2009) *Down to the Wire: Confronting Climate Collapse*. New York: Oxford University Press.

Orwell, G. (2008[1949]) *Nineteen Eighty-Four*. London: Secker and Warburg.

Owen, D. (2011) *Green Metropolis: Why Living Smaller, Living Closer, and Driving Less Are the Keys to Sustainability*. London: Penguin.

Owen, R. (1970[1813–14]) *A New View of Society*. Harmondsworth: Penguin.
Parenti, C. (2011) *Tropic of Chaos*. New York: Nation Books.
Parsons, T. (1968[1937]) *The Structure of Social Action*, 2 vols. New York: Free Press.
Paterson, M. (2007) *Automobile Politics: Ecology and Cultural Political Economy*. Cambridge: Cambridge University Press.
Patterson, R. (2003) *Dereliction of Duty: Eyewitness Account of How Bill Clinton Compromised America's National Security*. Washington, DC: Regnery Publishing.
Pearce, F. (2006) *When the Rivers Run Dry*. London: Transworld.
Pearce, F. (2007) *With Speed and Violence: Why Scientists Fear Tipping Points in Climate Change*. Boston: Beacon Press.
Peels, J. (2011) 'How soon before we get "green" 3D printing?' *Quora*, www.quora.com/How-soon-before-we-get-green-3D-printing.
Perez, C. (2002) *Technological Revolutions and Financial Capital: The Dynamics of Bubbles and Golden Ages*. London: Edward Elgar.
Perkins Gilman, C. (1892) 'Yellow wallpaper', www.publicbookshelf.com/romance/wallpaper/yellow-wallpaper.
Perrow, C. (1999) *Normal Accidents: Living with High-Risk Technologies*. New York: Basic Books.
Perrow, C. (2007) *The Next Catastrophe*. Princeton: Princeton University Press.
Peters, M., Fudge, S., Jackson, T. (eds.) (2010) *Low Carbon Communities*. Cheltenham: Edward Elgar.
Pfeiffer, D. (2006) *Eating Fossil Fuels*. Gabriola Island, BC: New Society Publishers.
Piercy, M. (1976) *Woman on the Edge of Time*. New York: Alfred A. Knopf.
Piketty, T. (2014) *Capital in the Twenty-First Century*. Cambridge, Mass.: Harvard University Press.
Pinder, D. (2015) 'Reconstituting the possible: Lefebvre, Utopia and the urban question', *International Journal of Urban and Regional Research*, 39: 28–45.
Platt, E. (2000) *Leadville*. London: Picador.
Polanyi, K. (1954[1944]) *The Great Transformation*. Boston: Beacon Press.
Popper, K. (1960) *The Poverty of Historicism*. London: Routledge and Kegan Paul.
Porritt, J. (2013) *The World We Made*. London: Phaidon.
Prigogine, I. (1997) *The End of Certainty*. New York: Free Press.
Prigogine, I., Stengers, I. (1984) *Order out of Chaos*. London: Heinemann.
Putnam, R. (2000) *Bowling Alone*. New York: Simon and Schuster.

Rand, A. (2007[1957]) *Atlas Shrugged*. London: Penguin.

Ratto, M., Ree, R. (2010) 'The materialization of digital information and the digital economy knowledge synthesis report', http://thingtanklab.com/wp-content/uploads/2011/02/SSHRC_DigEcon_DDF.pdf.

Rees, M. (2003) *Our Final Century*. London: Arrow Books.

Reid, C. (2015) *Roads Were Not Built For Cars*. Washington, DC: Island Press.

Rial, J. A., Pielke, Sr, R. A., Beniston, M., et al. (2004) 'Nonlinearities, feedbacks and crucial thresholds within the earth's climate system', *Climate Change*, 65: 11–38.

Ricca-Smith, C. (2011) 'Could 3D printing end our throwaway culture?' www.theguardian.com/technology/2011/nov/17/3d-printing-throwaway-culture.

Rich, N. (2013) *Odds against Tomorrow*. New York: Picador.

Riedy, C. (2007) *The Eye of the Storm: An Integral Perspective on Sustainable Development and Climate Change Response*. Saarbrucken, Germany: VDM Verlag.

Rifkin, J. (2000) *The Age of Access*. London: Penguin.

Rifkin, J. (2002) *The Hydrogen Economy*. New York: Penguin Putnam.

Rifkin, J. (2009) *The Empathic Civilization: The Race to Global Consciousness in a World in Crisis*. Cambridge: Polity.

Rittel, H., Webber, M. (1973) 'Dilemmas in a general theory of planning', *Policy Sciences*, 4: 155–69.

Rodin, J. (2014) *The Resilience Dividend: Being Strong in a World Where Things Go Wrong*. New York: Public Affairs.

Rogers, R. (1997) *Cities for a Small Planet*. London: Faber and Faber.

Romm, J. (2004) *The Hype About Hydrogen: Fact and Fiction in the Race to Save the Climate*. Washington, DC: Island Press.

Rosenthal, E. (2013) 'The end of car culture', *New York Times*, 29 June, www.nytimes.com/2013/06/30/sunday-review/the-end-of-car-culture.html.

Ross, B. (2014) *Dead End: Suburban Sprawl and the Rebirth of American Urbanism*. Oxford: Oxford University Press.

Royal Academy of Engineering (2010) *Electric Vehicles: Charged with Potential*. London: RAE.

Rutledge, I. (2005) *Addicted to Oil*. London: I. B. Tauris.

Saunders, S. (2010) 'Consumer-generated media and product labelling: designed in California, assembled in China', *International Journal of Consumer Studies*, 34: 474–80.

Savage, M., Williams, K. (eds.) (2008) *Remembering Elites*. Oxford: Blackwell.

Sayer, A. (2015) *Why We Can't Afford the Rich*. Bristol: Policy Press.
Schmid, H. (2009) *Economy of Fascination*. Berlin: Gebrüder Borntraeger.
Schneider, K. (2005[1971]) *Autokind vs. Mankind*. Lincoln, NE: Universe.
Schumacher, E. (1973) *Small is Beautiful*. London: Blond and Briggs.
Schumpeter, J. (1942) *Capitalism, Socialism, and Democracy*. New York: Harper.
Scranton, R. (2013) 'Learning how to die in the Anthropocene', *New York Times*, 10 November.
Sekula, A. (2001) 'Freeway to China (version 2, for Liverpool)', in Comaroff, J., Comaroff, J. (eds.) *Millennial Capitalism and the Culture of Neoliberalism*. Durham, NC: Duke University Press.
Sells, E. (2009) *Towards a Self-Manufacturing Rapid Prototyping Machine*. Ph.D. dissertation, Bath University.
Sennett, R. (1977) *The Fall of Public Man*. London and Boston, Mass.: Faber and Faber.
Sennett, R. (1998) *The Corrosion of Character*. New York: W. W. Norton & Co.
Sennett, R. (2009) *The Craftsman*. London: Penguin.
Shankland, S. (2010) 'HP joining 3D printer market with Stratasys deal', http://news.cnet.com/8301-30685_3-10436841-264.html.
Sharon, D. (1983) 'Drive-by-wire', *Futures*, 15: 491–8.
Shaxson, N. (2012) *Treasure Islands*. London: Bodley Head.
Sheller, M. (2004) 'Automotive emotions: feeling the car', *Theory, Culture and Society*, 21: 221–42.
Sheller, M. (2015a) 'Will "connected transmobility" hasten a sustainable mobility transition?' Keynote address, Eindhoven University of Technology, March.
Sheller, M. (2015b) 'Racialized mobility transitions in Philadelphia: connecting urban sustainability and transport justice', *City and Society*, 27: 1–22.
Sheller, M., Urry, J. (2006) 'The new mobilities paradigm', *Environment and Planning*, 38: 207–26.
Shelley, M. (1826) *The Last Man*. London: Henry Colburn.
Shelley, M. (2000[1818]) *Frankenstein*. London: Macmillan.
Shepard, M. (ed.) (2011) *Sentient City: Ubiquitous Computing, Architecture and the Future of Urban Space*. Cambridge, Mass.: MIT Press.
Shove, E. (2010) 'Beyond the ABC: climate change policy and theories of social change', *Environment and Planning A*, 42: 1273–85.

Shove, E., Chappells, H., Lutzenhiser, L. (eds.) (2009) *Comfort in a Lower Carbon Society*. London: Routledge.

Sieberg, D. (2010) 'World News America: 3D printing creates "something out of nothing" ', http://news.bbc.co.uk/1/hi/programmes/world_news_america/9318390.stm.

Silver, H., Arrighi, G. (2011) 'The end of the long twentieth century', in Calhoun, C., Derluguian, G. (eds.) *Business as Usual*. New York: New York University Press.

Silverman, M. (2012) 'Mashable tech how does 3D printing work, anyway?', http://mashable.com/2012/08/01/how-does-3d-printing-work.

Simmel, G. (1910) 'How is society possible?', *American Journal of Sociology*, 16: 371–91.

Sinclair, U. (2008[1926]) *Oil!* London: Penguin.

Slaughter, R. (2003) *Futures beyond Dystopia*. London: Routledge.

Slaughter, R. (2012) *To See with Fresh Eyes: Integral Futures and the Global Emergency*. Brisbane: Foresight International.

Sloman, L. (2006) *Car Sick: Solutions for Our Car-Addicted Culture*. London: Green Books.

Smil, V. (2008) *Global Catastrophes and Trends: The Next Fifty Years*. Cambridge, Mass.: MIT Press.

Smith, A. (1979[1776]) *An Inquiry into the Nature and Causes of the Wealth of Nations*. Oxford: Clarendon Press.

Son, H. (2015) 'The history of Western future studies: an exploration of the intellectual traditions and three-phase periodization', *Futures*, 66: 120–37.

Spence, A., Poortinga, W., Butler, C., Pidgeon, N. (2011) 'Perceptions of climate change and willingness to save energy related to flood experience', *Nature Climate Change*, 1: 46–9.

Srnicek, N., Williams, A. (2015) *Inventing the Future: Postcapitalism and a World without Work*. London: Verso.

Standing, G. (2014) *Precariat – the New Dangerous Class*. London: Bloomsbury.

Stedman Jones, D. (2012) *Masters of the Universe*. Princeton, N.J.: Princeton University Press.

Stemp-Morlock, G. (2010) 'Personal fabrication: open source 3D printers could herald the start of a new industrial revolution', www.economist.com/node/18114221.

Stengers, I. (2015) *In Catastrophic Times: Resisting the Coming Barbarism*. London: Open Humanities Press.

Stern, N. (2007) *The Economics of Climate Change*. Cambridge: Cambridge University Press.

Stiglitz, J. (2004) *The Roaring Nineties: A New History of the World's Most Prosperous Decade*. New York: W.W. Norton.

Stiglitz, J. (2007) *Making Globalization Work*. Harmondsworth: Penguin.

Storper, M. (2013) *Keys to the City*. Princeton: Princeton University Press.

Strahan, D. (2007) *The Last Oil Shock*. London: John Murray.

Strogatz, S. (2003) *Sync: The Emerging Science of Spontaneous Order*. Harmondsworth: Penguin.

Szerszynski, B. (2010) 'Reading and writing the weather: climate technics and the moment of responsibility', *Theory, Culture and Society*, 27: 9–30.

Szerszynski, B. (2016) 'Acting ahead of the future: towards an embodied, cognitive, social theory of anticipation' in *Futures in Question*. Special Issue of *Sociological Review*.

Szerszynski, B., Kearnes, M., Macnaghten, P., Owen, R., Stilgoe, J. (2013) 'Why solar radiation management geoengineering and democracy won't mix', *Environment and Planning A*, 45: 2809–16.

Tainter, J. (1988) *The Collapse of Complex Societies*. Cambridge: Cambridge University Press.

Taleb, N. (2007) *The Black Swan*. London: Penguin.

Tett, G. (2010) *Fool's Gold: How Unrestrained Greed Corrupted a Dream, Shattered Global Markets and Unleashed a Catastrophe*. London: Abacus.

Thackara, J. (2015) *How to Thrive in the Next Economy*. London: Thames and Hudson.

Theroux, M. (2009) *Far North*. London: Faber and Faber.

Thompson, E. P. (1968) *The Making of the English Working Class*. Harmondsworth: Penguin.

Thompson, M., Beck, M. (2014) *Coping with Change: Urban Resilience, Sustainability, Adaptability and Path Dependence*. Foresight Paper from 'The Future of Cities' Foresight Programme. London: Department for Business, Innovation and Skills.

Tilly, C. (1992) *Coercion, Capital and European States: AD 990–1992*. New York: Wiley–Basil Blackwell.

Timmons Roberts, J., Parks, B. (2007) *A Climate of Injustice*. Cambridge, Mass.: MIT Press.

Tita, B. (2014) '3-D printer makers get reality check', *The Wall Street Journal*, 7 April.

Toffler, A. (1970) *Future Shock*. London: Bodley Head.

Tuomi, I. (2003) *Networks of Innovation: Change and Meaning in the Age of the Internet*. Oxford: Oxford University Press.

Turner, F. (2006) *From Counterculture to Cyberculture: Stewart Brand, the Whole Earth Network and the Rise of Digital Utopianism*. Chicago: University of Chicago Press.

Tutton, R. (2016) 'Wicked futures: meaning, matter, and the sociology of the future' (under review).

Tyfield, D. (2014) 'Putting the power in "socio-technical regimes" – e-mobility transition in China as political process', *Mobilities*, 9: 285–63.

Tyfield, D., Urry, J. (2014) *Energy and Society*. Special Issue of *Theory, Culture and Society*, 31: 3–226.

UN-Habitat (2013) *Planning and Design for Sustainable Urban Mobility: Global Report on Human Settlements 2013*. London: Routledge.

Urry, J. (2000) *Sociology beyond Societies*. London: Routledge.

Urry, J. (2002) 'The global complexities of September 11th', *Theory, Culture and Society*, 19: 57–69.

Urry, J. (2003) *Global Complexity*. Cambridge: Polity.

Urry, J. (2005) *Complexity*. Special Issue of *Theory, Culture and Society*, 22: 1–274.

Urry, J. (2007) *Mobilities*. Cambridge: Polity.

Urry, J. (2011) *Climate Change and Society*. Cambridge: Polity.

Urry, J. (2013a) 'A low carbon economy and society', *Philosophical Transactions of the Royal Society A*, 10.1098/rsta.2011.0566.

Urry, J. (2013b) *Societies beyond Oil*. London: Zed.

Urry, J. (2014a) *Offshoring*. Cambridge: Polity.

Urry, J. (2014b) 'The problem of energy', *Theory, Culture and Society*, 31: 3–20.

Urry, J., Birtchnell, T., Caletrio, J., Pollastri, S. (2014) *Living in the City*. Foresight Paper from 'The Future of Cities' Foresight Programme. London: Department for Business, Innovation and Skills.

US National Intelligence Council (2008) *US Global Trends 2025: A Transformed World*. Washington, DC: US National Intelligence Council.

Vance, A. (2010) '3D printing is spurring a manufacturing revolution', *New York Times*, www.nytimes.com/2010/09/14/technology/14print.html.

Verne, J. (1996[1863]) *Paris in the Twentieth Century*. New York: Del Rey Books.

Verne, J. (2005[1865]) *From the Earth to the Moon*. New York: Barnes & Noble Publishing.

Verne, J. (2008[1873]) *Around the World in Eighty Days*, www.gutenberg.org/ebooks/103.

Von Hippel, E. (2006) *Democratizing Innovation*. Cambridge, Mass.: MIT Press.

Walby, S. (2009) *Globalization and Inequalities*. London: Sage.

Walby, S. (2015) *Crisis*. Cambridge: Polity.

Wallerstein, I., Collins, R., Mann, M., Derluguian, G., Calhoun, C. (2013) *Does Capitalism Have a Future?* New York: Oxford University Press.

Watson, R. (2008) *Future Files*. London: Nicholas Brealey Publishing.
Watts, D. (1999) *Small Worlds*. Princeton: Princeton University Press.
Watts, D. (2003) *Six Degrees: The Science of a Connected Age*. London: Heinemann.
Watts, L., Urry, J. (2008) 'Moving methods, travelling times', *Environment and Planning D: Society and Space*, 26: 860–74.
Weber, M. (1948[1919]) 'Politics as a vocation', in Gerth, H., Mills, C. W. (eds.) *From Max Weber*. London: Routledge and Kegan Paul.
Weinberg, M. (2013) 'What's the deal with copyright and 3D printing?' *Public Knowledge*, 3 March.
Weiss, C. C. (2012) 'The Double turns you into a video-calling, iPad-faced robot', *Gizmag*, www.gizmag.com/double-robotics-double-video-calling-robot/23783.
Weissman, J. (2012) 'Why are young people ditching cars for smart phones?', *The Atlantic*, 7 August, www.theatlantic.com/business/archive/2012/08/why-are-young-people-ditching-cars-for-smartphones/260801.
Wells, H. G. (1914) *An Englishman Looks at the World*. London: Cassell.
Wells, H. G. (2005[1898]) *The War of the Worlds*. London: Penguin.
Wells, H. G. (2011[1905]) *A Modern Utopia*. Boston, Mass.: Digireads.com.
Welsh, I. (2010) 'Climate change: complexity and collaboration between the sciences', in Lever-Tracy, C. (ed.) *Routledge Handbook on Climate Change and Society*. London: Routledge.
Whitehead, A. N. (1929) *Process and Reality*. Cambridge: Cambridge University Press.
Wilde, O. (2001[1900]) *The Soul of Man under Socialism and Selected Critical Prose*. London: Penguin.
Wilkinson, R., Pickett, K. (2009) *The Spirit Level: Why More Equal Societies Almost Always Do Better*. London: Allen Lane.
Williams, H. (1991) *Autogeddon*. London: Jonathan Cape.
Williams, R. (1977) *Marxism and Literature*. Oxford: Oxford University Press.
Williams, R. (1983) *Towards 2000*. Harmondsworth: Penguin.
Willis, R., Webb, M., Wilsdon, J. (2007) *The Disrupters: Lessons for Low-carbon Innovation from the New Wave of Environmental Pioneers*. London: NESTA/Demos.
Wollen, P., Kerr, J. (eds.) (2002) *Autopia: Cars and Culture*. London: Reaktion Books.
Woodbridge, R. (2005) *The Next World War: Tribes, Cities, Nations, and Ecological Decline*. Toronto: Toronto University Press.
Worldwide Fund for Nature (2008) *Plugged In: The End of the Oil Age, Summary Report*. Brussels: WWF.

Wright, E. O. (2010) *Envisioning Real Utopias*. London: Verso.
Wyndham, J. (2008[1951]) *The Day of the Triffids*. London: Penguin.
Wynne, B. (2010) 'Strange weather, again: climate science as political art', *Theory, Culture and Society*, 27: 289–305.
Yar, M. (2015) *Crime and the Imaginary of Disaster: Post-Apocalyptic Fictions and the Crisis of Social Order*. London: Palgrave Macmillan.
Young, M. (1968) *Forecasting and the Social Sciences*. London: Heinemann.
Žižek, S. (2011) *Living in the End Times: Updated New Edition*. London: Verso.

Index